D0081631

# AN ASSEMBLY OF GOOD FELLOWS

*Jack C. Ross*

# AN ASSEMBLY OF GOOD FELLOWS

*Voluntary associations in history*

**GREENWOOD PRESS**
WESTPORT, CONNECTICUT   ●   LONDON, ENGLAND

Library of Congress Cataloging in Publication Data
Ross, Jack C
  An assembly of good fellows.

  Bibliography:  p.
  Includes index.
  1.  Associations, institutions, etc.  I.  Title.
  HS35.R67          060          75-35355
  ISBN 0-8371-8586-6

Portions of Chapter 3 are reprinted by permission of the publisher from *Studies in Social and Economic Process*, edited by David Horton Smith.
Portions of Chapter 4 first appeared in the *Journal of Voluntary Action Research*.

Library of Congress Catalog Card Number: 75-35355
ISBN: 0-8371-8586-6

First Published in 1976

Greenwood Press, a division of Williamhouse-Regency Inc.
51 Riverside Avenue, Westport, Connecticut 06880

Printed in the United States of America

Club: ". . . an assembly of good fellows
meeting under certain conditions."

*Samuel Johnson, 1755*

# Contents

PREFACE                                                          xi


1.  The Study of Voluntary Associations in Other
    Places and Times                                              3

    *Definitions*                                                 5
    *Explaining the Existence and Prevalence of*
        *Voluntary Associations*                                 14
    *The Methods of the Study*                                   20


2.  Primitive Societies                                          27

    *Ascribed Associations in the Primitive Band*               28
    *The Tribe: Flourishing Voluntary Associations*
        *in Relatively Simple Societies*                         31
    *The Chiefdom: A Roman Empire in Tropical*
        *Paradise*                                               43
    *The Primitive State: Mixed Evidence on*
        *Voluntarism*                                            51
    *Peasants: Residual People*                                  60
    *Summary and Conclusions*                                    64


3.  Voluntary Associations in Ancient Societies                  71

    *China: Lower-Class Voluntarism*                             72
    *India: Caste and State*                                     85
    *Athens: The City-State*                                     91
    *Rome: The Military-Bureaucratic State*                     100
    *The Voluntary Associations of Ancient*
        *Judaism*                                               117

4. **English Voluntary Associations: From Religious
   Fraternity to Secular Club and Religious Sect**      135

   PART ONE: *Comparative Study of Major Types*
   *Introduction*                                        *135*
   *Methods of Research*                                 *137*
   *The Major Contrasts Between Fraternity and Club*     *140*
   *Comparative Membership Motives, Ethics, and*
       *Organizations*                                   *143*
   *Member Identity and Organization: Existence*
       *of the Fraternity*                               *144*
   *Member Identity and Organization: Existence*
       *of the Club*                                     *152*
   *Member Identity and Organization: Existence*
       *of the Sect*                                     *157*

   PART TWO: *Religious Organizations in Social*
       *Change*
   *The Monastery: Quasi-Voluntary Association*          *159*
   *The Emergence of Fraternity and Gild*                *163*
   *Differentiation in the Mature Phase of the Gild*
       *and Fraternity*                                  *175*
   *The Fraternity Idea: Special Applications*           *191*
   *Jewish Gilds*                                        *197*

5. **English Clubs and Social Change**                   205

   *The Emergence of Clubs*                              *205*
   *Drinks and Voluntary Associations*                   *208*
   *Coffeehouses and Political Clubs*                     *215*
   *Hedonism, Voluntarism, and Scientific Societies*     *217*
   *Voluntary Associations in Sports, Music, and*
       *Drama*                                            *221*
   *Deviants and Extremists in Clubs*                     *237*
   *Operative and Accepted Masons: Residual Gilds*        *243*
   *New Forms in the Eighteenth and Nineteenth*
       *Centuries*                                        *244*

6.  Restatement of the Model                                    254

        *Communication*                                         *255*
        *Goals and Interests*                                   *257*
        *The Collective Action Orientation*                     *259*
        *Variety, Purpose, Consequences*                        *263*


APPENDIX                                                        267
    Interdisciplinary Search on Voluntary Associations

            *Annotated Bibliography to Appendix*              *283*

BIBLIOGRAPHY                                                   285

INDEX                                                          297

# Preface

Ⅰf *An Assembly of Good Fellows* were a history book in the strict sense, it would be easily placed in the "revisionist" category. Despite heavy reliance on historical materials, it is, nevertheless, primarily sociological in character, and sociology has not elevated a similar neologism to prominence. The nearest thing to a label would be "historical sociology," even though my sentiments are all with the revisionists.

Both my method and my topic were strongly influenced by my mentors at the University of Minnesota. Arnold M. Rose and Caroline Rose interested me in voluntary associations in community life, both as teachers and exemplars. I had the good fortune to study with Arnold Rose and then, as a community social worker in his neighborhood, to get a deeper sense of his understanding of the importance of voluntary associations in social life. Caroline Rose was my mentor in neighborhood as Arnold Rose was in university.

My indebtedness to Don Martindale is of another sort. He contributed a sense of excitement about sociological inquiry and made evident in his social behaviorist method a way to go about macroanalysis of other civilizations. His continuing interest in and support of my work has been deeply satisfying.

One major theme of this book is that voluntary association studies have been strongly biased toward an American view of things; I hope to correct this bias by a new self-consciousness, a broader scope, and a greater depth in time. I would be less than candid, therefore, if I did not point out my own biases. For, as many a traveler in foreign lands has remarked, "strange that everybody here has an accent except me."

The first of my accents is that, like the majority of modern middle-class adults, I am and have been a participant in voluntary associations, and this participation has shaped my view of things. Belonging to something demands a commitment, and commitment affects one's life course. Let me illustrate with an incident that happened thirty-five years ago that is still vivid to me.

My fellow crew member in a labor gang was an aged Pole, who retained the strong accent of his homeland. One sweltering August day, after we had taken quite a lot of abuse from an unsympathetic boss, we withdrew to talk about home and things that were important to us. He suddenly put down his pick, took a dirty wallet from his pocket, and with loving care showed me a membership card. "There. I am Eagle. Franklin Roosevelt is Eagle too." Words cannot describe the emotion that accompanied his declaration. From time to time I have pondered over the event. What is the source of such a powerful emotion about a "mere" organization? Though I have never been a lodge member, I have had such feelings about some of the voluntary associations I have been part of, and such experiences eventually led me to choose to study membership organizations.

The story of another influence on my research also presents the opportunity to acknowledge a debt. Ray Wheeler was my co-worker on *Black Belonging* (Greenwood Press, 1972), which was the result of field research on membership in voluntary associations of black people. His commitment to objectivity always set a high standard. But I was left with more questions than I began with. Was the rest of the world like that single community? I felt I ought to write further but I didn't know how to start the awesome task that seemed so imperative. Then one day in 1972, this incident occured.

I was seated by the window reading the evening paper. My wife was cooking supper and the children were playing—a classical evening scene. My oldest daughter, aged 11, entered.

"Daddy, how do you make a statue of an elephant?"

"Ask your mother."

"Daddy! It's a riddle. How do you make a statue of an elephant?"

With that air of paternal indulgence that all interrupted-fathers-reading-paper must master, I replied. "All right. How do you make a statue of an elephant?"

"Well, you take an e-e-e-eNORMOUS piece of rock, and chip away everything that doesn't look like an elephant." Sigh.

"Go ask your mother."

I comfort myself with the thought that few people are asked to prove the validity of their reasons for research. So I began, chipping away everything that didn't look like voluntary associations. There has been a lot of chipping.

On a more formal note, I would like to acknowledge the assistance given to me by the staff of the Guildhall Library, London, where I did most of my British research. Their eagerness to help and the skill with which they did their work was always heartening. I wish to thank the Nuffield Trust for a grant that made my study in England possible. I am grateful to the Mayor and Archivist of the ancient city of Winchester for access to their vaults. Christopher Pickvance of University of Manchester spent many long hours discussing and criticizing. To my colleagues M. M. Lazar, Raoul Andersen, and George Park, I am also indebted for numerous kindnesses. David Horton Smith, of Boston College, has helped in numerous ways. May Kennedy and Sandra Doucet have tirelessly typed and retyped the manuscript. Finally, to my family, gratitude for so many things that I could not possibly think of them all.

As my father dedicated his work to us, I dedicate this work to him. Harold S. Ross (1893-1975).

# AN ASSEMBLY OF GOOD FELLOWS

# 1 *The study of voluntary associations in other places and times*

Contact with voluntary associations is part of the daily experience of the majority of modern adults and of many children. Sociologists and other social scientists now routinely inquire about voluntary associations in their community research as readily as they ask about education, sex, age, race, and income. The literature is voluminous and rich with data. It is common to assume, therefore, that we know a great deal about the subject. Recent inventories of knowledge about voluntarism, however, are more critical. A number of deficiencies are pointed out by Smith and Freedman, Palisi, and Warner.[1] Criticisms are made of definitions, theories, and validity of data. More to the point in regard to this study, the sociological works also tend to be limited to contemporary industrial society and are focused extensively on the United States to the exclusion of other countries.

This study does not correct these deficiencies through direct criticism. The intention is, rather, to expand the knowledge of voluntary associations to a more general level by examining societies that have been previously ignored so that existing research may be viewed in context. Accordingly, a selection has been made of societies that, while not representative of all theoretically conceivable kinds, will serve to raise a number of the more important issues.

3

An ancillary matter is the use of methods of research in historical sociology, a discipline that is often discussed but not often practiced.

If the purpose of the study were merely to demythologize the American view of things, it could be more simply done, because the basic facts are already available, even if they are not readily accessible to the average reader. For example, though the common view is that the United States is a nation of joiners, many modern societies have as many voluntary associations and probably a higher proportion of members.[2] And if we like to think of the Midwest as the heartland of America, we might ponder the irony of the fact that a greater proportion of the aborigines who lived in the same area, two centuries previously, belonged to voluntary associations, and in addition they probably used them more effectively in government and public affairs. The army that beat General Custer at Little Big Horn was a collection of voluntary associations.

Or consider another icon, that of the affinity of voluntary associations for industrial societies; in fact, the nonindustrial ancient Greeks and Romans belonged to many and used them extensively. Even farther back, early Mesopotamians probably had voluntary associations. The Old Testament has many references to voluntary organizations.

What aspects of voluntary associations should be selected for attention if we are seeking a wide range of societal types? Existing empirical research may assist in the identification of topics, but it is not a reliable guide because the body of research reports emerges from a very limited number of research perspectives and biased value assumptions. Attention must, therefore, be directed toward more universal and general ideas that are not culturally restricted.

The issue with which each study of a society will begin is simply the *existence* of voluntary associations, and the factors in each society that are correlated with that existence. This identification of course presupposes precise definitions of the nature of voluntarism and voluntary associations.

A closely related issue is *prevalence*. That is, if the necessary conditions of existence are present, what further things are associated with limitation or proliferation of voluntary associations?

The question of prevalence implies the question of variety or differentiation since "more" can mean increases in kind as well as increases in number.

A voluntary association is, by its very nature, a human collectivity that stresses an identified purpose and the association of members who seek to achieve it. It is a certain kind of relationship between ends and means. Inquiry will, therefore, be made into the *purpose* of the organization and why the members seek to achieve it through a particular kind of affiliation. This implies selection of some systematic criteria for classification of members and purposes.

It would be desirable to evaluate the results that the voluntary associations obtained by their actions. In some instances this will be done, but more often it will prove to be beyond the scope of the study.[3]

The reader who is interested in a review of the facts that are the basis of the selection of the topics for this study is referred to the definitive article by David Sills in the widely accessible *International Encyclopedia of the Social Sciences*,[4] to the work of C. Smith and A. Freedman,[5] or to the annual series *Voluntary Action Research*, edited by David H. Smith.[6]

## Definitions

A well-known English gentleman and clubman has given an apt working definition with which to begin. A club, Johnson says in his dictionary, is "an assembly of good fellows meeting under certain conditions."[7] Another English clubman added a note of realism with his own definition: a club is "the only place in London where my wife cannot get at me."[8] The observation would hold for most of the organizations to be depicted: to include some "good fellows" makes it necessary to exclude some who are not so good. Throughout history, one of the main kinds of exclusion has been that of opposite sex, epitomized in the definition of yet another English clubman: "Club—a weapon used by savages to keep white women at a distance."[9]

The restrictive or exclusive club is only one species of voluntary association. Many, in fact, stress open membership. Nor is a club necessarily a place or residence. Some even seek to enroll as many members as possible, regardless of status or identity, or may not, like the club, primarily seek conviviality or sociability. Paradoxically, most such organizations end up with a membership that is quite homogeneous anyway. Analysis, therefore, must consider not only stated purposes or principles but identification of actual behavior, and chosen definitions must make it possible to keep this issue clear.

The voluntary association is a phenomenon of variety and diversity. Before proceeding further, therefore, let us expand the scope of the working definition to more general and abstract terms.

A commonsense conception of the subject matter is inherent in the two words that compose the term.[10] "Voluntary" refers to individual action without coercion. It is typical to imply that this idea of voluntarism also excludes direct profit-seeking or work for full pay. "Association" refers to an organization. So a voluntary association is an organization of people who participate without coercion or direct profit. And that tells us a great deal about what we are concerned with. Unfortunately, as reference to the previous paragraphs will reveal, the apparent simplicity of this sort of definition is deceptive. When we begin to try to fit cases to the definition, a great many problems arise. Let us illustrate this problem with a sample dialogue of a sort that has occurred over and over during preparation of this volume.[11]

The experience is that of trying to explain what one is writing about to any interested person.

"What sort of work do you do at the university?"

"I am doing research on voluntary associations."

"I see. That's interesting. Could you give me an example of a voluntary association? You mean like the Boy Scouts?"

"Yes." So far, so good.

"Would you say that a union is a voluntary association?"

"Some of them are."

"How about the Catholic church?"

"Well, some scholars feel that . . ."

The apologies have begun. Only three questions and the so-called scientist is in trouble. Typically, the next ploy is to evade the issue or to move to some other level of discourse, in which marginal kinds of association are defined, impure motives are accounted for, sub-classifications are made, hyphenated terms invented, and so on. One learns to fight back. In dyspeptic mood, an effective option is to inquire about the *other* person's work, preferably asking for definitions whenever possible. Perhaps we need not be apologetic. Chemists and physicists can't define their fundamental terms to satisfy both themselves and the public either.

The problem here, of course, as suggested before, is that voluntary associations are part of anyday discourse, and communication between John Doe and the Specialist in such situations proceeds most easily from concrete examples of the sort mentioned above. Reviews of the history of sociological research show that a great deal of sociological defining work is done in just this way.[12] One reason for the survival of this operationalism is apparent to anyone who has ever attempted field research. It is very difficult to communicate with the individual who is a subject of the research, or simply interested in what the results are, in any way other than by giving examples. It is sometimes the best that can be done. Operationalism obviously fails, however, when the examples are not known or do not apply in the circumstances of the sample. Smith and Freedman, after a review of the field, pick a partially operational definition that illustrates this approach: voluntary associations are "organizations that people belong to part time and without pay, such as clubs, lodges, good works agencies and the like."[13] "Belong to" is a crucial term, which is different from "are employed by," or "are in favor of" or "are born into" or any other signification of association. Under the open-ended phrase "and the like," one is free to include almost anything and thus the way is cleared for ethnocentric localism and eventual parochial research. This cannot be the road to science.

We must, therefore, seek a more stringent standard. If a person takes Smith and Freedman's option, would it occur to him to include Cheyenne warriors or the voluntary armies of Gideon? It is not likely, and it certainly has not happened in sociological literature up to this point. An orientation is required that does not exclude things that the culturally biased imagination fails to conjure.

The only other simple choice in field research in most cases is to develop an abstract definition, perhaps modified by operational specification, which means the same thing to all members of a sample. This proves difficult in practice, if the universe covers a wide variety of social types, and it tends to bad results with uninterested or poorly educated respondents.

In the study presented here, there is no single set of "respondents," but simply documents that are the result of inquiry by uncoordinated investigators from other times and places. The theoretical problem of operationalism then gives way to the methodological one of the mute record.

Each of the societies studied here involves a different set or combination of kinds of documentary sources, but the definitions must apply to all of them. The first study, of primitive societies, draws on material by anthropologists, or directly on nonscholarly records of ethnographic sources such as Indian agents, missionaries, explorers, or merchants. The second study, of ancient civilizations, relies mostly on work by historians, classical scholars, and archaeologists. The third, of medieval and post-Elizabethan England, is even more eclectic, with work from lawyers, religious writers, journalists, economic historians, amateur local historians, political scientists, and official chroniclers. With such diversity, what formal definitions, concepts, and related techniques of research should be used so that the results can be cumulative and sensible?

The problem of diversity of sources is discussed in detail in a methodological appendix titled "Interdisciplinary Search on Voluntary Associations." The method may be briefly described as an epistemological classification of stimulus terms, which assures a correction of systematic biases, in information retrieval.

Smith, Reddy, and Baldwin note that there are two main definitional strategies in treating "voluntary association"—"that concerned with the individual, and that concerned with the association itself."[14] Each strategy has strengths that the other lacks. Definitions that center on the voluntarism of the organization, as measured or indicated by its purposes or typical actions, leave the voluntarism of the participants as a residual matter. The opposite approach starts from the criterion of voluntary action by members, whether or not the goals or typical actions of the association actually reflect members' voluntarism. To define voluntary associations as those organizations that act voluntaristically *and* whose members are volunteers would be the most restrictive criterion. Empirical reality would deviate from it in a great many cases. Before proceeding to such a pluralistic definition, let us illustrate some more typical definitional attempts of the two kinds in modern sociological work.

An example of the organizational-purpose type of definition is that of Sherwood Fox. Voluntary associations are "private, nonprofit organizations not engaged directly in any activities that are functional prerequisites for the on-going social system, that is, not directly producing goods or supplying a service."[15] The definition is also useful to illustrate the kinds of biases that enter work when one assumes, without checking facts, that no one would voluntaristically supply services or produce goods for a social system. The fact is that such systems are rather frequent in some societies; the *kula* ring economy described by Malinowski is an example.[16] Fox's criteria, if adopted here, would eliminate a large number of our examples, incorrectly, I believe. It is necessary, in the long run, to deal with productivity of organizations such as consumers' or producers' cooperatives that have voluntaristic components but enter into typical market situations with nonvoluntary organizations.

Arnold Rose, whose work on voluntary associations was seminal in the theoretical development of the sociology of voluntarism, gave a definition that may be used to illustrate the individual-voluntarism kind of approach. He saw voluntary associations in terms of the functions they served "in supporting political democracy in the United States."[17] "They distribute power over social life among a very large proportion of the citizenry. . . ." They also "provide a sense of satisfaction with modern democratic processes because they help the ordinary citizen to see how the processes function in limited circumstances, of direct interest to himself." They also provide a mechanism for social change. Despite these functions, which refer to both individuals and groups, Rose's actual definition is based on the strategy used to satisfy individual interests. "A small group of people, finding they have a certain interest (or purpose) in common, agree to meet and to act together in order to try to satisfy that interest or achieve that purpose."[18] In spite of their different emphases, the definitions cited share an assumption that the voluntary association is socially functional. There is certainly no proof that this is true: any such assumption may introduce an empirical error of truly enormous proportions, and there is no place in sociology for Polyanna beliefs like this. The definitional choice of Smith, Reddy, and Baldwin has no such assumption and meets the stringent pluralistic criteria developed above (a theory construction strategy that has unique problems, which will not be considered here).[19] The care and completeness with which the authors develop their definition commends it as a basis for one to be adapted to the purposes of this study.

The authors first define a group as "(1) the largest set of two or more individuals who are jointly characterized by (2) a network of relevant communications, (3) a shared sense of collective identity, and (4) one or more shared goal dispositions with associated normative strength."[20] A voluntary group is one whose goals involve voluntary action (defined later). Groups vary in degree of formality, as indicated by the extent of "formal leadership structure." The authors then make a distinction that is useful in dealing with the phenomenon of the varying reasons members have for membership. They define "analytical group members" as "persons or groups who conventionally provide services primarily aimed at accomplishing one or more of the group's goals." The organization may then be defined as "the largest set of analytical group members of an organized (formal) group having essential sovereignty and policy control over their own objectives and modes of accomplishing them."[21] The idea of "analytical group member" takes the place of the conventional concept of a status or position in a collectivity, but in addition, it highlights the fact that a member of an organization has group statuses at the same time. This set of definitions emphasizes a common feature of voluntary organizational life: there are frequently a significant number of people on an organizational roster who are inactive, beneficiaries or sycophants, part of the audience, casual associates and the like, who are not formally involved in goal accomplishment but nevertheless are significant parts of the scene. In the studies that follow we shall frequently encounter such issues. The authors have successfully defined the boundaries of the organization.

When an organization is defined in this way as an aspect of a group, there must be some additional account of the fact that groups are frequently altered or destroyed by removal of members, while it is conventional to think of organizations as having long life or perpetuity, and therefore having provision for replacement of members in a routine fashion. An approach in which organizations are defined independently, with component groups, seems to better account for the empirical realities of ongoing organizations such as the case of deactivated organizations, or annual voluntary associations that are active only when contingent events so indicate. The definition by Smith, Reddy, and Baldwin seems quite appropriate to the origination phase when specific analytic charter group members do act as a unit, but not to organizational maturity in which the abstract thing called "the organization" endures and the members are replaced or recruited to it. This is merely another instance of the long-established debate in sociology on the reality of the social level of analysis. The organization "exists," in the interaction of members of germane collectivities, and this perception of reality cannot be ignored.

The definition does not require fundamental alteration in order to be used systematically, but merely a notation that successfully functioning groups develop operative provisions for member replacement, recruiting, and identification of the person as an "analytical group member." Sometimes this occurs through the group and sometimes it happens by recruitment to the organization itself; either mode is possible, but the one used makes a difference. Whether the originating analytical group members are the focus or whether the organization is the focus is a choice to be made in research. They are separate things and must not be confused.

For the sake of contrast with a more conventional concept of association or "organization," Etzioni's definition may be cited as a typical example: "By organization we mean, following Parsons, social units devoted primarily to the attainment of specific goals."[22] Another typical approach, which will not be exemplified here, begins with the means or the mode of distribution of resources rather than with goals.[23]

Formal voluntary organizations in Smith, Reddy, and Baldwin's conceptual system are "organizations" (rather than simply groups) whose goals primarily involve voluntary action and the majority of whose members are engaging in voluntary action when they act as group members.[24] For the authors it is autonomous control or sovereignty that distinguishes the formal voluntary organization from the group. They give the example of an organization like the Boy Scouts, which is a formal voluntary organization at the national level, but in which each local troop would be a group. This distinction is valid, given the authors' stipulations, but leaves out the fact that organizations have degrees of partial autonomy at the various hierarchical levels, within the framework of the higher units. Ignoring some further minor distinctions that will not be important in this study, *the formal voluntary organization is equivalent to what is commonly called the voluntary association.*

The nature of voluntarism is the remaining issue. It has been kept to last to afford extensive analysis of the most troublesome factor in the definition.[25]

Voluntary action refers to the "primary emphasis on psychic rewards and commitment to larger goals, whether or not there are also monetary rewards."[26] A voluntary role is a "role, the majority of whose [sic] normative expectations involve engaging in voluntary action when performing the role."[27]

"Voluntary refers to the quality of having been chosen freely and consciously from among two or more alternatives without any substantial compulsion or coercion being applied."[28] A further distinction, which proves important in practice, is that between choosing membership and choosing to act voluntarily when one has become a member. This issue is highlighted in several of the historical societies to be studied. The monastery, for example, often involved voluntary joining followed by extreme discipline within the monastery having no semblance of voluntarism. So far as the act of joining is concerned, the two alternatives may simply be to join or not, rather than to choose between two organizations. There may even be a situation the opposite of that depicted above, involving coerced joining followed by voluntary participation. For example, many modern employers who believe that enthusiastic community participation is a good thing, coercively use participation in community life as a criterion of employment or job evaluation, but they don't much care what a person does if it is consistent with the general values of the firm. In the same sense, it is thought to be a good thing to belong to a church, regardless of which one it is. This activist orientation makes it necessary to distinguish, as has been done here, between voluntarism in joining and participating, if anything is to be learned about the total significance of voluntary associations in society.

The number of kinds of variation that are possible is obviously quite large, and in the study of this length, many subtleties will be overlooked. One of the variations, however, is sufficiently common to require a unique term. When either one of the two criteria of voluntary joining or participation is modified by coercion or direct seeking of rewards for some of the members, or for some of the time, the term "quasi-voluntary association" will be used. The quasi-voluntary association involves a relatively enduring kind of organization, sufficiently established as an ongoing affair because of relatively permanent conditions. It is permanently a partial voluntary association. The operational distinction regarding compulsion or coercion in joining or acting is whether pressures or inducements, if applied at all, ultimately respect an individual's ability of self-determination and self direction. The person must have the will and the ability of self-assignment.

The operational criterion regarding rewards is whether the rewards a person gets from participation are achieved or received in a separate social or cultural system from that in which the person's services or contributions are made. Rewards, to be considered voluntary, may not be contractual. Remuneration, if any, is accidental or incidental. "Psychic rewards" involves feelings of satisfaction that are the indirect result of activity that is consistent with one's ideals or values. In the authors' terms, the activity is concerned with "larger goals." The implied comparative is pettiness, smallness, or narrow self-interest.

It is tempting to turn the analysis to the history of philosophy in order to trace the numerous relevant attempts to define freedom and voluntarism. That will not be attempted here. Perhaps the work of the philosopher-turned-sociologist Georg Simmel would prove analogous to the position taken here. Simmel defined freedom as "transcendence of teleology."[29] That is, action is free when it is not based on a necessary relation of ends and means. In this sense, voluntarism is free action.

## Explaining the Existence and Prevalence of Voluntary Associations

The list of topics that were selected for attention may now be identified for reference by the key words *existence, prevalence, variety, purpose,* and *consequences.* Among these topics, existence of voluntary associations is not only temporally prior to the others, but also the most useful to analyze first because the concepts that are necessary to understand it readily apply to the others. The object of this section is a parsimonious general model of voluntary association existence that may be used in examination of each of the societies to be studied. Although the reasoning used in establishment of a model regarding voluntary association existence may be extended to explain prevalence by a few added assumptions, this will not be done systematically; nor will an attempt be made to develop any theoretical basis for explanation of variety, purpose, or consequences. Such attempts would be premature, given the nature of the available data. Rather, these topics will be explored where possible in light of the study of existence in each case.

Smith has developed a model regarding existence and has tested it with a contemporary sample of societies.[30] The model has the merit of definitional consistency with the work of Smith, Reddy, and Baldwin used above.

Smith makes the commonsense assumption that prevalence of voluntary associations is correlated with greater development of the same conditions that are necessary for existence itself. He says that "there will be a greater prevalence of FVO's in societies (or intercommunications networks) characterized (1) by greater *per capita* interior volume, permanence, and connectivity of intercommunication networks, (2) by greater differentiation of goals and interests, and (3) by greater permission, instigation, resources and payoffs for FVO's."[31] As previously, we may read "FVO" (Formal Voluntary

Organization) as voluntary association. Smith applied this model to secondary analysis of survey data from a number of societies having various levels of development, and obtained general confirmation.

Smith makes further distinctions and definitions regarding each of the three main criteria. The per capita volume of the internal communications network "may be defined as the ratio of the total number of intercommunications initiated and received by members of the network to the total number of individuals comprising the network."[32] This obviously is a consequence not only of the possibility of communication ("connectivity"), but of some other kinds of factors that stimulate communications once they are possible. For example, the existence of telephones or roads, or conversely the absence of physical barriers, must be accompanied by the cultural appropriateness of their use for voluntary associations. In primitive societies, kinship structure is a major criterion of who will talk to whom. Obviously, this is not a matter of arranging societies on a continuum from simple to complex, because some of the simplest societies have notably high volumes of communication. The idea of volume, then, may be seen both as a matter of significance in itself and as a measure of other factors, including connectivity and "permission." Smith has essentially coupled two different levels of analysis.

Smith then considers the significance of connectivity. "The greater the connectivity of the network, the fewer the number of communication links . . . necessary to reach any individual in the network starting from any other individual."[33] Although the statement is logically circular (i.e., it should be a definition rather than a hypothesis), it serves a useful purpose. Connectivity is the structural condition of communication efficiency. In high connectivity situations, not only are the minimum conditions of communications existent, but it is possible to avoid conditions of strain that threaten the links themselves. An individual may, for example, be able to reach some specific other not only through alternate intermediary persons, but through alternate role relations with the same persons. Having both possibilities makes the likelihood of successful communication higher, either on the basis of probability that a completion will result from an attempt to communicate, or on the basis of not overloading a heavily used role relationship.

"Permanence" refers to the endurance of communicative relationships. It is obvious that communication must endure long enough to make possible the kinds of relationships that are necessary for creation of voluntary associations. If the organizations in question are concerned with development of new experience and stimulation, long endurance may be associated with desuetude and apathy. Most modern empirical studies, however, show that the number of memberships increases with length of residence.

"For a group to exist there must be shared goals among the members; for many groups to exist . . . there must be a variety of goals, each one shared distributively within various subsets of individuals of the network."[34] Smith goes on to point out that if there is too much goal differentiation, there may not be enough consensus to permit group formation. To permit examination of primitive societies, this criterion must be qualified by yet another caveat. Though a primitive society may have relatively few *kinds* of goals, it may still have a large number of voluntary associations that form with similar goals but different personnel. The criterion, therefore, must stipulate a distinction between plurality of goals and plurality of kinds of goals. The latter tends to be the situation in modern industrial society; the former in primitive societies. In modern industrial societies, a typical middle-class man may belong to several kinds of narrowly defined organizations to accomplish what he wants for himself or his community; the modern African villager may belong to only one organization, but it is multipurpose and pervasive. To simply measure the number of memberships (that is, to practice typical modern empirical survey research) is to ignore major historical realities. In application of this criterion, then, attention will be given to both distinctions and to the significance of each. The importance of this distinction must be stressed. The criterion suggested by Smith leads to evaluation of the importance of voluntary organizations by the number of memberships; the alternative leads to evaluation of the importance of the organizations themselves, and to equate the two is to obscure a major part of the data.

Smith labels the third criterion "the collective action orientation" of the members of the communication network.[35] Voluntary action prevalence will be greater for increases in at least four important elements of collective action orientation: (1) the degree of permission of collectivities by the larger social system; (2) the degree of instigation of collectivities with the communication network; (3) the average resources of collective action of individuals of the network; (4) the net payoffs for collective action to individuals of the network.[36]

The "degree of permission" is another term for freedom of association, a major issue in Roman and Anglo-Saxon political philosophies and in the constitution of the United States of America. The issue takes two forms: civil liberties and civil rights. Civil liberties concern the right to the different, civil rights concern the right to be the same. Both are necessary in a functioning democracy. But again, the terminology of the approach seems to orient us to modern materials. Both "civil liberties" and "civil rights" fail to suggest the social structure of primitive societies in which there is no state that is the ultimate authority for citizens. "Permission" implies an independent authority, and that of course is only one way that humans regulate their relationships.

Smith's way of putting the problem of permission highlights a crucial issue in the analysis of voluntary associations, that which Keith Warner calls their "secondary nature."[37] The problem is this: how can something that is so important historically be secondary sociologically? The paradox might be cavalierly dismissed by noting the necessary but not sufficient nature of associations, but this is not enough. Voluntary associations are secondary in that they may usually be crushed by power (e.g., Nazi Germany), bypassed by efficient administrative staffs, or modified into nonvoluntary associations by numerous means. In another sense, however, they are not secondary, because healthy democracies have all proved to need them, and this study will show in addition that many other kinds of societies also find them indispensable. It seems to be the case that modern societies need some sensible balance and some significant relation between voluntary and nonvoluntary associations. Just what this balance might be is a matter for political philosophers. Smith is talking about existence and prevalence, and he has correctly isolated "permission" as a criterion. But so great is our (and the author's) commitment to freedom of association, that analytical isolation of part of the concept of freedom of association seems alien. He is talking about freedom, and freedom is assumed as a basic right, not a grant of permission. We would rather die for it in front of the enemy than define it in front of our friends. In one sense, *voluntary associations* (in nations that vote) *permit rule,* since voting research reveals that members are more often voters, and voluntary associations are also instrumental in formulating issues, evaluating candidates, and supporting the value of political participation.

"Instigation" of collectivities refers to the tendency and ability of individuals and organizations to form more—the voluntarism virility variable. "Resources for collective action" include "persons' facilitative cognitions (perceptions, beliefs), motivations, affections (sentiments, feelings), their facilitative capacities and skills, the time available to them, and the financial and material resources they have available."[38] These are very closely interrelated. There is a practical difficulty in using these variables in this research, since they involve different levels of analysis, some being personal subjective factors and others being social system qualities or resources. A full model, as Smith implies, would be quite intricate and is premature, since a great deal of research needs to be done before the variables can be made operational. In other works, I have treated similar problems as purely structural matters.[39] In the structural method, use is made in research of the idea that personal characteristics and resources are themselves caused by or developed through individuals' membership in other collectivities or systems. In historical research, we will more often be able to find out about such structural issues as a typical voluntary association member's other system affiliations, than about his subjective dispositions. On the whole, the matter of instigation will necessarily be slighted.

"Payoffs," or its less barbaric equivalent, rewards, are "what an FVO can do that individuals alone or informally organized could not do, together with the disadvantages such collective action incurs for its participants."[40] The idea of rewards is a crucial variable in the exchange theory of organizations. A recent anthology of voluntary associations uses this idea of organizing the research of many authors.[41] The concept obviously presents some practical difficulties here, by contrast with its use in analysis of nonvoluntary associations where some idea of reward might be obtained in more easily calculable measures such as money or some formal indication of power. One useful way of getting around this difficulty of measuring voluntary action rewards is to estimate opportunity costs, or the financial or material value of things one might have done instead of volunteering. Again, the idea is one that is better adapted to research in modern societies that provide for rational calculation of human effort than in earlier civilizations that did not. As noted before, research in voluntarism brings the need to account for subjective satisfactions, which must in cases of bygone times be estimated indirectly.

In the chapters that follow, inquiry into existence and prevalence will be the starting point in each analysis. The inquiry will be conducted with the definition and the model that have been proposed as a basis of analysis. It is obvious from the outset that the study of a number of societies using the elements of the model (volume, permanence, connectivity, differentiation of goals and interests, permission, instigation, resources, payoffs) and the two-part definition (with specified assumptions) would result in a very complex presentation, and probably tiresome reading as well. It is perhaps of greater importance to recognize that it is claiming too much to call the thing Smith has proposed a "model," when it only specifies a number of conditions and not the dynamic relations that are necessary among them. The identification above of a number of nonlinear elements in the relation between existence and prevalence makes this clear. He has identified and defined some of the important variables, but there has not been sufficient research to develop process models from them. The use he makes of his proposals was not that of a model but of sets of hypotheses of two or more colinear terms that appear to be valid when tested on modern international samples and with tolerant probability levels. Since the "model" itself was found to be ambiguous on several counts, and since the samples to be used here differ from Smith's, what use is to be made of it?

The elements will be used as a provisional model, to be applied to a series of case studies. The concrete historical situations under which voluntary associations occurred will be used to change the provisional model into a more precise one in Chapter 6. In those societies that had a high magnitude of prevalence, an attempt will be made to show how voluntary associations actually functioned; that is, how the more fugitive variables like instigation, sentiments, and so on, operated in the historical situation. To complete the analysis, some societies will be analyzed in which there were few or no voluntary associations. Several examples are available in a single society in which the organizations were terminated abruptly (Rome at the start of the empire; England *ca.* 1550) or stimulated suddenly (England under William I), and these add interesting diachronic evidence of the same phenomena.

### The Methods of the Study

Since the study is concerned with expansion of the field of voluntary association research, it is helpful to identify the reasons why the focus has previously been too narrow and to stipulate what is necessary to correct this deficiency. Some of the issues have been identified above. They may be summarized by simply noting that the study of voluntary associations has been concentrated in the United States (followed by Great Britain) and that the biases of the topic are those of American sociology itself. Two of these biases will concern us here. The first is that American sociologists have not been, like their European counterparts, forced to take account of other nations, languages, and cultures. Foreign languages are required of some American graduate students, who, however, rarely learn to use them adequately. American sociologists have simply not often taken other societies seriously, and this is particularly evident in voluntary association research. The British have studied Great Britain and the African colonies or former colonies.

The second issue is that historical sociology is given lip service in publications and graduate curricula, but it is likely taken to be irrelevant or simply a ritualistic matter of exquisite torture of graduate students to learn something about the European origins of the discipline. Americans generally lack a sense of history, perhaps because the present is so good and the future has always seemed so bright. At any rate, historical sociology is usually dismissed with only a passing genuflection to Max Weber or Karl Marx. Historical sociologists have extraordinary difficulty in getting their work published and recognized in the academic community.

The writer is a product of the American system, and therefore it has seemed desirable to be rather formal and methodical, both in my requirements of myself as a scholar venturing into strange territory, and in regard to a field that in itself has few guidelines and checkpoints.

The first of these formalities was mentioned previously: the methodological study "Interdisciplinary Search on Voluntary Associations," which is included as an appendix. The purpose of the methodological study was to make an analysis of the nature of the sources involved in the process of information retrieval, by a scholar from one discipline working in several others. This was necessary simply because the social organization of the modern university leads to parochial isolation of departments and disciplines, and hence vocabularies of the literature of each field become specialized and it is rather common to overlook important material. In order to stimulate further work along these lines, a special annotated bibliography is adjoined to the appendix.

The second methodological problem resembles the first. Once a decision is made to investigate voluntary associations in some society, say ancient Rome, one becomes aware that the people who did the original reporting or investigation had interests or biases not only of an academic discipline or even a nation, but of a certain era as well. For example, the late nineteenth century was a time of great concern about English gilds and the voluntary associations from which they had emerged; neither before nor since has there been such concern about the topic. Therefore most of the material that is accessible about gilds is heavily laden with the ideologies of the era, prominent among them British Liberalism and Guild Socialism. To carry the national example farther, it is hard to believe that the mass of English workingmen had no formal organizations for social purposes between the start of the morbidity of the gilds in the late sixteenth century and the nineteenth-century workingmen's clubs. But that is the conclusion one would reach from the major sources in clubs and gilds. There were in the literature some condescending clues that there existed a large number of workingmen's copies of upper-class organizations, but they were too trivial to be concerned with. So extreme were these biases that unless the researcher proceeds with a formal list of things to look for by means of secondary and often obscure evidence, a negative report would be made where none was due.

A similar bias, though not assignable to any nation or era, is concerned with ideological disinterest in certain kinds of activity. Ideological disinterest is the opposite side of the coin of ideological interest. If a way of seeing is a way of not seeing, as philosophically minded psychologists have noted, a way of ideological thinking is a way of not thinking; that is, of deciding to ignore classes of value as if they were not-value. The example that has most frequently come to light here is that regarding leisure activities. Games and sports were typical of all of the societies with which the study is concerned. Intense search has not revealed the existence of academic concern with the formal organizations that are constantly implied, and that must have been necessary, for the events that are mentioned to have taken place. The associational aspects of drama and music present problems of this sort. Most modern musicology is concerned with individuality of the composer and, to a lesser extent, the performer and listener. Nevertheless, some of the things that were done must have been organized by voluntary associations of some formal collectivity. Another bias has been that of religion. Protestant writers typically ignore sociological aspects of Catholic religious orders and monastic establishments. Jews are easily overlooked in analysis of medieval gilds because the necessary documents are to be found under Jewish library classification and not under sociological listings.

The biases of anthropological research are of yet another kind. Until recently, the field worker simply ignored associations, in favor of investigation of kin, which came forceably to attention since it was different from the culture of the researcher. A recent review of anthropological contributions to research on voluntary associations began with "materials written as early as 1949."[42] The studies existed in the libraries, nevertheless, but filed under other names such as club, sodality, society, or indigenous vocabularies.

It can only be hoped that these biases have been dealt with adequately, but yet not overcompensated. At the least, the more extreme ones have been recognized and identified. Much remains to be done; it can only be hoped this is a satisfactory beginning. The net result of this study will obviously be recognition that the voluntary association has been greatly underestimated in most previous societies.

Where direct records were lacking, the research was carried out by means of accumulated knowledge about the culture. Some seemingly unlikely specialties were used, such as theater costume, compilations of street cries, tavern signs, folklore collections, architectural studies, drama and literature, biography, and visits to some of the relevant areas in England. By contrast, social histories of the specific societies were significantly lacking in utility.

Proving something by the absence of data is not one of the accepted methods of scholarship. There are risks of that sort here. The result, no doubt, is to err as to the associational life of those people who were not literate or very visible, and whom no one at the time thought worth attention. Where such issues can be identified, the suitable notation has been made and perhaps better methods will be devised in the future.

The societies are presented in roughly the order of amount of literature about them, least first, most last. This is accidental and has no theoretical relevance. This makes it possible to acquaint the reader with the general nature of relatively simple voluntary associations before introducing a great deal of detail. Because of the extreme variation in the quality of the sources, it has been deemed advisable not to take up the topics in a rigidly systematic nature, resulting in endless null entries. The reasons for the choices will, it is hoped, be evident from the text itself.

## Notes

1. Constance Smith and Anne Freedman, *Voluntary Associations* (Cambridge, Mass.: Harvard University Press, 1972), pp. 1-23; Bartolomeo Palisi, "A Critical Analysis of the Voluntary Association Concept," in David

H. Smith, Richard D. Reddy, and Burt R. Baldwin, eds., *Voluntary Action Research: 1972* (Lexington, Mass.: Lexington Books, 1972), pp. 39-50; W. Keith Warner, "Major Conceptual Elements of Voluntary Associations," in Smith, Reddy, and Baldwin, *Voluntary Action Research: 1972*, pp. 71-80.

2. A recent edition of Lexington Books' annual series on voluntary action research is devoted to a review of voluntarism around the world. David H. Smith, ed., *Voluntary Action Research: 1974* (Lexington, Mass.: Lexington Books, 1974).

3. The difficulty of evaluative research may be seen in the problems encountered in political science studies of pluralism, which have frequently ended in theoretical rather than empirical disputes.

4. David Sills, "Voluntary Associations: Sociological Aspects," in David Sills, ed., *International Encyclopedia of the Social Sciences*, 17 vols. (New York: Macmillan Company and The Free Press, 1968), Vol. 16, pp. 362-79.

5. Smith and Freedman, *Voluntary Associations.*

6. The series began in 1972 and has appeared each year, published by Lexington Books, Lexington, Mass.

7. Samuel Johnson, *A Dictionary of the English Language*, 2 vols. (London: W. Strahan, 1755), no pagination.

8. Denys Forrest, *The Oriental: Life Story of a West End Club* (London: B. T. Batsford, 1968), p. 119.

9. Ibid.

10. Warner, "Major Conceptual Elements of Voluntary Associations," approaches the problem in germane fashion with a review of common meanings or characteristics attributed to voluntary associations in research literature.

11. A similar comment is made by James Luther Adams, "Foreword," in Smith, Reddy, and Baldwin, *Voluntary Action Research: 1972*, pp. xiii-xvi.

12. A discussion of similar issues is contained in Jerry G. Bode, "The Voluntary Association Concept in Twentieth Century American Sociology," in Smith, Reddy, and Baldwin, *Voluntary Action Research: 1972*, pp. 53-56.

13. Smith and Freedman, *Voluntary Associations*, p. viii.

14. Smith, Reddy, and Baldwin, *Voluntary Action Research: 1972*, pp. 175-76.

15. Sherwood Fox, cited in Smith and Freedman, *Voluntary Associations*, p.3.

16. Bronislaw Malinowski, *Argonauts of the Western Pacific* (New York: E. P. Dutton and Co., 1961).

17. Arnold Rose, *Theory and Methods in the Social Sciences* (Minneapolis: University of Minnesota Press, 1954;, p. 51.

18. Ibid., p. 52.

19. Smith, Reddy, and Baldwin, *Voluntary Action Research: 1972*, p. 197.

20. Ibid.

21. Ibid.

22. Amitai Etzioni, *A Comparative Analysis of Complex Organizations* (New York: The Free Press, 1961), p. xi; Talcott Parsons, *Structure and Process in Modern Societies* (Glencoe, Ill.: The Free Press, 1960), p. 17.

23. This kind of definitional strategy is used in Paul E. White, "Resources as Determinants of Organizational Behavior," *Administrative Science Quarterly* 19 (September 1974): 366-79.

24. Smith, Reddy, and Baldwin, *Voluntary Action Research: 1972*, p. 176.

25. The idea of voluntarism, as we know it today, is essentially a contribution of humanism, and less than half of our study is based on eras in which the concept was known or significant. The problem can easily be exaggerated, however. I contend that the basic issue so far as membership is concerned, is the ability of the individual in the concrete situation to make an assignment of self to a collectivity, and this was conceivable, if not practical, at all times. Rose excludes gilds, knightly orders, and other collectivities of the Middle Ages as voluntary associations on the grounds that they were at once "a community, governmental unit, and a religious unit." Rose, *Theory and Methods in the Social Sciences*, p. 52n. We agree on their nature and their significance, but I see this as a remarkable aspect of the variations to which voluntarism may be put, and Rose saw it as a definitional matter. The problem of the freedom of will in the Middle Ages will be dealt with in detail.

26. Smith, Reddy, and Baldwin, *Voluntary Action Research: 1972*, p. 168.

27. Ibid., p. 174.

28. Ibid., p. 167.

29. Georg Simmel, *The Sociology of Georg Simmel*, trans. and ed. Kurt H. Wolff (Glencoe, Ill.: The Free Press, 1950), pp. 100n-101n, 392-95. Simmel's treatment of the way that altruism creates indebtedness that cannot be repaid is a stimulating cue for further theoretical development.

30. David H. Smith, "Modernization and the Emergence of Volunteer Organizations," in David H. Smith, ed., *Voluntary Action Research: 1973*, (Lexington, Mass.: Lexington Books, 1973), pp. 49-73.

31. Ibid., p. 59.

32. Ibid., p. 58.

33. Ibid.

34. Ibid.

35. Ibid., p. 59.

36. Ibid.

37. Warner, "Major Conceptual Elements of Voluntary Associations," p. 73.

38. Smith, "Modernization and the Emergence of Volunteer Organizations," p. 59.

39. Jack C. Ross and Raymond H. Wheeler, "Structural Sources of Threat to Negro Membership in Voluntary Associations in a Southern City," *Social Forces* 45 (June 1967): 583-86; Jack C. Ross, "Toward a Reconstruction of Voluntary Association Theory," *British Journal of Sociology* 23 (March 1972): 20-32.

40. Smith, "Modernization and the Emergence of Volunteer Organizations," p. 59.

41. John N. Edwards and Alan Booth, *Social Participation in Urban Society* (Cambridge, Mass.: Schenkman Publishing Company, 1973).

42. James Nwannukwu Kerri, "Anthropological Studies of Voluntary Associations and Voluntary Action: A Review," *Journal of Voluntary Action Research* 3 (January 1974): 10.

# 2 *Primitive societies*

In this chapter the model presented in Chapter 1 will be used to analyze the nature of voluntary associations in a representative set of primitive societies. The societies chosen are arranged in order of increasing complexity, starting with band, then tribe, chiefdom, primitive state, and peasant village. A single society will be first described in detail in each case, followed by discussion of variations in similar societies.

The continuum of complexity is one used by Elman Service.[1] By complexity, Service means "more parts to the whole, more differentiation or specialization of these parts, and firmer integration of these parts to the whole."[2] He sees complexity as a correlate of increasing economic productivity. Productivity, however, obviously does not mean the same thing as availability of goods for consumption, since the peasants whom Service sees as having the mostcomplex society among primitives are known for the prevalence of starvation. The differentiation that makes high productivity possible also makes possible separation of production from consumption rights. In societies of great complexity, we will, therefore, give attention to differentiation in political and other institutional realms as well.

Other bases of classification could have been selected. In particular, the variables of the model itself are obvious choices. The complexity continuum has the advantage that it utilizes societal types that are well established in anthropological literature. No single-variable classification of societies is wholly satisfactory, since there are so many variables to choose from, each of which highlights only one feature of interest and subordinates others that may be significant. The complexity criterion has two things to be said for it in relation to this study: it encompasses more of the variables in the model than any other choice, and it has frequently been used in previous research as an explanation of voluntary association existence. Therefore, by using the typology of complexity, we may at the same time test the complexity thesis and tie the use of the model to existing literature in anthropology.

The complexity theme was stated as an hypothesis by Banton: "Voluntary associations become more common and significant as societies advance in technology, complexity, and scale."[3] S. M. Lipset has made a similar argument in several publications,[4] though he has been more oriented to the functions of voluntary associations in the growth of political democracy, a theme that may be traced to the Tocqueville tradition in American political and social thought. A preliminary test of the complexity thesis may be made here in passing, before turning to details: neither the authoritarian primitive state nor the peasant village in the modern state, the two highest in the complexity scale, typically have many voluntary associations, the first because of lack of permission, and the second for similar and additional reasons. To be fair to the cited authors, their arguments would have to be taken up in detail; obviously, however, a simplistic complexity-voluntarism correlation is insufficient.

### Ascribed Associations in the Primitive Band

We begin analysis with a baseline study of societies of least com-plexity, with the objective of explaining the *absence* of voluntary associations. The primitive bands, though they had special orderly arrangements for purposes of religion, hunting, or war, never formalized them into permanent organizations, nor did they ever develop a normative value of voluntarism. The absence of a social phenomenon, of course, involves speculation rather than proof. What is lacking? What activities or goals that are pursued in more complex societies by means of voluntary associations are lacking or reached by other means? The description of the primitive band also allows illustration of some of the abstract definitions from the first chapter. Obviously, the significance of this section is not manifest until the more complex examples are analyzed—we shall, therefore, not tarry long here.

The small size of bands is due to location in places in which sustenance is obtained by hunting and gathering over large territories in which food is relatively scarce. Bands are found in deserts (such as with the nineteenth-century Central Australians to be depicted here), the arctic, the southern tip of South America, and various other places where climate or lack of materials inhibits development.

The Arunta (also spelled Aranta) of Central Australia inhabited a vast arid area characterized by high temperatures in the day and cold nights.[5] Rainfall is seasonal, resulting in rapid growth of vegetation followed by long dry periods. Availability of game was likewise erratic. The Arunta lived on a variety of plants, animals, birds, rodents, and often encountered long periods of famine interspersed with occasional periods of surplus. They developed no means of food storage and had little variety in preparation. As a consequence of these features of sustenance, climate, and terrain, their economic system was oriented to immediate consumption. They did not develop a rational or authoritarian hierarchical system of food distribution through chiefs or functionaries. Direct giving and receiving of food and other gifts was customary and done with little ceremony or display. The economy, therefore, may be classified as partially voluntaristic but not associational.

Marriage was band exogamous, virilocal, and the descent sytem was patrilineal. Cross-cousin marriage was preferred.

The Arunta did not have a chieftainship or system of central authority. Attempted control over frequent feuds was exerted through kinship obligations, intense concern for etiquette, consultation or advice of elders, sorcery, and through the secret society of the totem.

The totem was an animal or other typical food object of the area of residence. The totem center was located in this territory. In the Arunta totem center (a guarded shelter) were kept the fetishes (*churinga*) of each individual, usually in the form of a bullroarer that was used to frighten noninitiates.

The secret society of the totem was the principal formal organization or association of the Arunta. All adult males of the band were members, provided they had successfully undergone the ordeals of membership—it would be stretching the definition to call it a voluntary association.

These ordeals were four in number and involved instruction and torturous tests. The first test began at puberty, and the last occurred in adulthood. Organizational secrecy was kept, and violators, even accidental, might be killed instantly.

Further socialization to membership was provided by means of the use of a secret name that each child was assigned at birth but which was not revealed to him until he had passed his last test of fitness.

A priest provided leadership of the totem center. He presided at ceremonies and feasts and was typically the most important member of that community, which otherwise had no ranking system by occupation.

The totem society was central in other ways. It exerted some economic control through organization of the feasts that celebrated adulthood. These feasts sometimes lasted several months, and hence the totem society became a key to the regulation of the economy and norms about sharing.

Hoebel says of the Central Australian "tribes" (a word he used to include bands) that "the initiated married men form a domineering, tightly knit group, possessed of much secret lore and enjoying many lordly privileges all of which indicates without doubt that here we have a true tribal association."[6] By "tribal association" Hoebel refers to associations or fraternities that "include all the adult men of a society. The adjective *tribal* serves to distinguish them from the more limited type of associations that are open to only a privileged few."[7]

The meaning of the statement can be made more clear by posing a hypothetical alternative. Among the Arunta there were many totem secret societies, as many as bands. If the Arunta people *as a whole* were considered as a society, then the *society* had many associations and proportionately more adults were members than, say, U.S. males in lodges and fraternities. However, since an Arunta was born to a specific band totem, that of his father, he had no choice between associations and so the idea of voluntarism was meaningless. His only choice, and the one seldom taken, was to become a deviant or an outcast. The sources do not, in fact, say what happened to those who failed the tests; if there were a significant number and they were still members of the band, the concept of voluntary association would apply. Hence the criterion, mentioned earlier, of a plurality of choices is highlighted. The Arunta adult had no real plurality of choices, and the secret society cannot be called a voluntary association.

The Arunta had other types of organized activity, none of which took associational form. Military activities, mostly vengeance raids, were carried out by groups organized afresh for each venture in traditional mode. Work was a family function, divided along sex lines. Sorcery was an individual role and did not take organizational form.

Two factors stand out prominently regarding absence of voluntary associations. The harshness of the environment led to the necessity for extreme forms of dominance in social relationships and for immediate rather than deferred gratification. Permission for association could not exist, if the idea would occur, not so much because of lack of will to do so, but because in a dangerous environment there was little leeway for cultural options. This same harsh environment resulted in a lack of permanent abode—the wandering hunter-gatherer could not experience a sufficient volume of internal communication to establish the minimum social base for association formation. The one organization, the totem association, developed around the locale of things, not people, and was a means of control through religion, not the shared development of pluralistic options.

### The Tribe: Flourishing Voluntary Associations in Relatively Simple Societies

The tribe is next in the sequence of societal complexity. The Cheyenne of the Plains Indians will be used to illustrate the voluntary associations of tribes.[8] The Cheyenne were typical of the Indians of the Midwest Plains in their level of voluntary association activity:

not so involved in dancing clubs as the horticultural people they left
behind in Minnesota and Wisconsin in the seventeenth century, but
more active than the small tribes of hunters that preceded them to
the west. They seem, therefore, to be a representative case.

The Cheyenne are a people of the Algonkian language group.
During the eighteenth and nineteenth centuries, they had extensive
contacts with many other tribes of the Plains Indians of Algonkian,
Athabaskan, Caddoan, Kiowan, Siouan, and Uto-Axtecan language
groups and shared with them many features of culture and social
organization. Statements about the Cheyenne are generally appli-
cable to the other Algonkian: the Arapho, Gros Ventre, Blackfoot,
Cree, and Ojibwa.

The Cheyenne hunting economy was organized with a rigid division of labor along sex lines. The men ranged far in the search of
game, while the women did virtually all the work of the
encampment. At home, the men scorned all work and spent their
time in ceremonial activity, storytelling, and other activities that
supported their principal productive and military roles.

The weather and location of game dictated the immediate size of
the band and its hunting strategies. In the summer the entire tribe of
ten bands gathered for the organized hunt, particularly of buffalo,
and for extensive rituals and governmental meetings. Band exogamy
was practiced, and the summer meetings offered necessary
opportunities for marriage negotiations and the intricate gift
exchanges that marriage required. The long summer assemblies
created the high volume of per capita communication that is a
necessary (but not sufficient) cause of association formation.

The Cheyenne kinship system was based on bilateral descent and
uxorilocality. Marriage was forbidden to defined categories of
relatives in either descent group. The purpose of marriage was said to
be favorable enlargement of the circle of relatives. Since a man who
married moved to his wife's band, his acceptability as a hunter and
warrior there became a factor in the formal organization of those
activities into associations, and no doubt his reputation influenced
the marriage itself. It is perhaps premature to speculate on the
formulation of a general hypothesis about kinship and association
existence, since there are so many possible alternative arrangements

for association formation. If the Cheyenne had practiced virilocality, would it not be reasonable to assume that kin ties (father-son, or uncle-nephew) would be strong enough to be the basis for hunting and war activities, and no voluntary associations would be necessary? It is not wise to argue the functional necessity of hunting and war associations among the Cheyenne simply because they were uxorilocal, but it can be said that uxorilocality of mobile bands undoubtedly contributes to this end.

Contact between families of a child's father and mother was an important occasion. Fathers' families (that is, outsiders to the mother and child) had important parts to play in child-rearing rituals, many of which occurred during the summer tribal gatherings.

The summer gatherings of the units were also a time for solemn deliberations of the tribal council. This was a group of forty-four male members who served ten-year terms. They governed secular affairs of the tribe as a whole, though band business was also influenced by family authority and by military associations. Council decisions took effect through the personal influence and standing of the members; there was no government bureaucracy or police. The men of the military associations, however, took an active voluntary part in carrying out the decisions. Thus there were no voluntary associations unique to government, but membership in a military association implied a duty to the tribe itself.

The Cheyenne adopted the horse, which diffused northward from the early Spanish explorers far to the south, and the action apparently changed their whole way of life. The horse enabled them to vastly increase their efficiency as buffalo hunters, not only in the hunt itself, but in the increased range of the bands of the tribe in the search for living and hunting grounds. In other words, the horse allowed periods of assembly for social life, as well as for an adequate economy. The horse did the same for other tribes, and the eventual result was crowding of hunting territory, with greater frequency of contact with other tribes under conditions of competition. The Plains Indians, therefore, became more and more warlike in the century preceding the actual encroachment of white settlers in the same territory. It is not surprising, therefore, that among the principal organizations of the Cheyenne were the military associations that united the fighting men of the several bands. It cannot be determined if the associations existed before the introduction of horses, nor if they were as active before actual white settlement, but whatever their history, they were extremely active at the time of the first white records which date to the early nineteenth century. The six military associations had members in each of the ten bands. Among the Cheyenne, the associations were ungraded or unstratified, while among other Plains Indians there were definite hierarchies and a warrior could pass through each rank as he became qualified. Among the Cheyenne, Crow, Kiowa, Wind River Shoshone, the ungraded associations were open to all men. A man needed a sponsor to join, and when invited, he merely distributed gifts to the members. A man usually selected the unit to which his father (who was in another band) belonged, though he might do otherwise.

The Dog Soldiers assocation was an exception to these generalizations. The Dog Soldiers were all members of one band. This apparently began before 1850, when all male members of the Flexed Leg band joined the Dog Soldiers. This exception is very instructive for this analysis because it appears to be the start of an alternate form of social organization. If it had endured, it would have meant that tension would be created between the kin principle of organization and the military association principle, possibly resulting in change from tribal democracy to band autonomy under military government. Llewellyn and Hoebel comment in this regard,

> This extraordinary feature endowed the Dog Society with a unique cohesiveness and gave rise to a situation pregnant with great—but largely unrealized—possibilities of governmental formation. One main problem of theory, had the times been less disturbed, would lie in how such a unit could escape developing new and dominant governmental aspects.[9]

In the Dog Soldiers, too, there was the possibility of a new kind of warfare, perhaps a change to rational-legal from the traditional organization based on individual process, and certainly a change from voluntary association to association.

The integrative features of the military associations, other than the Dog Soldiers, became effective because uxorilocality and membership in the father's association led to a net of relationships in which each band was reciprocally obligated to men of all other bands and all other associations in a diffuse arrangement that lent stability and continuity. In this case, uxorilocality led to complexity, and thus relative complexity is, under these conditions, correlated with prevalence.

With this distribution of members, the military association could not easily be an army. When men of one band of the Cheyenne went to raid the horses of another tribe, or to seek vengeance, both of which they did rather frequently, they selected suitable companions on the basis of their ability and religious appropriateness, and there would not be an opportunity, usually, for the military association to gather as a unit.[10] Summer made for other opportunities. The summer was like the annual convention of the American Legion: they did not get together so much to go to war but to talk about what they did in the last one, to conduct a bit of business and to have one hell of a time. The summer might be war time, but its routine was the coordinated hunt, government, dancing, and ceremony.

Another reason that the military voluntary association was not a fighting unit lay in the meaning of fighting for the Cheyenne warrior. War for the Cheyenne was a loosely coordinated collection of individual exploits, not a rational venture with political-military goals. The highest objective of a warrior was to touch a live enemy—the scalp was proof that he had done it and a souvenir that allowed convincing coup counting.

Among the Cheyenne there were women's clubs that supported the men's military voluntary association—a sort of Legion Auxiliary. The most important association was the Quill Decorators. These women decorated robes with traditional or contemporary creative designs. The clubs were long-lived affairs, with the younger women initiated by the old into the time-honored ways of skilled work. The women's organizations were taken very seriously by the men, who gave them considerable deference. James Mooney, cited by Lowie, reports a large variety of Cheyenne women's craft clubs, each specializing in some particular skill, and requiring heavy entrance fees.[11] Mooney's contact was with the southern bands, and fees are not mentioned by other writers.

In addition to the integrative effects of the military associations between bands, the men's and women's voluntary associations had a custom that apparently was of significance in uniting men and women in bands. Each men's military voluntary association had four female functionaries. They played an integral part in ceremonies. They were picked for their beauty and could not marry while they held office, though they might resign to marry and frequently did so. Conversely, men had specific roles in the Quill Decorators. The club was private, but it provided for men to make contact through an intermediary male who was chosen by men for his bravery! His contact with the club during meetings was highly stylized and formal, and his deference to the club assured it of its place in the Cheyenne scheme of things. Thus, although there was no reason to assume that it was done intentionally, both men and women maintained the right to organize privately to assure their interests but still provided for a defined relationship with the opposite sex and for efficient communication with them. It is hard to imagine how a modern sociological consultant could have intentionally designed a better or more efficient communication structure. The Cheyenne culture stressed differentiation of men's and women's activities and had values of mutual support for the activity of each. Though it is nowhere recorded specifically in anthropological literature, the Cheyenne obviously had a custom or principle of freedom of association.

The predominant part played by the military association made it the basis for the development of two kinds of contranormative roles, which served the purpose of highlighting and defining the significance of militarism and the military voluntary association. The *contraries* were a small number of especially brave men. "As the name suggests, these men always do the opposite of what is said: that is, they say *no* when they mean *yes*, approach when asked to go away, and so on."[12] Being a contrary was seen by contraries as a burden that they would gladly surrender, but before they could do so, someone had to take their place.

The *berdache* provided another kind of contrast. These were transvestite males who were led by a validated vision to reject the military role and participation in military association. They donned women's clothing and took on many aspects of feminine roles. They were not, however, deviants in the morally pejorative sense to which we are now accustomed regarding homosexuality, since the vision, once validated, was not open to question.

In neither case did the role lead to associational form, though the contraries might in some cases act as a group. Both the contraries and the *berdache* were few in number in each band, perhaps too few to sustain voluntary associations even if they had felt reasons to organize them.

Dancing played a central part among the Cheyenne, as among all of the Plains Indians, and was especially important during the summer encampment. Much dancing was directly related to the activities of each military association. Dancing was not the special purpose of the military association, but only an integral activity. The Sun Dance, important to all Plains Indians, and later forbidden by the white man's law, was an activity of the whole tribe and not one of a military association or band.

Neither Cheyenne religion nor magic took independent organizational form. Individuals practiced religion and the medical-magical arts, and the shaman emerged as a specialist in the band. The most honored of the fetishes was the Medicine Hat, which was kept in a special lodge. The fetish lodge did not become a permanent temple with a membership, just as the Sun Dance lodge did not become a source of crystallization of a Sun Dance voluntary association. Spier, however, speaks of a "fraternity" of former sponsors of the Sun Dance, who shared control of a medicine bundle that was necessary in the dance.[13]

In the case of the Cheyenne, we see several examples of how multiplicity of goals, pursued through role differentiation, can lead to formation of associations or voluntary associations. Too few cases have been presented, however, to attempt a theory in this regard. It can be noted that each adult male had two principal occupational roles, which were closely related: the hunter, and the warrior. Only one, the warrior, led to formation of a voluntary association, which then took on added duties in the hunt. Among women, only one of their many activities led to voluntary association formation, that of decorator and sewer. To systematically ask why each of the other separable activities of males and females did not take voluntary association form would be an important theoretical exercise but shall not be attempted here. Certainly band size would be critical. Role and status differentiation led to the *possibility* of assocation and voluntary association formation, but not to their necessity.

Analysis is now turned to other tribes among the Plains Indians, in order to examine contrast and variations. The secret religious association of the bands (and primitive states to be examined later) were in strong contrast to the secular organizations of tribes. As Hoebel says, "purely secular organizations given to furthering nonmystic interests and not concerned with terrorizing women and children, have no compulsive need to surround themselves with secrecy. Such were the military and dancing clubs of the Plains Indians."[14] The Cheyenne military assocations were fairly representative of all Plains tribes except that in some Plains tribes the associations had formal age ranks rather than achieved prestige arrangements, or had whole associations for young boys. Clubs devoted solely to dancing (as formal voluntary associations) were more frequent among most other Plains Indians than among the Cheyenne. In all cases, military associations were at times concerned with dancing, but among the agricultural tribes like the Hidatsa and Mandan, clubs evolved that were centered almost exclusively on dancing. A basic difference was, of course, that cultivators had a more stable residence.

Age grading among tribes, as in the chiefdom and primitive state, was a basis of common interest and identity but did not by itself necessarily lead to an association. The age grading of the dancing clubs was not so much a matter of pure chronology. The age grades are similar to the analytical construct that demographers call a "cohort"—a set of people of specified similar age who are followed through their life cycle. The cohort is more, however, than an intellectual construct here. A local cohort of Plains Indian youth could either be united by experience of a compelling vision by a leading member that resulted in creation of a dance, or more typically, they purchased an established dance from the next older cohort, which then had to buy one from its elders. The meaning of the procedure can be seen by contrast with the American plan. Let us suppose that the Harding generation purchased the Charleston from the Woodrow Wilson people, who thereupon purchased the tango or the turkey trot from Teddy Roosevelt's bully chums, and so on. On the contrary, in North America, the youth tend to be inventors, not purchasers, of new dances, and tend to keep them, with associated language and romantic sentiments, as they age. The Plains Indians conceived of a dance as alienable property, owned either by a specific age set of a tribe or by a voluntary association, or in some cases by an entire tribe. The dancing associations would not have existed without the salience of cultural realism for all of the tribes. This may be seen in two senses. The Plains Indian concept of material property was casual or nominal—land did not belong to persons but had religious standing as a source of valuable things. Conversely, the spiritual was real, and one danced in order to partake of that reality. Dancing was not leisure or recreation, unless we wish to alter completely the conventional meanings of these terms. The dance could be property because it was spiritual and spirits were real. To return to our model, goal differentiation existed for groupings of the Plains Indians to a marked degree regarding religion, and therefore became the object of association formation, while goal differentiation in economic activity was rather slight. We experience something near the exact reverse, making the material real and the holy abstract. Voluntary associations may be adapted to either epistemological orientation; it is plain, however, that the epistemological assumptions of our daily lives are very different from those of the Plains Indians and that we would gain a great deal of understanding of our organizations by examining our philosophical roots more closely.

Among the Cheyenne, the voluntary nature of the associations is not in question, but among other Plains tribes the evidence is not so clear. As long as people who were qualified by identity had no choice but to join, there were no true voluntary associations. Information about degree of compulsion is confusing. Lowie gives an example of virtually compulsory advance from a children's to an adult club in the Kiowa, which had one child's club, four adult clubs that were about equal in standing, and one elite club of the best warriors. [15]

By contrast, Lowie's data on the Arikara tribe show latitude for choice. "Arikara organizations were neither arranged in an age series nor graded in any other way." [16] Most Arikara clubs were for dancing and charity, but some of the organizations were specifically military. The Arikara adults could join any of their dozen clubs at will or leave as desired, though being invited by members was preferred. Clubs competed for members and often tried to use compulsion to get individuals to change membership. Among the Iowa, a man joined as many clubs as he could afford. [17]

The Arikara case is particularly instructive for this study of voluntary associations and type of society, because it reveals the process of emergence of multiple voluntary associations at single status levels. The phenomenon is apparently the consequence of fusion in the Arikara at the time of their northward migration (*ca.* 1734 in one estimate) of two elements: the concept of the dance as alienable cultural property, and the idea of dance associations (not necessarily voluntary at that time) as age-grade strata from the Hidatsa and Mandan with whom they came in contact. The Arikara apparently adopted the multiple dances of the stratified Mandan and Hidatsa (as did others) but without their age grading. The result was an array of clubs with membership practices that would seem familiar to the modern American middle class. One different feature is the practice whereby an Arikara brave would give his wife to the head or sponsor of the club he wished to join as a part of his entrance fee.

It has been seen that dancing clubs and military associations were organized in such a way that they served (in conjunction with marriage customs) to integrate the several bands or villages or tribes. Integration here refers to reciprocal obligations between social units. We have also seen that the Plains Indians had relatively frequent contact between tribes or their messengers, both friendly and warlike, and considerable similarity of structure. Integration within tribes was accomplished in a variety of ways, but the military associations and dancing clubs seemed to have some part. They were organized in a wide variety of combinations ranging from the dual organizations of the Cheyenne (regular versus elite warriors, plus contraries), to the age-graded Mandan and Hidatsa, the egalitarian diffuseness of the Arikara, the preparatory youth, adult, and elite clubs of the Kiowa. To these should be added the dual system of the Pawnee, which was even more complex.[18]

The Pawnee were organized into four sets of tribes. The Skidi, the largest set, had an intricate arrangement of sacred medicine bundles that were the symbols of each village's separation and unity. The bundles were hostages, in a sense. A series of associations of chiefs and officials united the villages and governed them. The main voluntary associations were official; that is, they had a mandate to act for the whole society through custodianship of the medicine bundles. These organizations were differentiated into purely hunting, hunting and war, and war only. There were also a set of functionally specific organizations of medicine men or shamans that tended to make performances very competitive.[19] In addition to these official organizations, there were "private" voluntary associations, which were organized by ambitious individuals or leaders, and which tended to be short-lived.[20] These organizations tried to gain recognition by superior performance in a particular field of endeavor. Among them were Children of the Aruska, which was a voluntary association of contraries. Another such organization was devoted to mischief and picaresque escapades, justified by a phallic religious cultic practice. There were several other organizations highly committed to virtually suicidal bravery, and a women's society that parodied men's regalia and had torture of captives as a chief function. Although it is difficult to evaluate the quality of a form of social organization, the tension between official and unofficial organizations appears to have served the Pawnee well and helped make them a vigorous and prosperous tribe by Plains standards, though some members obviously paid a high price.

Another variation of the familiar basic elements was found among the Iowa.[21] The Iowa had a stratified society of hereditary chiefs, a parvenu nobility of virtuoso warriors, and a lower set of braves or commoners. Each stratum (the term is appropriate if "class" is conventionally reserved for an economic set) had its own voluntary associations that no other might enter.

The mode of organizational change among voluntary associations varied from tribe to tribe. There were tribal differences in whether the need to change led to preserving goals and changing members, or the reverse, as circumstances called for adaptation or invention. Where voluntary associations were official and their goal activity was important to survival, we might expect membership to be changed, if needed, to assure reaching important ends; where goals were vital only to members and not to larger collectivities, we might expect a wider range of variation. Military association leadership among the Cheyenne ordinarily was terminated as a warrior aged. But since the leader was chosen to die in battle and expected to, old age was unusual. The term of office was also loosely related to the expected ten-year service on the tribal council. But any time a man could no longer exert leadership, he was expected to give up office. By contrast, the contraries (a group in Cheyenne; a voluntary association in some other cases) actively sought their own replacements.

At the other end of the scale, the unofficial voluntary associations of the Pawnee more often sprang from the unique event that occurred to a charismatic leader or founder, and in this case the original membership was of greater importance. Any organization that is the result of the routinization of charisma encounters problems of adopting to change in leadership. Where age cohort was a criterion of membership, a short membership was often expected. Another dimension is seen in the women's societies, which more often involved lifelong membership and helped establish regular relationships in a separately articulated female prestige system. In the women's case, the goals appear to have remained the same and performances were quite stable over time, though full data are lacking.

Leadership of tribal voluntary associations was almost uniformly based on demonstrated ability to lead, which is less often a characteristic of groups in Western civilization. Only one example of systematic change of leadership was found. There was a routine leadership change among the Pawnee each year at the time of the first thunder in the spring.[22]

Most of the Plains Indians encountered seasonal variations of weather and food availability, which resulted in very different activity levels during the year. War was intermittent. Since voluntary associations played such a large part in meeting these problems, we would expect to find stress on the organizations to adapt. This adaptation took several forms. There might be specialization between organizations or within each one, though, as pointed out in Chapter 1, primitive societies as a whole, in contrast to modern industrial societies, tended to have relatively few kinds of organizations concerned with similar goals. Both patterns were encountered in degree, with no tribe following an extreme. Most voluntary associations combined dancing and war or hunting in some way. Some, as mentioned above, had voluntary associations devoted solely to dancing, which could be a year-round activity; some were devoted solely to hunting or war. Shamanism was usually an individual role, practiced as needed, but the Pawnee shamans had a sort of annual fair where tricks were competitively exhibited, and shamans were organized into a voluntary association resembling a gild.

Each tribe found it necessary for some military or hunting association to have superior authority during periodic marches and the hunts and at other times of danger or high stakes. These police or military elite functions (e.g., those of the Cheyenne Dog Soldiers) were never allowed to become despotic, and their opportunities for power were checked in some way by the tribe or council. As Wissler points out, "the performing of police duties by a society was an accidental association and . . . such a factor can scarcely be considered as contributory to the formation of a tribal system of societies."[23]

## The Chiefdom: A Roman Empire in Tropical Paradise

The chiefdom is described by Service as a society that has "reached a productivity which permitted large populations and a hierarchical form of centralized leadership."[24] This type, although found in other areas, is practically universal among South Pacific Melanesian and Polynesian groups. This kind of organization is apparently well adapted to the island environment featuring small land areas of residence, highly productive vegetation, adequate animal and virtually inexhaustible resources of fish, and the uneven distribution of some other materials that supports a high rate of trade between residential units. The ecology of the small island society is admirably suited to organizational centralization, since the food is necessarily centrally consumed but diffusely sought. Outside of some units in a few large land areas such as New Zealand and New Guinea, these societies all encountered the same geographically determined problem of social organization: a high rate of interaction within a residential group with a relatively fixed residence, coupled with the problem of regulation of relations between units by means of norms as to trade, religion, and political military dominance.

Throughout Polynesia and Melanesia, the economy typically took the form of production by a family or small territorial units of families, with centralized distribution through a chief who, in varying degrees, thereby amassed wealth and political-military power.[25] This relative similarity of culture and social structure makes possible some comments that are rather more general than in the previous cases and presents an interesting problem: Why do some of the island societies have many associations, some of which have voluntary aspects, and others almost none?

Tahiti, in the Society Islands, has been selected as a representative case.[26]

Goldman reviewed the historical and archaeological evidence and concluded that Tahiti was settled sometime prior to 950 A.D.[27] Thus the society was well developed when a Portuguese vessel under Quiros first made contact in 1606, followed by Wallis in 1767 and Cook in 1769.

Kinship was traced in the father's lineage, and in the mother's father's line. Some people were found by Ellis who could repeat their genealogies of nearly fifty generations *from memory*, which would take them back to about the time of first settlement. Lineage established social rank, with highest rank associated with an unbroken lineage of firstborn sons. Later in Tahitian history, firstborn females attained high standing. Similarly, rank within a family was based on ordinal priority. This family standing was held to be valid regarding relations between families—a firstborn son of one family had precedence over a second-born of another. Marriage rarely took place outside of rank. Kin groups were stratified in a permanent class system, which roughly corresponded to ranks of chiefs, sub-chiefs, and commoners. In addition, there was a category of people who were outclassed, including deviants, slaves, and miscellaneous others. The stratification system obviously bears comparison to the Hindu caste system, which will be examined in the next chapter—a society that also had few voluntary associations but for reasons that are different.

Economic production, consisting of care of pigs, cultivation of breadfruit, yams, and other tropical crops, was a family endeavor, with the help of magical specialists. Produce was partly consumed directly, but a major portion was given to the subchief or to the chief, who distributed it through feasts and other payments. Thus there was a highly integrated social and economic system, with three-class stratification, which was extremely cohesive and normative and permitted little or no mobility or deviation.

Power of the chiefs was made even more effective by negative religious sanctions controlled by the chiefs in hierarchical order. The basis of the sanction system was the *tabu*, which was a religious prohibition related to rank. Every object touched by a high-rank person was tabu to those of lesser rank. Religion was based on ancestor worship, and the major activities took place in an open family shrine where ancestors were buried. Polynesians believed in a generalized spiritual substance or power called *mana. Mana* was the spiritual quality of persons, related to their rank, and was poison to lesser persons. It is doubtful if such a reified idea of quality in persons would be possible if ranking systems in economics, religion, and the purely social realm were in any degree separable. The Tahitians, in sum, are a particularly forceful example of absence of the differentiation of goals and interests that the model of voluntary association existence and prevalence specifies, and consistent with the theory, there is little resembling voluntary association life. The contrast to the Arunta is startling—they had virtually no vertical hierarchy, and the Tahitians a very elaborate one.

This issue of lack of differentiation may be examined further in regard to activities common to every society, which are usually separately institutionalized. Occupation, for example, did not appear to be the basis of formal organization in Tahiti. The high level of craftsmanship found among Tahitians was accomplished with only a small number of specialists, who performed their tasks according to religious ritual, and therefore under royal dominance. Each major craft had a god and a family religious shrine. Some sources speak of a gildlike organization of craftsmen, but I can find no further information on the nature of these associations and must assume that the word "gild" was used in a careless manner that is typical of too many analyses. The gild, as we shall see later, depends wholly on the separate institutionalization of religion and economics and provides a meditating mechanism between the two. Religion and economics were too integrated in Tahiti for a true gild to develop. It may be, however, that there was a voluntary association of some sort in operation. It was probably minor if it existed at all.

Warfare was organized directly by the chiefs on each occasion, and all ablebodied persons took part in some way. It was informal rather than voluntaristic.

There was no real army, but merely a general societal mobilization. Neither were there any specialist military roles. Instead, there were heroes among the survivors, who best exemplified the courage and service to the king that were held in such high esteem.

Music, art, and athletics were avidly practiced but were apparently casually organized as group activities. Even wrestling matches, which attracted mass audiences of thousands, were traditionally organized and gave rise to no associations. Organization was always spontaneous and occurred only under royal guidance.

With such total organization of society, it is hard to imagine what added purpose voluntary associations could serve in economics, religion, or politics, regardless of whether they were permitted. It is unlikely, in any event, that the chief would have permitted any semblance of challenge to his divine authority that private associations might develop. His ability to destroy individuals or their property at will for the slightest infraction of tabus was virtually unchallenged, and except for an occasional instance of discussion with advisers, there was little potential source of opposition.

One association, however, did exist, and it was an organization of men (with a related women's branch) that provided, with the blessing of the king, an obscene and irreverent entertainment reversing sacred values. This group, the Ariori, was organized as a permanent traveling troup of performers. They took the God of War as their patron. The members were adults who were childless (except for the highest ranked member) and owned no property. In addition, they were usually youngest offspring and hence categorically and permanently low in rank, regardless of their lineage group. The arrival of the Ariori in the settlement was the occasion of a feast and a series of performances watched by large crowds in a sort of Mardi Gras atmosphere. Goldman identified the Ariori as "an agricultural fertility cult elaborating the familiar theme of sexual licentiousness."[28] The organization had a ranking system similar to that of the parent society, except that it was morally inverted. Higher rank was *achieved* by greatest skill in violating the important values, through play acting. Thus, in a society where ascribed rank was dominant and mobility rare, a source of achievement was offered in an alternative system under control of the chief.[29] The Romans themselves never did a more thorough job of bread and circuses.

Was the Ariori a voluntary association? Banton includes it as such in his analysis.[30] The most crucial doubt has to do with the fact that the role of the Ariori member was full-time (which does not necessarily disqualify it) and one from which the performer gained his sustenance, though from gifts and not from contractual services. There is no evidence that the performers were forced into the role, though their permanent low rank in the stratification system would provide an obvious incentive. It is hard to know from the available information how the individual Tahitian viewed his ordinal rank in a family: one can know that he has older siblings, but there is less certainty that one is the last (of a living mother) that will arrive, in a society noted for a high birthrate. The Tahitian's view of an occupation was not the same as ours, in which occupational and nonoccupational roles are clearly distinguished. The Ariori performers got the most significant part of their sustenance from the king, and so did everybody else. In this sense, voluntarism did not exist (regarding the vocation-avocation distinction). The example of the Ariori again highlights the need for specificity of the context of the definition. In this case there are no data to use in a decision.

In summary, Tahiti was a chiefdom in which there was minimal associational development. Attention is now turned to chiefdoms in which there was somewhat less authoritarian control, and more associations, some of which were voluntary.

The reasoning followed so far has stressed the relation between the economy and social organization. This is, however, not an argument based on economic determinism. Though the chiefdoms of Polynesia were similar ecologically, there were apparently alternate ways the food and material resources could be organized. Let us review some of the relationships between economy and organization in order to identify these alternatives.

As was found when the band was analyzed, where institutions concerning "mastery of nature" require constant emphasis, socialization to sex and age role performance is vital.[31] The more primitive the society, the more important the physical strength and skill of the males is for actual survival, and the more males typically dominate females and the young. The physical requirements and skills of hunting are similar to the skills of warfare, and use and control of weapons supports the institutionalization of male dominance. Some of the ways this dominance is socially carried out are through male control of assiciational religion by means of secrecy, control of defini-tion of what is sacred, and monopoly of access to sacred objects, coupled with the use of violence to punish deviation. Under such circumstances, we would certainly not expect to find existence of associations to promote women's interests,[32] and youth interest associations only as they pertain to socialization to adult male roles. In the more complex tribes and chiefdoms, where mastery of nature is less problematic, age and sex principles of associational formation are still important, but with a growing elaboration and variety of arrangements, and some participation or representation is permitted to women. Age and sex are still the basis of the strongest cleavages in social structure, but since other means of control over these matters are well established, some variety is possible and we find clubs that are concerned with dancing, ritual, religion or ghosts, and just sociability, and that have greater freedom of association.

This reasoning is consistent with the complexity thesis presented above. But it has already been seen that one chiefdom, obviously higher in productivity than the tribe and wanting nothing by way of subsistence, nevertheless had little association activity. Why the failure? It was suggested that the integration of the society under absolute rule prohibited such development. Then do associations develop in the chiefdom when power is shared?

The answer is that where royal dominance is limited, diffuse male dominance seems to take over. In the chiefdom, these institutions of male dominance are often implemented by use of a separate house or reserved place in a general communal lodge, and these may become headquarters for voluntary associations. Eighty-seven of the primitive societies mentioned by Codrington[33] and Webster[34] had men's houses of some sort. Thirty-three of these were primarily bachelor houses for residential purposes, or bachelor houses combined with some other function. Five of the bachelor houses were also guest houses. In some cases, married men also slept in the bachelor house. The bachelor house was a political club or center for community decision-making. Such quarters were not often shared by younger men, who were usually excluded from decision-making. Among the Naga of Assam, the Mois of Siam, and several tribes of Anam and Cambodia, a compromise was reached by use of a bachelor house, with an open platform nearby where older men sat to discuss affairs.

Among the more stratified chiefdoms typical of Polynesia, the council house was the location of solemn deliberations of the nobility, which in some cases included women. Where men's clubs were age-graded, compartments for separate groupings were sometimes made within dwellings.

In this sample of eighty-seven societies, in only one case, the Batak of Sumatra, was the men's house shared by the women who formed an autonomous group. Formal or clandestine visits by women to bachelor houses are another matter. This appeared in many cases.

The correlation of secrecy with the use of a clubhouse is far from complete. Secrecy required physical barriers, and where no edifice was devoted entirely to their use, the secret associations shared one or made use of controlled-access territories. This applies to bands as well.

One of the most consistently encountered mechanisms of secret organizations among chiefdoms and bands was the use of a noise-making device, either the bullroarer (a flat stick or stone swung rapidly on a string) or a stiff stick scraped on a rough surface. The scenario consists of a barrier penetrable by audio but not visual communication, privileged access to the enclosure, and training to interpretation of the sounds as divine manifestations. Attempts to penetrate the secret area were punished severely, often by instant death. So complete was the socialization of youth and women to the set of meanings associated with the secrets of the associations, that even when bullroarer devices were readily visible, they were not perceived. Similarly, people from other chiefdoms who frequently visited each other treated the visibility of the sacred objects very differently—what was "seen" one place was not in another, by the same persons.

Other uses to which the clubhouse was put also show that it was a convenience, rather than a necessity for secret organizations. The house was frequently used for puberty rituals or isolation of male youth from female. It was often the place where men stayed or cooked their meals when their wives were ritually impure and sex or even social contact was forbidden. It might serve as a repository of skulls or relics of enemy victims, or as a storage place of trophies of hunts.

In general, the clubhouse in its several forms was a wholly male affair and usually closely related to control over decisions by means of secrecy and exclusive control of religion. Although the data are not completely satisfactory, it seems safe to conclude that the clubhouse was rarely the premises of a strictly voluntary association, not so much because the clubhouse was incompatible with the voluntary association but because the club so often occurred in a chiefdom in which the chief did not tolerate voluntary associations. There were, however, some cases in which a voluntary association of a sort existed, particularly where the guest quarters were regularly used by outsiders or where several clubhouses were accessible to men who, therefore, had a choice. Banton includes the Banks Islanders among the Melanesians having voluntary associations. In this case, there were both "secular and . . . ceremonial" organizations.[35]

In summary, the chiefdoms in which power was shared resulted in the distribution of that power among other males, typically through means of the clubhouse and related organizations that had only an occasional secondary voluntaristic aspect. The reasons why secret societies were rarely voluntaristic will be considered again in the next section on the primitive state, and also when peasant societies are analyzed.

## The Primitive State: Mixed Evidence on Voluntarism

The primitive state is higher than the chiefdom in the scale of complexity. It differs from the chiefdom in its larger territory of dominance and because of the means of control necessary to achieve that dominance. These means typically include a state bureaucracy or other mode of central administration, plus a military force, under central control.

The word "primitive" seems also inappropriate when used to describe some of the states that will be used as examples. Many reached a high level of culture, as exemplified in surviving archaeological artifacts. The societies involved are those in which the people lived by hunting, limited agriculture, or husbandry, had a relatively simple technology, and in which literacy was limited or confined to elites. Residence was in relatively small villages and a few cities that grew as the result of commerce or as royal residences. The examples selected were in Africa. We begin with the historical context of political and economic growth, since it is in relation to these affairs that the voluntary associations of the primitive state must be explained.

Perhaps the single most significant source of state dominance of African peoples was the discovery of iron and its use to make tools and weapons. Hull says that on this basis, kingdoms began to appear at various places in sub-Saharan Africa around the start of the Christian era.[36] He suggests the date of 500 B.C. for the upper Nile, however. Some of these areas of dominance were relatively stable and isolated; some were used to expand into southern territories. Bantu expansion to the south may be dated at about 700 A.D. There was a powerful central government in the Katanga area in the eighth century. The

Sefawa dynasty of Bornu lasted for about one thousand years, starting in 846. About 1000, the Yoruba settled in West Africa and created the sacred city of Ile Ife with its myth of the sacred leader Oduduwa. The material culture of these earliest times suggests that there was a high level of skill in metalworking in small villages, and possibly the workmen were organized into gilds. Such gilds existed previously in several Mediterranean countries, and probably here as well. Not enough is known of these gilds to determine their voluntarism; certainly the gilds were small organizations in which organizing skills were learned along with cultural norms of obligation and authority, which are frequently accompanied in other societies with emergence of mutual aid and fraternal organization in general.

The Islamic dominance of the Mediterranean accompanied the growth of Islamic cities on the African shore, well before the reawakening of city life in Italy and the rest of Europe. Commerce across the Sahara existed throughout the eighth to eleventh centuries. Empires established during this era grew not only on the basis of local iron technology, but on trade as well, and cities grew up along the major trade routes south into central Africa as well as the east and west coast ports. Major empires are recorded in Mali (eleventh century) and Songhai (fifteenth century). The Songhai empire was complex and integrated more effectively than any existing in Europe at the same time, having provinces, governors, imperial mayors of cities, a central court, and a standing army. The empire of Gana (modern Ghana) grew wealthy on the taxation of trade. At its peak it is said that it could assemble an army of 200,000.

The trade that nourished the cities of the interior was of two major kinds. The first, persistent but of minor consequence, was the trade in manufactured salt from the coast to the interior. Other products moved along the same routes. Since salt was also mined in the interior, the coastal trade was never decisive.

The second kind of trade involved northward movement to the Mediterranean of slaves, gold, ivory, pepper, and other goods that could still bring a net return after the long trip. This trade may have existed for 1,500 years. The goods received in return by Africans in the interior cities were manufactured items, copper, and horses.

Based on this exchange, major cities grew at Kano, Bornu, Kanem, Timbuktu, Taghaza, and a host of minor cities and towns spaced throughout North Africa. Islam was spread along the same route.

It is not, however, safe to assume that the associational life necessary to sustain the organization of marketing must have been similar to that of large cities of like function elsewhere, and that there were, therefore, gilds in the market cities. There is ample evidence that the exchanges were oriented to accumulation of royal rather than merchant wealth, and this may mean that public markets did not necessarily result in a merchant stratum organized into gilds or other fraternal voluntary associations. Let us turn to the limited direct evidence.

The first good documentary source which has survived is the journal of Leo Africanus, which tells of the author's tour of central and west African kingdoms in the early sixteenth century. He found a great deal of wealth and vast royal stores of goods, indicating a high level of craftsmanship. He does not, however, directly record anything about gilds.

Whether or not there were gilds, this prosperity did not endure long. The first major blow was the military conquest by El Mansur of Morocco in 1591, which began the destruction of Sudanese empires. At about the same time, European traders began to arrive more and more frequently at west African ports, seeking slaves and luxury items such as spices or ivory and offering European goods in exchange. The process hastened the destruction of African empires in several ways. First, since slaves were typically acquired in war, the increase in price of slaves probably stimulated conflicts. In the eighteenth century, and particularly in the early nineteenth century, when American plantations greatly increased the market for slaves, the traders pressed the African empires for more and more human commerce, and then began direct raids. Second, the destruction of salt manufacture at the seacoast during slave raids disrupted inland trade. Slave traders gradually gave way to traders in other goods, and Europeans established in the port areas pressed growth of trade in European terms; this led eventually to the transformation to wage labor and a money economy. The final addition was the introduction of missionaries in the nineteenth century, seeking men's souls where traders had enslaved their bodies. The missionaries found mostly savages—the great early interior cities were almost gone.

The parallel with the fall of the Roman Empire is interesting. In both cases, the barbarians (what other word is so appropriate?) came to the heartland of the great civilization, destroying more by the imposition of their way of life and their destruction of rule than by the warfare that guaranteed their presence. And as in the Roman Empire, the remnants of the cities formed the eventual basis of new societies, drastically changed but surviving on the same ground. Kano, Timbuktu, Ibadan, Ile Ife were still there, but it was centuries before they again began to grow and prosper.

Most of the African empires of the colonial era were empires of indigenous military leaders who necessarily established virtually despotic rule over their territories. Voluntary associations that could become independent sources of power could not be tolerated under such circumstances. Such empires probably dominated markets as well and inhibited growth of the institutions of an independent merchant stratum. Military conquest was often an indirect product of European influence, as native leaders adopted military tactics from settlers and applied them to conflicts between native peoples. Conquests of this sort resulted in rapid consolidation of territory and imposition of new political forms from above. Existing age-set mutual aid organizations and tribal fraternities typically responded by going underground. The secret society is a product of this set of forces; it will be described in detail later.

There were, however, areas that had no despotic kings, either in the colonial era or before, and we might, therefore, expect a possible growth of voluntary associations. Hull says that the Abashieni of Kenya had an elected "great ruler" as early as the sixteenth century.[37] The Ibo had many tribes with democratic governments of assemblies of village males. "Commonly, African societies that did not experience sudden traumatic infusion of alien peoples continued to exist within an uncentralized political milieu."[38] Social control was based on common religion, tradition, secret societies, age sets, and kin relations. These, too, were primitive states, though the lack of centralization leaves some doubt about the use of the term.

The Karmathian brotherhood of Islamic nations was encountered by medieval Christian traders in the Mediterranean. Islamic doctrine has no place for secret societies, and the openness of the Karmathians to Christian members suggests that it was a flexible form of fraternal organization. Islamic villages in sub-Saharan Africa that were visited by early missionaries and then by anthropologists in the twentieth century, had strong fraternal organizations and gilds, which indicate that this organizational form was widespread. This intrusion of Islam must be considered as a positive force in permission and instigation of voluntarism. Modern craftsmen in Islamic villages of various tribes assume that their craft organizations are very ancient ones. These gilds have the usual ascriptive membership principle, the sons following their father's trade, and single gilds might be composed entirely of kin. However, certain aspects of voluntarism remained, such as purchased membership, leagues of gilds, affiliated voluntary mutual-aid activities, and so on. The gild in this instance seems to fit the definition of the quasi-voluntary association. It should be pointed out that the information on which this is based originates in the twentieth century, though there is little reason to doubt its applicability to previous centuries, since such arrangements apparently existed even before the Roman Empire.

To analyze the voluntary associations of a primitive state in detail in a single case, the Nupe have been chosen. The choice has several merits for the purpose of this study. It is the subject of one of the few thorough anthropological studies done on African kingdoms before World War II, in which voluntary associations were considered. The other major choice would be Herskovits's work on Dahomey, which is equally voluminous and also focuses on relevant topics—but is, in my judgment, an inferior work as far as organization study is concerned.[39] The major source on the Nupe is the work of Nadel, *A Black Byzantium.*[40] In addition to its excellence as anthropology, it has the added value of having become the point of reference for a number of subsequent works on the same area, in which voluntarism is also considered. Although the study is rather recent, compared to our previous analyses, there is evidence of considerable continuity with the past, and the label of primitive state seems to apply, even though the changes due to colonialism must be accounted for.

The Nupe resided in Nigeria, an area of ancient settlement. The age-grade association was the most important form of organization of the villages. Almost every adult and many children belonged to one, though there was no compulsion to do so. Failure to join was seen as a rather curious thing, since there were so many rewards from membership.

The voluntarism of the Nupe villager was consistent with a general support for individual choice. This freedom extended to the actions of the associations too, and the various villages freely developed many variations in style of organization.

The age-grade organization was called the *ena*. Most *ena* had specific age limits. Typical ones were 10-15, 15-20, and 20-30 years. A person might stay in an organization for varying lengths of time. The youngest *ena* in a community might be mimicked by a still younger group in play.

There were separate *ena* for males and females. The male *ena* contained both single and married men. Married women did not belong. The family system was loosely related to the age-grade organization. Parents did not intervene in affairs of younger *ena*, but might give material support for such events as festivals.

The *ena* was organized as a lifelong age cohort. The association was promoted to a higher rank as a unit, at a time selected by the village, usually fixed by the agricultural season.

Leadership in the *ena* was a source of prestige. The leader was usually better educated than the other members and possessed various perquisites. He was involved in all sorts of social and political contacts and negotiations. Leaders were free to pick their own titles, which they often did with a flare for publicity or for flattery of more prestigious people.

The *ena* tended to homogeneity of membership. Members were of similar social standing or reputation, and this was in part determined by the occupation of the member's family. Members also tended to be similar in political affiliation. In small villages there was only one *ena* to each age cohort; in towns there could be several, which served to further emphasize status distinctions.

The *ena* was a multiple-purpose organization. It served as a way of organizing many kinds of collective activities in a village. The *ena* also organized recreation: there were feasts, parties, naming ceremonies, weddings, and funerals. Dancing and music were always important, and the accomplishments of each *ena* in this regard was a thing of pride to them.

The *ena* of boys and girls were formally related. This relationship resulted in regulation of premarital sex and contact. The *ena* functioned to control behavior in regard to the activities mentioned above. The members could ostracize their fellows for misbehavior. The original songs and dances of each *ena* were often based on proverbs, or developed admonitions and advice.

*Ena* for females were limited to the youngest set. Girls dropped out when they married, at fifteen or sixteen years. The absence of *ena* for married women diminished women's influence—males thus had an organized voice in politics and public affairs, but women did not.

The Nupe were strongly committed to collective work. Though much of their collective work involved agriculture, it was not limited to it. Members of work organizations would cooperate in labor on houses, roads, public facilities, walls, ditches, and so on. The two systems of collective work were called *egbe* and *dzolo*. *Egbe* was general collective work of all kinds. It could be done through an *ena*, or through a spontaneous group for a single project. *Egbe* thus did not take voluntary association form directly, but was a festive occasion. A farmer whose land was being worked might provide a drummer and a flutist. He would furnish food and drink. Workers competed with each other to be known as the best workers. Farmers likewise competed for the title of best farmer—the *Sode*. Not all farmers could get *egbe* work done. Those who qualified were usually related by kinship in some way and were older men. The younger men did the work and hoped to qualify later in life for *egbe* work benefits. The *egbe* was thus a strong force in social integration, which could work well as long as there was little migration. When migration was high, because of urbanization or wage labor (e.g., mining), the system began to break down, and derivatively the *ena* began to change function.

The second form of collective labor was the *dzolo*. *Dzolo* work was intended to provide large amounts of labor during peak demand periods, such as harvests. There were no exchange devices, such as the music and feasts of the *egbe*. The *ena* were not involved. *Dzolo* work was simply another instance of the general cultural value given to collective activity.

Many nonagricultural occupations were organized into gilds. Membership was hereditary and certain families controlled the occupations for generations. The gild was very involved in the attempt to maintain its standing in the Nupe prestige system. The stakes were high because the gild represented multiple interests: family and kin, their typical occupation and its standing, social ranking in community life, ceremonial rectitude, and political affiliation. The political advantages were developed through systematic collaboration with gilds of the same occupation in other villages. The collective gilds negotiated their privileges directly with the king. This system differed from the medieval European one, which grew directly out of feudalism, and involved town gilds that individually negotiated locally with the king's agent, either the bailiff or the sheriff. The result of this European articulation to government, to be described later in detail, was that there was never a national gild system. The Nupe system seemed to offer a greater chance for eventual national economic power of local community workers.

The gild had certain voluntary features over and above the ascriptive membership rule. The members worked together in a common shop under leadership of a senior family member. They shared the cost of certain items of capital equipment such as a forge. There were various practices of cooperative work, depending on the occupation. Individuals worked for themselves, as entrepreneurs, in a collective environment. The head of the gild would pay taxes for individuals. There were numerous mutual-aid features. The Nupe gild seems to fit the concept of quasi-voluntary association.

Some occupations were not engilded. It is hard to see why they would not be, since they seem as economically well adapted to it as the others. In this category were tailors, embroiderers, leather workers, indigo dyers, hatmakers, mat and basket weavers. Perhaps it was simply an historical matter of the way the status sytem worked out—the gild workers were definitely higher in social standing than nongild workers, and occupations often derived their standing from religious or traditional importance. For example, grave diggers were high on the prestige ladder because of the importance of burial customs.

It was mentioned that some primitive states were relatively democratic, and some not. In contrast to the Nupe, obviously one of the former, were many in which all age-grade associations were ruthlessly suppressed because they represented potential opposition. The complexity thesis of voluntary association prevalence obviously is inadequate on the basis of this fact alone: primitive democratic states had voluntary associations, and primitive nondemocratic ones of similar complexity did not. To complete the presentation of the primitive state, an examination of such a nondemocratic society is necessary. Good materials are lacking, however. A brief summary may be made to at least indicate some of he issues involved.

African secret societies were—and still are—active in control of behavior that is beyond the easy reach of the law. Because the secret societies made certain kinds of social order possible, leaders were willing to accept them and even allow them some say in official matters. The *Ogboni* association of the Yoruba could punish certain criminal offenders.[41] The Poro of the Mende of Sierra Leone had the power to remove chiefs. Other secret societies were more simply functional in community life: they treated insanity, provided aid, regulated disputes, and so on.

It is obvious that the secret societies are an extension of the general sort of cooperative activity mentioned previously. What is it, then, that happens when the state becomes despotic? Evidence is scanty regarding the precolonial states, and much of what is known is derived from the contemporary activities of associations like the Mau-Mau, which became active in struggles for independence. It can be surmised that the secret society in the precolonial primitive despotic state acted as a political counterforce to preserve order among the people and to bring ulers to heel. The nineteenth-century rulers, for example, typically formally prohibited all societies, and then negotiated with them in private to gain their cooperation to keep power more easily.

The meaning of the secrecy of the fraternity is highlighted by the case of Dahomey, where the *gbe*, a fraternity, was permitted by a strong king but only with the stipulation that it not be secretive.[42] The *gbe* was a mutual-aid organization that regulated weddings, funerals, and engaged in social activities. The secrecy being absent, the organization was no longer totally an agency of male control and women belonged or organized similar sororities.

In functional terms, the secret societies provided an organized threat to strong leaders, in some senses as the always potent threat of the military revolt does in Africa today. The secret societies, however, always had a dual orientation; they aided the needy as well as punishing wrongdoers. The secret society, like the other voluntary associations of the primitive state, was still a citizen's interest organization, mediating the institutions of the community to solve problems that everyone shared.

It is not correct, then, to see "permission" as a one-sided affair, a grant by a ruler to organize. The secret society again illustrates the dual nature of "permission." The secret society permits the ruler to function, and he in turn facilitates their community activity and accomplishment.


## Peasants: Residual People

Service lists the peasantry in the modern state as the most complex kind of primitive society.[43]

The peasant village in the modern state presents an instructive negative example for analysis, though the reasons for the absence of voluntary associations are different from those of the chiefdom.

Anderson, writing about *preindustrial* states, says "peasants rarely formed voluntary associations of any kind."[44] Anderson's evidence is convincing. Even when more inclusive criteria are used so that isolated villages in *modern industrial* states are considered, voluntary associations are rare. Evidence to be presented in Chapter 3 about the numerous voluntary associations in ancient China may be considered an exception, depending on the definition of peasantry. The definition proves to be crucial, because there are instances of quite isolated rural people, not peasants, who do in fact have a high rate of voluntary association participation. The peasant is not just the end of some scale of a rural-urban continuum, but is a person who lives in and is part of a very specific kind of social organization that is decisive regarding nonparticipation. In contrast to the idea of the stable, population-exporting territory used here, Kirby views peasantry in the context of development toward modernization, and thus finds among them that "true voluntarism begins to develop on a broad scale in peasant societies, whether ancient or modern."[45] The key word is "begins." Following the orientation used here, the beginning is slight, and certainly in clearly peasant societies like those described by Redfield, there are no voluntary associations at all. How, then, does the social organization of peasantry inhibit voluntary associations?

Peasant villages or folk societies are "dependent parts of larger national states."[46] Robert Redfield, from whose work much of contemporary thinking about peasantry stems, says that "the investigator sees a small society that is not an isolate, that is not complete in itself, that bears not only a side- by-side relation but also an up-and-down relation to more primitive tribal peoples, on the one hand, and to towns and cities on the other."[47]

This characteristic of multirelatedness would at first glance seem to present a favorable condition for formation of voluntary associations among peasants. Chapple and Coon emphasize this aspect when they conclude that "whatever the other characteristics of an association, it is always formed at the point of tangency of several institutions, or of subsystems within an institution."[48] This point of view is certainly consistent with the complexity thesis, and the model of prevalence that forms the orientation of this study. Why then, if Chapple and Coon are right, do peasants typically not form voluntary associations to deal with their "points of tangency" of institutions?

First, peasants do not form voluntary associations because the need for a relation between institutions may be met in a variety of other ways, many of which are more favorable to the more powerful state. One means is the role of boundary management or relation between insiders and outsiders. In numerous studies we encounter the schoolteacher, doctor, merchant, priest, government agricultural agent, political party organizer, or even anthropologists as agent or patron.[49] The radio and newspapers, powerful agencies of relationships between social systems, are in the hands of outsiders and do not serve as points of crystallization for organizational efforts but only as one-way communication. Peasants thereby have their own development limited and their own control apparatus usurped by outsiders or those within with divided loyalties.

Second, peasants are almost wholly agricultural people with traditional or sacred rather than rational-legal land use orientation. They do not use land for capital. Typically, they market only a small portion of their produce and consume the rest or exchange it locally. The market is not crucial to them, or where it is significant it is in the hands of outsiders, and does not lead to the attempt to form associations to control it. Leadership that would assist in such transformation rarely arises from within—more often, the discontented and ambitious migrate to the city in their own interest, and the village becomes a residuum of traditionalists and failures. Where modern states attempt to organize peasants for development with such devices as cooperatives and development councils, voluntary associations may emerge. More often, new forms of dependency are the long-run result.

Third, the points of tangency between institutions represent social barriers that are difficult to penetrate. Peasants are a stratum in the modern state and are typically very isolated from the middle and upper classes who may form organizations among themselves. The result is that the traditionalists continue their defensive ways: magical-religious practice, ceremonies, and familism. They are left-overs, in a world of change. By way of contrast, the peasant who moves to the city may form voluntary associations to assist in transition to urban life.

Fourth, and closely related to the preceding point, the peasant village is involved in a stratification system in which the upward mobility, adaptation, or integration potential of voluntary associations has little meaning. The peasantry is distinguished from the more primitive tribes or bands from which it may have sprung, and also from the urban dwellers who have perhaps similar origins but who have changed their ways as well as their residence. Either of these two comparative groups may have a place in a stratification system in which there are heights of respect and prestige to claim, and depths to which a failure can descend. The peasant is in a relatively complete stratum of families of the same occupation. To make the comparison more concrete, rapidly urbanizing societies such as the African Mende, Temne, Yoruba, Ibo, Bamako, and numerous others, have voluntary associations that provide a means of accomplishment, respect, and prestige for the migrant to the city. Such organizations are possible because members have had similar experiences in mutual-aid organizations in villages at home, such as those of the Nupe described previously. These people come from a multioccupational village in which voluntary associations are means of crystallization of the stratification system. It is, in fact, easier to make the move from the tribal village to the city than from the peasant village, which is, following Service, more complex.

According to Hobsbawm, secret societies were common among peasants in the nineteenth and twentieth centuries.[50] The types that he traces, located in Sicily, Italy, and Spain, originated among tradition-oriented rural people whose local societies are regulated by absentee governments in whose origin they did not participate and whose operations they do not understand. The secret societies of such peasants typically originate in action defined as criminal by the state for which action there is a traditional peasant remedy that the state forbids. Many of the crimes are against officials or property of absentee landowners. The criminal becomes an outlaw and gathers a small group that may find shelter and help among the peasants. Some such secret organizations take a religious orientation, often in opposition to a church that seems as remote as the state.

Secret societies of peasants of this sort are the very antithesis of voluntary associations. They arise precisely because the state does not provide a legitimate scope for voluntary associations. They often flourish in the same environment as violent factional politics, another indication of lack of intermediate political systems that tie peasants or urban minorities to the national political centers. In several cases, national police were stationed in each district, having the purpose of control of the populace by military force.

The nineteenty-century *mafia* were such outlaw secret societies, as were the *fasci* from which fascism emerged. Their outlaw status and the correlated discipline which they underwent certainly made these nonvoluntary associations, even though many of them acquired mutual-aid and charitable functions.

It is the absence of mutual-aid fraternities *prior to* outlawry that distinguishes the *mafia* and *fasci* from African secret societies in primitive states. The African secret societies were fraternities driven underground, or founded underground, when tyranny was imposed on a truly fraternal people. Hobsbawm did point out that in some cases in Italy and Spain there were mutual-aid fraternities attached to Catholic churches, but these may have been in towns among nonpeasants.

The secret society, then, is not *necessarily* nonvoluntary. The circumstances need to be examined in each case before a decision. The major issues: permission, and instigation capability, here primarily previous experience with voluntary associations, usually mutual-aid fraternities.

## Summary and Conclusions

Voluntary associations were found in primitive society in considerable number and variety. The representative societies, however, were sharply distinguished as to existence of voluntary associations: tribes had many; chiefdoms and primitive states few; bands and peasants almost none. The findings may be represented in a chart. If the complexity thesis is valid, the ranks should correspond.

The rank score of 4.5 indicates a tie. For this table, Spearman's rank order correlation coefficient is 0.125, which is not statistically significant at the conventional 0.05 level. Of course, the selection of societies and the judgment about rank lack a rigorous basis, and this must be seen as only a crude test of the complexity thesis.

The reasons for the absence of voluntary associations could be established directly in some cases where they were specifically forbidden; in other cases speculation about their absence can be suggested with due caution. In the chiefdom, integrated and comprehensive authority suppressed individuality, and the notion of voluntarism could have never occurred. In the peasant village, emigration of the most ambitious, dependency, high-stratum barriers

| Rank of Complexity | Rank of Prevalence |
|---|:---:|
| 1. Bands (least complex) (Arunta) | 4.5 |
| 2. Tribes (Cheyenne, other Plains tribes) | 1 |
| 3. Chiefdoms (Tahiti, Polynesian clubs) | 3 |
| 4. Primitive states (Nupe, other African states) | 2 |
| . Peasants in modern states (most complex) (Sicily, Italy, Spain, etc.) | 4.5 |

and imposed authority prevent the formation of associations. In the primitive band, the small size of groups coupled with extreme diffuse dominance by males through monopoly of force and religion left no room for voluntarism.

Where voluntary associations flourished, among tribes, they took on a wide variety of instrumental and expressive activities. In integral relation with (rather than substitution for) the kinship system, they established a network of obligations and responsibilities between band units, resulting in coordination of activities, and similarly of values and norms. They provided for enactment of sanctions as an agent of government, motivated and regulated economic and military life, standardized cultural activities including religion, entertainment, medicine, and magic.

The voluntary associations were significant as a mechanism of social differentiation wherever they were found. They united people of the same standing or identity and served to establish and maintain the prestige claims of those people as a unity, against competing claims. In this process, they were vital in establishing and ranking of members in the stratification system. There was some indication of *internal* stratification in the organizations, provided by leadership in organization affairs, but it was comparatively slight. The voluntary association was an association of equals.

Primitive voluntary associations were articulated with the major statuses of societies, among which the most frequent bases of membership were sex and age. Age-grade associations were more numerous among males and were concerned with narrow age ranges; female age-grade organizations tended to be fewer and covered wider age bands.

Where residence was stable or the traveling unit was not changeable, socialization to voluntary associations took place. There were some play groups modeled after older youth or adult organizations.

Secret societies were found principally in primitive states and among peasants, under conditions that were unfavorable to voluntary associations, either because of lack of permission or because of the authoritarian nature of the society. Most secret societies were not voluntary associations.

The most conspicuous example of the prevalence of primitive voluntary associations was seen among the American Plains Indians. If membership of modern American adults in voluntary associations is taken as a midpoint between various survey results, a level of about 50 percent is a good approximation. The Plains Indians, then, belonged to close to double—almost 100 percent membership of the adults. Maybe Tocqueville was right that Americans were a nation of joiners, but was it the red or white Americans?

### Notes

1. Elman Service, *Profiles in Ethnology* (New York: Harper & Row, 1971), pp. xii-xiii.

2. Ibid., p. 491. Complexity does not necessarily imply firmer integration, which seems like a spurious issue here.

3. Michael Banton, "Voluntary Associations: Anthropological Aspects," in David Sills, ed., *International Encyclopedia of the Social Sciences*, 17 vols. (New York: The Macmillan Company and The Free Press, 1968), Vol. 16, p. 358.

4. Seymour Martin Lipset, *Political Man* (Garden City, N.Y.: Anchor Books, 1960); Seymour Martin Lipset and Reinhard Bendix, *Social Mobility in Industrial Society* (Berkeley and Los Angeles: University of California Press, 1960).

5. The main descriptive sources are Elman Service, *Profiles in Ethnography;* idem, *Primitive Social Organization* (New York: Random House, 1971); Baldwin Spencer and F. J. Gillen, *The Northern Tribes of Central Australia* (Oosterhout, Netherlands: Anthropological Publications, 1969); W. Lloyd Warner, *A Black Civilization*, rev. ed. (New York: Harper 1958). Warner's work was first published in 1937; Spencer and Gillen's in 1904, when reference was available to times when the Arunta were relatively uninfluenced by invasion. In this and examples to follow, a typical fiction will be usually pursued—the society will be depicted as if at a normal time, without the rapid changes that invasion may have in fact posed.

6. Adamson Hoebel, *Man in the Primitive World* (New York: McGraw-Hill Book Co., 1958), p. 404.

7. Ibid., p. 403.

8. The main descriptive sources are George Bird Grinnell, *The Cheyenne Indians*, 2 vols. (New York: Cooper Square Publishers, Inc., 1928); Karl N. Llewellyn and Adamson Hoebel, *The Cheyenne Way* (Norman, Okla.: University of Oklahoma Press, 1941); Robert H. Lowie, *Societies of the Arikara Indians* (New York: The Trustees, the American Museum of Natural History, Anthropological Papers, 1915), XI, 8; idem, *Plains Indians Age Societies* (New York: The Trustees, the American Museum of Natural History, Anthropological Papers, 1916), XI, 13; idem, *Societies of the Kiowa* (New York: The Trustees, the American Museum of Natural History, Anthropological Papers, 1916), XI, 11; idem, *Primitive Societies* (London: Routledge, 1921), Chapters 11 and 12; James R. Murie, *Pawnee Indian Societies* (New York: The Trustees, the American Museum of Natural History, Anthropological Papers, 1914), XI, 7; Alanson Skinner, *Societies of the Iowa, Kansa, and Ponca Indians* (New York: The Trustees, the American Museum of Natural History, Anthropological Papers, 1915), XI, 9; Clark Wissler, *General Discussion of Shamanistic and Dancing Societies* (New York: The Trustees, the American Museum of Natural History, Anthropological Papers, 1916), XI, 12. The time is dictated by the data: after first contact with white invaders from the Atlantic coast and long

after introduction of the horse from Spanish settlers to the south. Aged informants interviewed by Lowie and Murie around 1915 prove to be an excellent source when supplemented by earlier written journals of explorers.

9.  Llewellyn and Hoebel, *The Cheyenne Way*, p. 100.

10.  Grinnell, however, gives examples which show that each band had a remarkable knowledge of where the oher was likely to be at any time, even in the vastness of the plains that range from Alberta to Oklahoma. Even in the winter there was occasional contact.

11.  Lowie, *Primitive Societies*, p. 192.

12.  Service, *Profiles in Ethnology*, p. 122.

13.  Leslie Spier, *The Sun Dance of the Plains Indians* (New York: The Trustees, the American Museum of Natural History, Anthropological Papers, 1921), XVI, 7, p. 481.

14.  Hoebel, *Man in the Primitive World*, p. 408.

15.  Lowie, *Societies of the Kiowa*, p. 845.

16.  Lowie, *Societies of the Arikara Indians*, p. 654.

17.  Skinner, *Societies of the Iowa, Kansa, and Ponca Indians*, p. 692.

18.  Murie, *Pawnee Indian Societies*.

19.  Wissler, *General Discussion of Shamanistic and Dancing Societies*, p. 858.

20.  Murie, *Pawnee Indian Societies*, p. 579. The idea is similar to the practice of national chartered voluntary associations in the United States and elsewhere. The Boy Scouts and Red Cross are the best-known examples. The charter gives recognition of special status, added prestige, and useful contacts for fund raising. Hoebel, *Man in the Primitive World*, p. 502, gives an example of a voluntary fire department, a voluntary association, that was an official government agency. A different pattern will be described, in the next chapter, of the coopted voluntary association in the late Roman Empire period.

21.  Skinner, *Societies of the Iowa, Kansa, and Ponca Indians*.

22.  Wissler, *General Discussion of Shamanistic and Dancing Societies*, pp. 858-59.

23.  Ibid., p. 875.

24.  Service, *Profiles in Ethnology*, p. xii.

25.  The clearest alternative is the case of the Trobriand Islands *kula* ring, in which gifts of significance were given without exchange, and received without repayment from another party. The gift without reciprocity in kind led to less power accumulation for the Trobriand chief. The *kula* ring is an example of a voluntaristic economy that leads to social solidarity through

normative obligations. In a peculiar sense, the Trobriand Islanders had more voluntarism in their total society than most of those we will consider. By comparison, the United States has a formal, nonvoluntary market economy, and some voluntary associations (cooperatives) within it. It does not follow that the Trobrianders failed to have voluntary associations because they had a voluntaristic economy. The Trobriand society is described by Bronislaw Malinowski, *Argonauts of the Western Pacific* (New York: E. P. Dutton and Co., 1961).

26. The time is the early nineteenth century. The main sources are William Ellis, *Polynesian Researches* new ed. (London: Henry G. Bohn, 1853); Irving Goldman, *Ancient Polynesian Society* (Chicago: University of Chicago Press, 1970); Felix M. Keesing, *Social Anthropology in Polynesia* (London: Oxford University Press, 1953); Hutton Webster, *Primitive Secret Societies* (New York: Octagon Books, 1968); Robert Henry Codrington, *The Melanesians* (Oxford: Clarendon Press, 1969); W. H. R. Rivers, *Social Organization* (London: Kegan Paul, Trench, Trubner and Co., 1929); Malinowski, *Argonauts of the Western Pacific*; Marshall D. Sahlins, *Social Stratification in Polynesia* (Seattle: University of Washington Press, 1958). Ellis provides the earliest reliable ethnographic source. Sahlins's work is a systematic study that allows some basis for generalizations to the other island societies. Codrington, Rivers, and Malinowski provide contrasts between Melanesia and Polynesia.

27. Goldman, *Ancient Polynesian Society*, p. 170.

28. Ibid., p. 191.

29. Ellis in *Polynesian Researches*, tells about the Ariori in detail but seems too horrified to tell what they actually did that was so obscene. Others tell us: it was s-x. Ellis was not above describing cruelty and violence at great length (e.g., decapitation in war, smashed skulls), but sex was too much for him. Missionaries often have a way of seeing that produces rather biased ethnography, and their work must be seen in perspective.

30. Banton, "Voluntary Associations: Anthropological Aspects," p. 358.

31. Don Martindale, *American Society* (Princeton, N.J.: D. Van Nostrand Co., 1960), pp. 298-356.

32. So much so that Heinrich Schurtz in his 1902 classic *Altersklassen und Männerbünde* (cited by Webster, *Primitive Secret Societies*, p. 7; and Lowie, *Primitive Societies*, pp. 284-85) assumed that women were inherently unsociable. Webster, writing in 1907, assumed a "consciousness of kind" theme, following the popular work of Franklin Giddings, which allowed only that women were sociable with women when they had a chance. From

Germanic sex determinism (Hoebel, in *Man in the Primitive World*, p. 402, called it "androcentric prejudice") to social instinctivism is mostly a change in the name of an intellectual error very common in the era from which the data for this study are drawn—hence the continual issue here of interpretation of materials.

33. Codrington, *The Melanesians*, passim.
34. Webster, *Primitive Secret Societies*, passim.
35. Banton, "Voluntary Associations: Anthropological Aspects," p. 358.
36. The facts in this section are from Hull and Mabogunje. Richard W. Hull, *Munyakere: African Civilization Before the Batuuree* (New York: John Wiley and Sons, 1972); Akin L. Mabongunje, *Urbanization in Nigeria* (London: University of London Press, 1964).
37. Hull, *Munyakere*, p. 16.
38. Ibid.
39. Melville Herskovits, *Dahomey: An Ancient West African Kingdom* (Locust Valley, N.Y.: Augustin, 1938).
40. S. F. Nadel, *A Black Byzantium: The Kingdom of the Nupe in Nigeria* (London: Oxford University Press).
41. Banton, "Voluntary Associations: Anthropological Aspects," p. 359.
42. Hoebel, *Man in the Primitive World*, p. 406.
43. Service, *Profiles in Ethnology*, p. xiii.
44. Robert T. Anderson, "Voluntary Associations in History," *American Anthropologist* 73 (1971): 214.
45. Richard M. Kirby, "Voluntary Action in Developing Countries: Types, Origins, and Possibilities," *Journal of Voluntary Action Research* 2, 3 (1973): 151-52.
46. Service, *Profiles in Ethnology*, p. 501.
47. Robert Redfield, *The Little Community, and Peasant Society and Culture* (Chicago: University of Chicago Press, 1960), p. 17.
48. E. D. Chapple and C. S. Coon, *Principles of Anthropology* (New York: Holt, 1942), p. 418.
49. It is not insignificant that anthropology graduate students may be surely identified as just returned from "the field" by the items of native clothing that they attempt to find market outlets for among their university friends and professors.
50. Eric Hobsbawm, *Primitive Rebels* (New York: Frederick A. Praeger, 1963).

# 3 *Voluntary associations in ancient societies*

In the previous chapter, associations and voluntary associations of primitive societies were examined. The societies that were used as a basis of analysis were arranged on a continuum of increasing complexity, and it was found that voluntary associations were frequent only at the level of medium complexity, in the tribes and in some primitive states. Complexity alone may therefore be abandoned as a sufficient explanation of voluntary association occurrence.

In this chapter, attention is directed to five ancient societies, each of which took state form and each of which was far more complex than primitive states. They may be characterized, with some simplification, as each having a single major feature that, when examined in conjunction with the common element of statehood, provides a source of insight into the nature of voluntary associations. The five are China, the familism state; India, the caste state; Rome, the military-bureaucratic state; Greece, the city-state; ancient Israel, the religious state of a chosen people.

In Chapter 2 the form of authority was found to be a major factor in the explanation of existence and prevalence of voluntary associations. In this chapter the common factor is the state—legitimated final authority. Considerable attention will, therefore, be given to the issue of permission. The choice of examples does not follow some

71

theoretical classification of states, but is based on societies selected for their historical significance. Analysis of some of them in several phases allows an approximation of a theory of types, however. Rome during the Republic and the Empire presents a study of change in type of authority; Greece before and after revolution presents some contrasts as well.

Analysis begins with China, in which the central feature of relevance is the social organization of the family, in tension with imposed rule of the dynasties.

## China: Lower-Class Voluntarism

To presume to make general statements of any accuracy about a subject as vast as the social life of China seems at the outset to be absurd. However, most scholars are agreed that there is a remarkable continuity to Chinese society and that in spite of successions of dynasties and the impact of invaders, the core features of Chinese life have survived with very little change. The successful reorganization under the present regime seems to have gained a great deal of its force precisely because its radical changes took account of the continuity of social institutions.

The consistency applies to associational life as well, down to at least the first half of the twentieth century, and even contemporary communes are said to bear some resemblance to earlier foundations. The primary association forms, those concerning the family or descent group, cooperative crop watching, mutual aid, credit assurance, harvesting, and theatrical performance, are still called in many instances by names derived from those of ancient times. To simplify matters somewhat, a period has been selected that begins after the end of feudalism and ends before the Maoist regime. Eberhard speaks of the Chinese medieval period—250 B.C. until the tenth century—and the modern period until the twentieth century.[1] Information is more readily available in the part of the modern period just before Japanese invasion, when sociology was relatively accepted and research permitted. After that time we have external documentary research by foreign and expatriot scholars, which largely ignores associations; before the sociological period (*ca.* 1900) our inquiry must depend on badly biased reports of missionaries, colonial administrators, and curious or sensationalist travelers. Evidence from the 1900-1940 period will be presented, and attempts made to estimate its applicability to earlier dynasties.[2]

Maybon says that "a community of residence, of profession, of political ideas or of religious beliefs, anything is a pretext for the Chinese to form associations."[3] The major forms of association shall be described, and the question to be addressed is: Why and under what circumstances did these associations take voluntary form? It is obvious at the outset that activities that took voluntary association form in many societies had, in China, virtually compulsory membership. The answer will also be sought, therefore, in the preference or necessity for compulsory participation.

The social organization of the family system is articulated about two sets of functions, the economic-procreative-affective, and the religious-lineage aspects. The first of these was institutionalized through the *chia*, a coresidential set of related families holding productive economic property in common. It usually consists of three or four generations under the leadership of an older male, but not necessarily the oldest. The relations among family members were formalized into expectations of filial piety following the hierarchy of five obligations of the Confucian code. Residence of women is virilocal, and hence the household contains people of the same family name, *hsing*, which is also usually typical of other households in the same village. In towns and cities this lineage village system breaks down and many family names are found.

The *tsu* is perhaps the most enduring and successful aspect of Chinese social organization.[4] The term is often rendered as "clan," but this obscures the fact that the *tsu* is a formal association, which elsewhere is not always true of clans. The *tsu* is a formally organized agnatic descent group tracing its origin in a certain locality to a specific ancestor. It is not, however, inclusive of all of the same *hsing*. The name *tsu* has been found as far back as the *Shang* dynasty (up to 1123 B.C.). It acquired its classical form under the *Sung* (960-1276 A.D.), and most available genealogies trace to this period. Thirty-five-generation genealogies are not uncommon.

The *tsu* had a shrine or ancestral hall. This was usually located in the site associated with the ancestor who was venerated. The hall was the place of preferred burial of descendants, and it also contained commemorative plaques and tributes. The shrine and the associated territory were considered sacred and were defended against encroachment.

The leader of the *tsu* was selected by a formula and was typically the oldest survivor of the oldest lineage. He might, therefore, be a young person, put under tutelage of a council of advisers. The leader had specified duties, involving maintenance and defense of the shrine, adjudication of disputes, ceremonial leadership, and control of funds.

The activities of most *tsu* included mutual aid and proper burial, care of the elderly, education, and other benevolent actions. The *tsu* was distinctly not an association for corporate profit or direct contractual rewards, nor was distribution contractual but according to need. "The member families own property in common, but this property is for religious, educational and relief purposes, rather than a means of livelihood."[5] By contrast, the *chia* or family organization held property in common as a basis of economic production and distribution.

On the basis of goals and means of distribution of rewards, the *tsu* fits the criteria for a voluntary association. But when the nature of membership and the implications of the means of behavior control are considered, doubts arise.

Each *tsu* attempted to keep all eligible persons in membership, no matter how far they might roam from the ancestral home. Some members would make pilgrimages from a great distance to annual meetings. There were limits, however, and members living at a distance might form a new *tsu* of the same *hsing*. Similarly, *tsu* might attempt to make peace with their neighbors by inventing a genealogical link to present a basis for amalgamation. In the ordinary course of events, some *tsu* might allow their membership lists to lapse, and then appoint a group to rejuvenate the organization, often beginning with appointment of a group of scholars to bring the lists up to date. At such times (one figure was every twenty-five years) there were advertisements and new members were screened and some accepted.

The rewards of belonging to a *tsu* were considerable. It presented the most acceptable and ritually pure way of ancestor worship, and at the same time it qualified a person for membership in an association that provided security and protection for its members, an organized voice in public affairs, and many other more or less tangible rewards. The cost might also be high: conformity to ethical precepts was expected, and the well-organized *tsu* sometimes punished its deviants with beatings or even banishment. It is hard to say if banishment was intended to accomplish internal discipline or was for the purposes of impressing the public; at any rate, a number of records show that punished members were often readmitted.

Unlike most voluntary associations that we shall examine, the *tsu* took into membership all males who were qualified by reason of birth. This is partly surmise, since records are unclear on such matters. At any rate, it is clear that the *tsu* did accept into membership people of very different economic standing, and in this regard it is distinctly different from most other voluntary associations, for whom common interest most often implies similar economic standing. There is no reason, however, that common interest cannot have some basis other than economic standing; it was indeed the fact that the ancestral relationship itself was of overwhelming importance, and this was deemed to be the basic determinant. There is no reason why esteem cannot be the salient criterion of common interest, though American research more often assumes that status is the most significant. We shall encounter such issues again regarding the English clubs, where common interest was ultimately evaluated in intellectual or character rather than class terms, the idea of "gentleman" being a rather flexible one. In this line of reasoning, personal status or esteem are qualifications for entrance, the personal goal being prestige; the organization may, to serve its own ends, give honorary membership to persons already having prestige.

Though the *tsu* accepted people of all economic levels, it made distinctions between them on an economic basis. The poor were often not permitted to attend certain meetings, and in some cases were only accorded the fundamental right of burial in the ancestral ground.

Now we may return to the question of whether the *tsu* was a voluntary association. Based on the evidence available, it is probably correct to assume that in the normal circumstance it was not, though the main reason for that judgment, that of ascribed membership, showed occasional phases in which members were sought and accepted in a typical flexible voluntaristic pattern. Certainly, the activities of the association, which were determined by the specific differentiation of the functions of the *chia* and the *tsu,* made the organization's actions typical of voluntaristic roles in conformity with the definitions adopted here. The voluntaristic phases of membership and the likelihood of expulsion and reacceptance all support the view that the *tsu* was a quasi-voluntary association as defined in this study; one in which partial voluntarism (on the phase basis here) was a permanent and stable aspect of the organization. The significance of the *tsu* for sociological theory should not be overlooked. It illuminates clearly the fact that we commonly accept uncritically the idea that voluntary associations are based on the rational mode in which ends-means calculations are the cultural norm. There is no reason why the traditional mode cannot be the basis for voluntarism as well, if the conditions arise that make the alternative of not belonging feasible—and such conditions do in fact arise with regularity, including such matters as war, migration, schooling.

The *she* was another form of social organization of ancient origin. Hsiao identifies the *she* as an administrative district.[6] In 1660 the *she* was a government-designated set of households, numbering twenty to fifty, so that each division could extend "mutual assistance in farm work, in the event of death or sickness occurring in any of them during the farming season."[7] The *she* in some places was coupled with another district, the *li,* or replaced it in still others. The term *she* can be found as early as 517 B.C.[8] Several centuries later it was found as a unit for worship or sacrifice to gods or land and grain. Kublai Khan (1270 A.D.) organized units of fifty households into *she,* each under guidance of an elder adviser. In the nineteenth century further attempts were made to use *she* for governmental purposes, and at times they were used as tax districts. Throughout its long history, one thing is clear about the *she*: it was a unit of community social life, sometimes a basis of worship, controlled by its members, and imperial administration attempted to make use of its solidarity for purposes of control. The relation of the *she* and the government is essentially that of conflict of traditional and rational modes of action, in which most of the initiative was from the government bureaucracy in the hands of Mandarin administrators representing a distant emperor, and personally foreign as well. It succeeded only when sufficient force and administrative skill could be marshaled to make it work. Unfortunately there is little record of *she* from the people themselves; most of what is known is from government decrees proposing its abuse. Under government abuse its potential voluntarism probably decayed, but like most Chinese institutions, it endured and appeared again as an indigenous enterprise. The *pao-chia* was another imposed rational scheme of administration, taking units of *chia* (families) as its basis.

The *tsu* and the *she* were typically perceived in quite different lights by the government. The *tsu* upheld the official virtues of Confucian orthodoxy and was seen by governments as a useful means of regulation of the populace. The *she*, and even more so the *pao-chia*, were spatially rational units designed to fit the purposes of orderly administration, and not necessarily adapted to the needs of the people. At times the *pao-chia* was even made into a unit of continual registration and surveillance of the populace, with a registration card on the door of the leader of a unit of ten households that recorded the coming and going of each member. The *she* was basically an indigenous social organization that was ingested by the state, the *pao-chia* was imposed on the people, and the *tsu* was an indigenous unit that was sufficiently orthodox to be let alone.

Another basic form of citizen's organization was the *hui*. Gamble found large numbers of *hui* and *she* in his early twentieth-century research in Shansi, Honan, Shantung, and Hopei. He believes that generalizations about them may be extended to a much earlier era. Here is Gamble's compact description:

> In the Peiping area there were the Green Crop Association (*ch'ing-miao Hui*) and the Public Association, the United Association, the Public Welfare Association and the Public Discussion Association.
> *I-po Hui*, the "Common Ground Association", or *Kung*

*K'an I-po Hui,* the "Cooperative Crop-Watching Association," was the most prevalent type of village association in
Shantung.

Some Shansi villages called their group the Field Patrolling
Association, or simply the Crop Association. Religious
associations took their names from the particular god
worshipped or the temple with which they were con-
nected. [9]

Gamble examined a large number of village associations and concluded that they could be grouped into three types, varying from the
purely social and traditional, to the later, more nearly political, type.
The "general association" took care of all interests of a village. [10] It was
a group of leaders, selected on the basis of ability or rotation among
families. Gamble's second type is the "specific association," of which
"some were purely religious, related to temple worship or temple
maintenance, watching, canal repair, or granaries." [11] Gamble's third
type is called "compound." "The compound association consisted of
an over-all association with semi-independent minor organizations
operating under it. The minor units generally were organized on a
territorial or clan basis." [12]

The associations described by Gamble had many kinds of membership criteria. Some religious associations were divided on a street
basis. Some were divided between tenants and landowners. Some
villages were divided into districts and had general associations in
each area. Some were *she,* named after the dates of the dramas that
they presented.

I have kept Gamble's term "association" in all of the foregoing. He
does not take up the issue of voluntarism, but his evidence suggests a
variation in degree of independent choice. A large amount of
voluntarism existed in the case of the amateur drama associations,
while the general village association represented virtually compulsory assumption of obligations on the basis of inherited identity.
Crop watching varied in its organization, depending on the village.
A. Smith, writing in 1899, reported that crop watching (i.e., prevent-
ing stealing) was a major activity, organized by families or under a

village headman, or by a cooperative association, or by hiring watchers, but there was no single traditional form.[13] Burgess stresses that crop watching was under authoritarian control.[14]

Conditions favorable to development of associations and voluntary associations are typical in cities, because of the multiplication of vocational roles and the usual emergence of a merchant class that has much to gain by organization. The ancient Chinese city, however, differed from the Occidental city in that it was bureaucratically administered by imperial government, and was not the primary locus of citizenship as in Europe. There was no sworn association of burghers, or a commune, which could be the fountainhead for further associational growth. The gild was a prevalent association in European cities.

Chinese gilds were similar to European gilds in that they set standards, controlled apprenticeship, and developed internal administration based on religion. However, their place in government differed from that of the European gilds, and they were different from the fraternal voluntary associations out of which the European gilds emerged. Their power was sometimes great and represented a force with which the emperors had to contend. Of particular interest is the gild of bankers, traced to 200 B.C., which asserted control over currency. Burgess surveyed the literature on Chinese gilds and identified seven types, several of which represent probably erroneous uses of the term.[15] The first is simply a religious fraternity to do honor to a god—this is perhaps a mistaken reference to a *she* or a *hui*. Professional gilds were those that sold services rather than goods. Craft gilds were associations of handworkmen. Commercial gilds were associations of merchants of one kind of goods, wholesale or retail. The provincial economic gild was an organization for promotion of commerce in an area. The gild merchant, a term modeled after the European general gild of craftsmen and merchants in political and economic affairs, was rare or perhaps an erroneous reference. From Burgess's data, it cannot be determined if these were voluntary associations, though I doubt it.

The last type, the provincial social gild, is probably a genuine voluntary association, one of the few not composed solely of peasants or villagers, and, therefore, worthy of extended discussion. Burgess identified 413 in Peking alone.[16] This type, the *hui kwan*, met the special needs for visitors of a certain identity, during residence in the city. (Chang translates the term as *hui kuan*.)[17] Many *hui kwan* had clubhouses that had been built during earlier dynasties as hostels for students taking their examinations. These later served the needs of commercial travelers and officials whose duties took them to cities— a sort of Oriental YMCA. There is no good reason to call them gilds; that term is best reserved for economic organizations.

Burgess notes that most Chinese gildsmen were illiterate, and since the literate ones spurned such people, there is little record by or about them.[18] Korean gildsmen, however, were often literate and copied Chinese practices, so most knowledge about Chinese gilds is from this secondary source.

Under feudal conditions peasants grouped themselves around a feudal lord for protection. In return, they owed him taxes and services. This sometimes resulted in a "joint liability association," a form of guaranteed mutual aid and required savings organization, probably a voluntary association.[19] The association differs from the celebrated English *frith*, a mutual-security organization, which had no savings provision.

The *tsu* and *chia* were doubtless the most decisive sources of financial security. Nevertheless there were numerous reasons for borrowing money outside of these sources, one obvious one being the limits of the *chia* itself and the frequent unsuitability of the *tsu*. It was undoubtedly thought to be preferred to borrow from sources having less ability to shame the debtor. The result was a large number of cooperative loan associations. Clifford Geertz has written a lucid theoretical treatise on the role of this "rotating credit association," and many of the findings of his work apply to China.[20] Gamble reports numerous "mutual savings associations" (*ca.* 1925) in north China.[21] Tsu, in 1912, wrote of "mutual loan associations" throughout China.[22] A. Smith identified the *ch'i hsien hui* as the generic type in villages and (by inference) cities as well.[23] There were innumerable formulae for the organizations. One simple form involved a group of seven members, in an order determined by lot. Each made a monthly contribution to the one at the bottom of the list, then awaited his own turn for a payment. Most of the organizations had some ceremonial aspect, such as a feast paid by the beneficiary or host. Some had bonds for the recipients, so they would not renege on their payments in turn.

Another form of credit association operated through membership subscriptions that were put out at high rates of interest, the proceeds sometimes being consumed in feasts.

The basic formula, once worked out, could be put to many uses. One interesting variant was that of mutual burial insurance on parents. A group of men would form a *hui* (or *pao-she*) for their parents, with yearly subscriptions. If the fund was not called for, annual feasts were held using the investment income. Weddings, unlike funerals, were postponable, and hence did not apparently generate credit associations.

Smith also notes the prevalence of *hui* as pilgrimage loan societies, called "mountain societies" because of the object of a visit to a sacred mountain.[24] One variant involved a "stationary mountain society," in which members represented the mountain symbolically, then stayed home and blew the savings on a big feast.

In each of these examples of credit societies, the data are relatively modern, at least from the nineteenth century. Some credit arrangements obviously were needed for times of increased commerce and city growth; others may be ancient. The data are not good enough to permit further judgments.

With the exception of the high-ranking members of the *tsu*, possibly a quasi-voluntary association, voluntary associations among the Chinese do not become more numerous as the status hierarchy is ascended. Voluntary associations are an activity of the lower levels. Since the empirical generalization that higher status is correlated with higher rates of voluntary association membership is one of the best-established findings in modern sociology, this calls for some explanation. How does such a striking contrast with other societies come about?

The gentry was the most significant upper stratum. Terminology here differs with the writer—but if the term "gentry" is reserved for the educated upper *class* whose source of wealth is land rent, then the term "literati" may be used when scholarship *role* is the focus, and "official" when the literate gentry were employed as government bureaucrats. All were of the gentry *class*; some also had the *roles* of official and scholar. The literati was composed of scholars who had passed a series of very difficult state examinations. All state officials were chosen from the certified literati. Some who passed the tests were not appointed to office and were sometimes found as secretaries to village associations or as private tutors. The gentry was a class that was constantly renewed by proven merit—this is decisive.

The character of the literati was salient as a determinant of their nonparticipation in communal organizational affairs. Not only did they not participate, but their conduct was exemplary for others, and they were authoritative in matters of interpretation of desirable behavior, as well as influential in making official policy. The scholar prided himself in purely individual accomplishment. The knowledge he sought was always of the past. In spite of the extreme difficulty and significance of the examinations (failures sometimes committed suicide), knowledge per se was not as important as other accompanying virtues: propriety, etiquette, poise, elegant expression, and piety toward authority. The Confucian scholar sought to become a paragon of indifference, the quintessence of involuted charisma. The religious ideal was acceptance of the world, not mastery of it. Among such people, a rational purpose for collective action was lacking.

Confucian ethics stipulated that there be a rank ordering of obligations. These duties were, in order, to master, father, husband, older brother, and friend. In effect, these obligations tended to bring about "rejection of other than purely *personal* ties among family members, and students as companions."[25] In the everyday life of peasants, however, practical duty toward neighbors was added to the five classical obligations, and this was the basis among villagers for formation of mutual-aid associations that united people other than kin.

One might well look at the practical as well as the theoretical impossibility of a voluntary association of Confucians. How, after all, could the Confucian ever get through a committee meeting or business session when his overwhelming commitment was to elegance of expression, ritual perfection, and indifference to the problem? Success for the Confucian depended on fate, not mastery.

The state religious cult was, over many centuries, orthodox (definitionally true, of course) and Confucian, while Taoism and Buddhism were heterodox. The typical tension between the palace courtier groups (including eunuchs and the harem) who were sometimes heterodox and the officials (Confucian scholars) often resulted in intrigues with the heterodox religions and their spokesmen. Heterodoxy did not imply anything like excommunication, however. The typical peasant, in fact, looked on religion as a practical matter and used various gods, regardless of the sect promoting them, for their efficiency. Thus the heterodox sects were infrequently the basis of association formation. At the same time, temples proliferated, each representing some aspect of religious action for which sponsors could be found. Priests in general did not form congregations but performed practical services for those who could pay for them. In their times, Jews, Christians, and Moslems were each the source of heterodox religions in China, and in such cases religious communities did form with voluntary associations as one possibility among them.

The remaining association of interest is the secret society, which was introduced in Chapter 2. Like the heterodox sects despised by the Mandarin scholars, the secret societies were written about with derision or simply ignored, and as Chesneaux points out, information is scanty and often of dubious veracity.[26] Chesneaux defines a secret society thus: ". . . It designates associations whose policies are characterized by a particular kind of religious, political, and social dissent from the established order."[27] The societies may be divided into two main kinds; the White Lotus group in the north, and the Triad societies in the south. All of them were characterized by stress on the Taoist sense of individuality, anticonventional asceticism as to sexual and dietary practices, mutual-aid programs, and utopian egalitarianism. Some of them were Buddhist millennarians.

> What the state found most intolerable was that these rebel groups were not founded on the acceptance of the natural condition of man, as were the family, the clan, the village, and the guild, but on voluntary initiative and individual choice. They were in effect surrogate kinship groups offering their outcast and rebellious members the

services commonly furnished to the orthodox by
their kinsmen.[28]

Secret societies were quiescent mutual-aid groups in peaceful times,
offering typical fraternal benefits to each other in time of need
through a local lodge.[29] Though they recruited their members heavily
from the peasants, they also gathered in from time to time certain
alienated urban workers who had been displaced from their traditional family groups, such as discharged soldiers, boatmen displaced
by technological advances, and certain petit bourgeois. Then when
they came in conflict with the government, they would become
outlawed, and on such occasions they became bandits (*fei*) or even
united in temporary armies to attack towns. The Boxer Rebellion was
headed by Boxer secret societies; the Kuomintang built on them, and
in the early phases of his work, even Mao found a place for them—
they too were oppressed workers of a sort.

The version that we have in the West of the secret societies comes
from Mandarin scholars in China who were wont to categorize all
secret societies as *fei* or bandits, and from knowledge of them acquired in the United States, where they were suspected of all manner
of crimes. The *Fu Manchu* terror movies of early cinema built
extensively on this set of myths. Some of the accusations were true,
for the foremost groups in the United States were representatives of
the Triad societies that during the nineteenth century were actively
engaged in revolutionary activity in southern China, and who
oganized a number of criminal activities in the United States. But it
should be stressed that basically the Triads and the White Lotus
societies were, in *peaceful* times, heterodox voluntary associations
maintaining mutual-aid activities that succeeded insofar as the
administration of the government was sufficiently inept or corrupt to
allow them to persevere.

The justification of the secret societies was the belief, widely held
by all Chinese, that the ultimate rationale for acts came from heaven.
People on earth who spoke for justice spoke for heaven, and
everyone could do so directly. One did not volunteer, in our modern
sense of the term; one sought to act in a certain obligatory manner.

In none of the English-language glossaries that accompany major scholarly works on China was there a word indicated for "voluntary." There were numerous variants for duty, respect, obligation, and the like. Perhaps only in the more individualistic and mystical writings of Taoism are there justifications for such acts, and significantly, Taoism was frequently the basis of secret societies and lower-class actions of all kinds; it was in these classes that the majority of voluntary associations were found. Perhaps the strongest claim that can be made is that, in Max Weber's phrase, Taoism and voluntarism had an "elective affinity."

To return to the formal language of the model concerning voluntary association prevalence, the Chinese at all times had an adequate level of per capita volume of interior communication; a fairly high level of differentiation of goals and interests in society, limited by formal integration of the religion and economy along family lines; specific limitations as to instigation, particularly religious-authoritarian; and definite restrictions regarding permission. In particular, the rewards to be obtained from voluntary association formation were sometimes insufficient, in that alternate or preferred traditional means were available. The result is that Chinese voluntary associations existed in a limited number of structural locations in society, prominently in lower-class or heterodox situations.

A parting thought on China. Does the complete absence of eroticism in Chinese religion have anything to do with the absence of voluntarism? In the next chapter, a connection between hedonism and social clubs will be traced; but in the section that follows this, Hindus, who had erotic cults, had little voluntarism.

## India: Caste and State

The gross chronology and sequences of development of China and India are similar in many ways; both began with tribal peoples, suffered numerous regional conflicts, invasions, and conquests, and went through similar feudal and city development stages.[30] Yet China produced numerous associations, some of which were voluntary, while India had fewer associations and no significant or enduring voluntarism. By identification of the associations of India before the caste system, and by analysis of the coercive nature of the associations that persisted during the caste period, further light may be shed on the conditions necessary for existence of voluntarism.

The general nature of the Hindu caste system is probably sufficiently known to most readers, that little space need be given to it. An excellent brief presentation of the sociological fundamentals of caste may be found in Martindale.[31] A widely used sociology text with a good discussion of caste is Rose and Rose.[32]

Three main kinds of formalization of institutional life through organization are most crucial for study of India: political, economic, and religious (including caste). Family organization through clan, sib, or phratry never took associational form of any enduring significance in India, in notable contrast to China.

Drekmeier identifies the precaste Veda era (that is, perhaps 700 B.C.) as a period with a "crude pluralism."[33] A prominent political aspect of this pluralism was the *gana*, variously translated as "republican community" or "armed organization." The *gana* may be analytically subsumed under the term *sangha* or group, which is comparable to the Chinese generic term *hui.*[34]

The *gana* was "an egalitarian tribal association, of an age before Brahman ideology consolidated society on the basis of varna distinctions."[35] The *gana* was perhaps an intermediate stage between the tribe and the small regional republics that existed in North India before conquest or consolidation into hereditary kingdoms. When Alexander the Great invaded India, he found it necessary to negotiate with numerous republican communities; later Greek invaders complained about the complexity of representative rule and even democracy that they found there. Was this "crude pluralism" consistently institutionalized throughout into intermediate associational forms? It is not possible to do more than speculate. We do know there were gilds then, but the gild is the form of organization that always leaves the most evidence, usually easily identified through archaeological remains (e.g., pottery, metalwork) or historical records of occupations in documents or on tombs.

The gild apparently began in villages and cities throughout India in early times and survives still. The name given to the gild form of economic organization was *sreni*. The *sreni* of the early eras were organizations, apparently of workers of single occupations, in the small number of crafts that the technology of the time required. Distinctions gradually arose between merchant gilds and craft gilds. Auboyer denies this distinction,[36] but Drekmeier's untangling of the etiology of the terms seems more convincing.[37] Most likely, a distinction emerged in major cities where importing and exporting grew in militarily favorable periods, or elsewhere, or through market or domination of fairs in trading cities under royal approval. It is clear that there was no elaborate development or diffusion of gild types as in China or Europe. In particular, what is missing in India was a form of general diffuse gild of several occupations like the *gilda mercatoria* in England or the gild-based commune of France and elsewhere. The practical difficulty of communication in a diffuse gild composed of several castes is obvious.

The craft *sreni* was usually the least powerful, found more often in villages, and perhaps was more consistently based on recruiting exclusively through family lineage.

India's gilds were powerful organizations, and their dual contribution to regal dominance and to the stabilization of villages, before and during the later eras, should not be overlooked as a causal factor in development of the caste system, though it is more common to see the influence of the caste system itself as an independent force.

The village crafts could consist either of single-worker shops or shops of several relatively autonomous workers in industrial manufacture. The later system was also found in Africa but was relatively rare in Europe except in the transitional phase before industrialization. Even in preindustrial Europe, the multiple-worker shop tended to be a group of employees under an owner-manager. The *sreni* in cities often grew to considerable size, and amalgamation of shops into large plural units was common.

As mentioned above, *sreni* membership was hereditary, through apprenticeship of sons. The European system, by contrast, allowed and sometimes even favored apprenticeship of sons to the highest-ranking occupation possible. Such ambition was practically unthinkable for the Hindu under the caste system; a person was fixed in his path by birth, which established his *dharma*, and his goal was to

properly fulfill those requirements. Change was rare, though upward and downward mobility did occur, particularly through entire
subcaste initiative.

The headship of the *sreni* was distinctly different from that of gilds
of other places and times, and was one important reason why gilds of
India may not be counted as voluntary associations. The headship was
rarely elective. Usually, the head had the power to select his
successor, and his sons were preferred. The head controlled the
finances of the *sreni* and was responsible for taxes and other external
transactions. The head was a disciplinarian and was often severe. He
made bargains with royalty, which were often remunerative. The
*sreni* sometimes had its own militia, which it was bound to furnish to
the prince.[38] The royal militia, during the caste era, was always
difficult to manage, since caste prohibited contaminating contact
between militia of the various *sreni* who would often be of differing
castes. Liturgical acts are typical of gilds everywhere. In this regard,
the foregoing description of India's gilds is not different. The distinction was that liturgy was channeled through the gild head in India,
which put him in an advantageous position.

Weber notes that the impossibility of fraternization between gild
members and others was a decisive distinction between Indian and
Occidental gilds.[39] What this means regarding the issues involved
here is that the relationships between the *sreni* and others was
necessarily managed through agent roles, primarily that of the leader, who thereby developed his own power to a greater degree. This
may be conceptualized as an example of a broker or gatekeeper role.
The gatekeeper may process news in either direction, in a manner
favorable to enhancement of his personal interests. He is a channel
between groups not having access to each other. As a broker, he may
tax the transactions of his clients (tax farming) and thus accumulate
fortunes. The caste system, in numerous ways, provided for growth
of such roles because of the impossibility or simple inefficiency of
cross-caste contacts.

This inability to fraternize was undoubtedly significant, but would
not by itself absolutely prohibit members from organizing to exert
control or to share the profits. What is more significant is that the
ethics of Hinduism during the caste era, and to a significant extent

previously, were oriented ultimately to nonearthly rewards. The really important rewards one achieved were to be realized in rebirth. It was not so much that *sreni* members lacked common interests, but that in the Hindu scheme of things the important interests were essentially not calculable in earthly terms.

Weber puts the point another way. Among Hindus, there was no basis for *ressentiment*.[40] *Ressentiment* refers to diffused generalized and cumulative repressed feelings of hatred, antagonism, or envy. Ressentiment was understood by Weber as the possible basis of collective retributive action under appropriate circumstances. "*Ressentiment* is not found among Hindus and Buddhists, for whom personal suffering is individually merited."[41] By comparison, the suffering of the Jews consistently led to a collective basis for action.

Neither was there any basis for rational action in development of a congregational form of religion. All action was evaluated subjectively, and hence religious collectivities had nothing mutual to offer. The relation between the *guru* and the devoted Hindu was one of personal instruction; even monks in monasteries had essentially the same approach. As Weber puts it, "In India the religious caste taboo rendered difficult the rise, or limited the importance, of any soteriological congregational religion in quasi-urban settlements, as well as in the country."[42]

In the previous section, it was seen that certain sects and heterodox developments were the basis of opposition ethics and association growth in China. In India, Buddhism, which was heterodox except under Emperor Asoka, was quite favorable to the growth of *sreni*, both because of its ethics and because of the favorable atmosphere for both Buddhism and economic associations in cities. Weber notes that the Vishnuite sect, the *Kartabhajars*, attempted to develop a commensal fellowship across caste lines.[43] Virtual worship of the *guru* eventually made associational form impossible. In each case, the commitments to *dharma* (ritually correct duty) and *karma* (the cycle of rebirth) were pervasive.

Many Hindu sects or cults were outgrowths of eroticized worship. Included were various forms of phallus worship and sublimated erotic fellowships. In contrast to Christian feasts, which were specifically oriented to *agape*, the Hindu feast was a collectivity of individual erotic actions. The resulting sects had collective aspects, but not the rational voluntary associational form. In many cases, the data do not reveal the collective nature of the sects. In any case, they were never numerically significant; Weber estimates that the total of sect members did not exceed 5 percent of the population.[44]

Throughout the era in which the caste system was dominant, certain typical community forms inhibited growth of associations. A very large proportion of Hindus lived in villages, and these villages were small. Most villages were populated by members of one sub-caste (compare Chinese villages, populated by bearers of a single family name). Like the principle of *sreni*, nonfraternization, this has obvious practical consequences for efficiency of communication—a higher rate of communication internally among caste compatibles, and a low rate externally. This in itself is consistent with association formation. But it also meant that the village council (the *panchayat*), the *sreni* leadership, and the subcaste *panchayat* tended to become an elite or, in some cases, the roles were held by the same individuals. The tight integration and lack of heterogeneity made association development, other than that of the *sreni*, meaningless or virtually impossible; on the other hand, *sreni* heads could and did develop regional control of shop production. So far as a single village was concerned, there was lacking the necessary plurality of goals of interests.

The homogeneity of the village was never complete, however. Certain service or professional castes were needed on a diffuse basis—for example, sweepers and barbers whose trade involved a regional clientele of several villages. But the dominance of each village by a certain group was typically clear.

The subcastes themselves, ironically, at times recruited members on a voluntary basis. Modern India, under the impact of industrialization, shows numerous instances of the attempts of whole subcastes to become upwardly mobile, and in cases of ambiguity, individuals may press a claim to membership in a higher caste. Usually the subcaste is governed by a ruling council, but individuals are not thereby members in the caste association.

India, like China, has always been tolerant of a plurality of gods. There have been small communities of Christians, Jews, and several other minority religions in India for many centuries. Finally, the concentration on Hinduism in this section does not abnegate the contribution of Islam and other minorities to the life of India; Islam, as noted in other chapters, has had a long history of fraternalism, and gilds have been particularly prominent.

India, like China, has had secret societies. They have not been so prominent as a political force nor so numerous. Perhaps the best known are the thugs (*thugee*), which was a secret society of robbers.[45] Perhaps the term "secret society," as used regarding China and Italy, is not wisely used here although it is common to do so. The thugs were a subcaste association of a low rank. Again, the pervasive integrating power of the caste system is evident—even robbers had a definite place in society, regulated by caste norms like every other set of persons. India is a fascinating subject, and there is a strong temptation to search for other reasons for the absence of voluntarism or for other minor quasi-voluntary associations and deviant cases. Space is better devoted, however, to other ancient societies with many voluntary associations. Appropriately, then, we look to Athens.

### Athens: The City-State

Athens is simply the most prominent of the numerous city-states that emerged in the 1,000 to 1,500 years before Christ from tribes that inhabited the valleys and mountains of innumerable islands and peninsulas in the eastern Mediterranean Sea. The city-state was typically composed of a fortified city that dominated a territory with prominent natural boundaries. Sparta represents the type that exercised domination through military, and Athens through naval, power.

In spite of the physical separation of the Attic city-states, they had a considerable cultural similarity and tended to think of the land as a Greek unity. The major gods were gods of all Greece; commerce among cities was normal, and there was constant borrowing of ideas, forms of government, art, and language. The voluntary associations that emerged among them, perhaps as early as the age of Homer, also reveal similar features, particularly among the religious associations that formed for worship of the more general deities. It was in Athens, however, that voluntary associations reached the greatest degree of development and there that they reveal most sharply the strengths and weaknesses of this means of corporate life. In another sense, the voluntary associations reveal the strengths and weaknesses of Athens itself, since they were so intimately involved in its great experiment in government as both positive and negative forces.

The main forms of voluntary association were the *thiasos*, *eranos*, and *hetairia*.[46] They were, so far as their primary ends were concerned, devoted respectively to religion, fellowship, and politics. This single distinction should not be taken as decisive, however, since all Greek voluntary associations were religious, and in the course of time any organization that succeeded tended to exand its activities to affairs that confronted it. In addition to the three mentioned, there were numerous gilds in Athens and wherever Hellenism spread. Gilds will be discussed separately. Throughout, the voluntary association was primarily a small organization of friends and it is through the meaning of this friendship that an explanation must be sought.

We may begin by noting that the Athenian family system was organized in a manner that was surprisingly similar to the Chinese *tsu*. The two important elements were the *oikos* or household, and the *genos* or family association. *Gene* are comparable to *tsu*. In both cases the family association was a source of power, encompassing only a fraction of the families; each regulated its members through worship of family deities and related traditional values, and supported them in time of trouble. Connor gives the following compact summary of the *gene*.[47]

All the families of the *genos* claimed descent from a common ancestor and were closely held together by six ties that may be summarized as follows.

1.   Common religious ceremonies.
2.   A common burial place.
3.   Mutual rights of succession to property.
4.   Reciprocal obligations of help, defense, and redress of injuries.

5. Mutual rights and obligations to marry in certain determinant cases, especially when there was an orphan daughter or heiress.
6. Possession, in some cases at least, of common property, an *archon* and a treasurer of their own.

The ancestor might in fact be a mythical or an apotheosized hero. The family association was effectively a formalized agnatic descent group making strategic use of real and fictive kin principles. Connor estimates that there were one hundred *gene* in Athens, encompassing one-fourth of the population.[48] The strategic nature of the association is revealed by the fact that the one-fourth were probably those highest in prestige and with the most to defend.

The *gene* tended to dominate the *deme* in which residences of *gennetai* were concentrated. The *deme* was probably originally a village. The *phratries*, more inclusive kin categories, also tended to be concentrated in certain *demes*. The *phylae*, or tribes, were ten in number and constituted official divisions of the *polis* (or corporate people of the city). In order to make exact statements about each of these elements and their relations, the era would have to be specified. In general, the tribe became less significant in time as a basis of loyalty and action, and the *phratry* became primarily the basis of military action. The most significant thing to point out is that. the city-state was very thoroughly and formally organized, with specified structures to represent each kind of interest. In this milieu, the individual found himself faced with numerous obligations, resulting in specific values about the relative significance of each possible type of relationship. How did the individual citizen respond to this complex associationism?

The obligations of an adult male were matched by a sense that every relationship presented an opportunity for getting help in time of need. A man who was a member of a *genos* could call on it for help and it would respond—the call for help held a very high priority for all members. One who was a member of a *genos* might seek help first from members of his phratry. Kin of some kind were thus the first refuge in time of need.

After the kin came loyalty to the *deme*, tribe, and *polis* in that order. Each relationship had its use and its place. Loyalty to the *polis*, though last, came to the fore when Athenians faced their common foes, and that was very often. Athenians, however, lacked a diffuse loyalty to their state; the duty to love one's friends and hate one's enemies was always foremost. It should be emphasized that opposition to enemies was a virtue of a good man, not a role that was assigned or that fell to certain categories of individuals in a social unit. The musings of the condemned Socrates about the obligation of the citizen to honor the judgment of the state were deviant in his time; the idea of love (*agape*) for mankind that Christianity featured was still centuries away.

It was, therefore, natural that man must be calculative about friendship. The Greeks conceptualized friends from the perspective of the person, as *philoi*, meaning roughly those who were affectively close to a man, his social circle. A more inclusive terminology was applied to describe the potential supporters of a prominent person: *hoi peri* or *hoi amphi*, meaning the groups (including *philoi*) around a man. The *hoi* might be all or part of a voluntary association.

Since there were ten *phratries* and many *gene*, politics in the *polis* itself required support from a plurality of these units. One of the more prominent of the ties that were sought for this purpose was exogamous marriage. Marriage strategies began with the assumption that preferred marriage was to a prominent *gene* and exogamous to one's own. The term *kedeia* was applied to a marriage link. Love or personal attraction was a pleasant surplus value, but not relevant to the decision to marry. In eighteenth-century English literature, the theme was satirized by Henry Fielding's Squire Western, who so eagerly sought advantageous marriage for his daughter that it did not occur to him to ask the sex of the other gentleman's child.

A kin grouping or association was the closest to a man's heart, and it was also usually the most significant religious organization for him. Religion for the Greeks was essentially ceremonial. It was not the ground of moral behavior nor of the relationship to a sacerdotal order of any kind except the *gene* itself. The family organization had such a sacerdotal authority over a person, but it was the authority of the family and not its gods or its priests that counted. Priests were functionaries who conducted ceremonies and interpreted natural events and signs. The most important source of religious interpretation, the oracle at Delphi, was advisory and nothing more.

Small religious associations grew in the *phratries*, probably as a convenience for the ceremonies regarding certain *phratry* deities. These *thiasoi* were guaranteed freedom under the law of Solon, which was perhaps merely a codification of accepted earlier practices. Under the guarantee they flourished and seem to have been the basis of worship of the most diverse possible range of deities. Lécrivain has identified the following categories of *thiasoi*:[49]

1.  The *eranoi*, considered as a category of religious organization. *Thiasoi* of priests were often called *eranoi*, perhaps in confusion or as a transitional form.
2.  The *synthytai*, which was a reunion of the faithful having a common sacrifice.[50]
3.  The *mystai*, an association or group of those faithful to certain mysteries. Some of them were indistinguishable from the public cults. Among the better known and more controversial were the cultic associations for worship of Dionysos.
4.  The chanters of praise for various deities. It is not clear from the text if these were found in Athens.
5.  Associations of strangers worshiping foreign heros or deities.
6.  Religious organizations of members of certain professions, such as merchants, some of which were also foreigners.

There were numerous variations in the practices of these organizations, but the differences were substantive rather than formal. It is also difficult to distinguish the point at which a purely religious organization became an *eranos* as in number 1, since both were religious. Analytically, the difference between the two forms has to do with the dominance of mutual aid in the *eranos*. The *thiasoi* were solely religious.

The *eranos* was referred to by Homer as a meal to which each contributed a share. The *eranos* is referred to in one source as a "convivial party"[51] or picnic—a kind of potluck supper like they have at the community church on Wednesday night where everyone brings a covered dish. In some cases the meal was catered and monetary contributions replaced the food offerings. The term *eranos* came then to mean a contribution or subscription.

The subscription idea was also applied to aid of those members in need. "The Athenian societies do not appear to have kept up a common fund by regular subscriptions, though it was probable that the sum which each member was expected to advance, in case of need, was pretty well understood."[52] A grant was considered to be repayable, and suit could be brought for recovery. It is doubtful that suit would often occur: not only does one not do such things against friends, but doing so makes a person an enemy, which would strain or destroy a club. *Thiasoi* also lacked regular budgetary control.

The *eranos* seems to be rather weakly developed as an associational form, though it is possible that the data, which are rather scanty, are at fault. It lacked the elaboration and mathematical-actuarial intricacy and comprehensive coverage of possible contingencies of which the Greek intellect was surely capable. The most likely explanation is that the institution of friendship, beginning in the kin and extending outside the *genos*, was adequate to meet most needs for security and welfare. For example, burial needs, which elsewhere were commonly met in such clubs, were not *typically* met through the *eranos*.

*Hetairiai* were associations of comrades. The best-known examples are those in which the comradeship has been put to use in politics. In the tense times in the later years of the Athenian democracy, *hetairiai* were extremely active among both the democrats and oligarchs, and were sometimes guilty of subversion or conspiracy. An oath of loyalty was sometimes required under such circumstances. The *hetairiai* as revoluntary conspiracies were known as *synomosiai*.

*Hetairiai* were most often formed from those best suited to be friends—members of one's own *genos* or *phratry*, but others could be chosen as long as they met the tests of friendship. They were put to uses that would be expected of friends: support in lawsuits, favorable testimony for friends before the courts, countersuits against a friend's enemy, and so on. Friendship always had higher priority than objective and impartial truth before the courts; hence a man active in public life needed organized friends and often used them aggressively. It is easy to overemphasize this, since the known examples are the dramatic ones. Nevertheless, some leading citizens were sued almost daily, and most Athenian citizens were more familiar with the courts than modern men.

Calhoun gives numerous examples of subversion of justice by *hetairiai.*[53] The methods used included attempted bribing of juries (a very difficult task because juries were selected by lot from a large pool), oratory and claque techniques in assemblies, false witnessing, aggressive rumor mongering, and even assassination.

The institution of ostracism was intended to be a way of exiling obnoxious figures who had not been convicted of crimes. Plutarch said that ostracism would "undo the *hetairiai.*"[54] But ostracism was a limited device and was only allowed each year by vote of the assembly. At least one instance has come to light in which an *hetairia* organized the ostracism of one of their enemies by influencing votes.

It seems quite likely that the generally bad reputation that the *hetairia* has had among scholars is exaggerated out of proportion by a relatively few cases. The majority of the incidents were concentrated in the last half of the fifth century B.C.; many of them concern the oligarchs themselves. Most prominent men belonged to several such clubs because it was a necessity, and they served the same relatively innocent purposes that they do now.

Some *hetairiai* were known for their penchant for boisterous behavior. There was one "club of wits" of sixty members.[55] Most others were smaller. The club names were often daring or sacrilegious. Some took the name of some public enemy or object of scorn. Some were openly licentious, a theme we shall encounter again in eighteenth-century England.

The club idea, once established, could be used by any people who had something in common and were permitted to do so. Thus there were *hetairiai* of professional sycophants, pettifoggers, and shysters.

The existence of gilds was mentioned earlier. None of the sources found have identified a unique generic name for the gild. The gild was apparently a religious association of a common profession, but the word "gild" (or "guild") is used for each of the three types of voluntary association that have been identified here. Unfortunately, the scholars who have written about gilds in classical times have never been very clear about the meaning of the term—this judgment may be applied to the work of such otherwise excellent scholars as San Nicolò, Boak, and those responsible for dictionary and encyclopedia reports. There are mentions of *emporoi*, associations of traders, and *naukleroi*, associations of shipowners.[56] Their corporate features need not include a voluntaristic element, though they may have had elements of ceremonial religion as in the *thiasoi*. San Nicolò also hints that the gilds were engaged in conspiracies as were the *hetairiai*.[57] The most likely conclusion is that the more important functions of economic life among the Athenians were absorbed into other institutions. The gilds probably did not have an economic monopoly under law.

There are several linguistic forms that have led to some confusion about Greek voluntary associations. The *hetairoi*, or companions, were military groups, mentioned in the *Iliad*. *Hetairiai* were courtesans, female companions, hostesses, entertainers, or sometimes prostitutes.

Females were sometimes members of religious organizations, and they were found as priestesses who formed professional voluntary associations. They were not ordinarily active in politics and hence not in political clubs.

Slaves were sometimes permitted to have their own *thiasoi*, to worship deities of their own. They did not have this right under all regimes, and the development was relatively minor.

Some summary comments may be made about the Athenian case before going on to materials about Rome, which it resembles in many ways. The city-state obviously offers the opportunity for a high volume of communication, which the model specifies for existence of voluntary association. There is ample evidence of permanence and connectivity, differentiation of goals and interests. The law of Solon established permission; there were ample skills for instigation, and numerous resources. In a sense, the voluntary associations of Athens were limited by the excesses of the democracy of which they were a part. By excesses is meant the (periodic) insistence that all public institutions be democratized, such as the practice that juries not only debated facts but matters of law; that offices such as that of army general were elective; that numerous officials were selected by lot rather than skill; that decisions were made in mass meetings too large for careful debate, leading to demagoguery (the modern sense); that there were no permanent political parties but merely coalitions or tendencies. These evaluative points have been argued at length elsewhere and would take excessive space if pursued here. The issue is that in the absence of administrative procedures through permanent structures, voluntarism was put to service and not always with good results. Of particular interest is the fact, which I think is indisputable, that in the absence of formally organized public political parties, *hetairiai* became conspiracies that destroyed their credibility as voluntary associations.

Second, and akin to the last point, the principle of a sharp distinction between love and hate, or friend and enemy, led to establishment of rigid boundary conditions for voluntary associations. Athenian voluntary associations thus failed to develop a range of kinds of interests, and variety of members, and thereby limited the contribution that might have been made to that already exceptionally vital culture. But who is to say whether it would have been better or worse? This finding provides the occasion to expand on the criteria of prevalence stipulated in Chapter 1. There was, in fact, adequate differentiation of goals and interests in Athenian society for development of many voluntary associations. The categorical nature of the idea of friendship simply limited their flexibility and effectiveness, but not their prevalence. Differentiation has a quality as well as a quantity dimension, which may be conceptualized as a problem of boundary maintenance.

Third, the Athenian stratification system was formalized on the basis of wealth. A man knew, and his friends knew, exactly which of four economic classes he fitted into and, therefore, to what kinds of political office he might aspire. The system may well have limited the desire of the lower classes to participate in society through political action. The *hetairiai* were found principally among the upper classes, indicating effective, if not intentional, limitation of social participation.

### Rome: The Military-Bureaucratic State

The most striking sociological fact about Roman voluntary associations is that they were so prevalent among the lower classes, apparently more than among the higher. They were also relatively uniform in organization and were confined to a limited number of kinds of goals, and had members of very unequal social rank in certain instances. A similar overall correlation of class and prevalence was found in China; this second finding may be taken as a general invalidation of what is widely accepted as the best-grounded universal empirical generalization in the research area, that higher class is correlated with more memberships. Much of the study will be devoted to description of the features of Roman social organization that are necessary to explain these unusual findings.

Let us begin by noting a paradox. When the new imperial government of Rome suppressed voluntary associations, the immediate result was obedience, but within a very few years, there were more of these small organizations than ever before. In the preceding two centuries (of the Republic), when the long class struggle resulted in some democratization of the civic culture, there was comparatively less voluntary association activity. We will find that some of these correlations are partly spurious, or simply accidental concurrences; the total explanation lies in the social changes that accompanied or caused these political acts of suppression. The explanation of existence and prevalence must, therefore, be sought in *change* in social organization, as well as in the more static structural descriptions.

Analysis of Roman life falls conventionally into the three epochs of Roman history: The Royal (to 509 B.C.) and Republic (to Julius Caesar), and the Empire. Although these categories are useful for analysis of political and military events, they do not prove very useful as the basis of analysis here. The *nature* of Roman voluntary associations changed very little over the centuries. The data, however, are scanty for the Royal period and even during the Republic. Therefore, most of the analysis will concern the contrast of the Republican and Empire eras; the major difference between the two being that of greater control over voluntary institutions during the Empire.

A brief description of the nature of the most significant Roman voluntary associations is necessary before turning to detailed explanation. The terminology is quite complex, but for sociological purposes the various terms can be reduced to a smaller number. The two major forms of Roman voluntary association were the *collegium* (plural, *collegia*) and the *sodalicium* (plural, *sodalitas*). The anglicized "college" and "sodality," still in use, derive from these terms.

The two terms were actually very much alike in use. *Collegium* is the most widely used Latin generic word for "association." Another term, *societas*, was applied to temporary gatherings, but probably not to associations. The modern use of "society" to apply to a formal organization, usually a voluntary association, implies a formal aspect that was lacking in Rome. *Fraternitas* was also found. *Sodalicium* refers to a group to provide regularity of sacrifices and sacred meals.[58] From Cagnat's text it seems apparent that "association" is more apt than "group" for *sodalicium*.[59] Gilds in Rome itself were called *corpora*, those in the provinces *collegia*.[60] *Collegia* will be used here, however, as the more general term. *Collegia fabrorum* may be taken as the equivalent to the trade gild; *Collegia opificum* as a noncultic professional corporation. For sociological purposes, there is little reason to keep the modifier terms. Other examples include the *collegia artificum, mercatorum, negotiatorum.*[61]

Waltzing (writing in French) takes "corporation" as the generic term, from *corpora*, and groups the several Latin words under it.[62] "Corporation" is common as a generic term in both French and translations from German to English. There is some sense in Waltzing's usage, though it is confusing to modern readers, for whom the word signifies a company or business firm. The Roman *collegium* was a legal person (sometimes the right was denied) entitled to sue and to be sued, and was quite specifically defined under law, and in this sense it might be equivalent to our idea of a *nonprofit* corporation or *eleemosynary* association. The term *collegium* acquired its meaning quite early in Rome. As early as the Royal period, and perhaps as early in that period as King Numa, the Roman voluntary association had this defined legal character, and this lucid designation was one reason why they were easily organized—but easily controlled when rulers needed. In terms of our basic model, instigation of associations was formally institutionalized very early, based on strong norms that supported the legal right.

In certain uses *collegia* were not voluntary associations. For example, the pontifical college was the corporate form of the official priesthood that, among other things, decided on the admissibility of new deities and cults. One writer lists four exceptions of this sort. With these exclusions, the *collegia* were all voluntary associations, until perhaps the third century A.D., when membership became compulsory in some gilds.

The earliest *collegia* of which there is record are those that refer to occupations. As mentioned before, the early appearance of economic associations is deceiving, since their records tend to be preserved better because of the enduring artifacts they leave. Roman legend ascribes the origin of the *collegium opificum* to King Numa, who, according to Plutarch, founded *collegia* of carpenters, dyers, shoemakers, tanners, workers in copper and gold, potters, and flutists.[63] Paul-Louis has rendered the list as "flute-players, gold-smelters, smiths, dyers, cordwainers, curriers, brass-workers, and potters."[64] Perhaps more important than the differences in the list is the fact that the occupations that were done in the home were not represented, such as weaving, spinning, baking, sewing, decorating, wine-making, and so on (a similar point is attributed to Theodore Mommsen). Later, baking, brewing, and the like, became men's occupations and *collegia* of their workers were formed. The implication is that around the eighth century B.C., industry was relatively undeveloped and still quite close to the home. Organizations of traders and navigators developed at an early date, as in Greece.

There is not any doubt that these early "gilds" were voluntary associations, though external control over their operations was quite close. Unlike the economic organizations of ancient China and India, those of Rome never autonomously undertook to organize a monopoly or restrict trade, to farm taxes, to govern the trade internally, or to govern the municipality as *gilda mercatoria*, nor did they typically organize shops on an industrial basis, to compete with the slave production units that did so. Under the Empire, late period, the *collegia* were used to enforce numerous state policies and became nonvoluntary. Thus their minimal autonomy and lack of enterprise, even before the Empire period, was probably due to the extent to which their operations were supervised by officials whose legal position as head of the voluntary association was subordinate to the official's role as a civic magistrate.

At the height of Roman prosperity the fragmentation of occupations was extensive. If we recall that Rome was bigger than all but our greatest modern metropolises this is not surprising. Since large-scale organization of production was exceptional, each product that was regularly used and processed in a city came to have its own small *collegium* of specialized workers. It is probable that the fragmentation of occupations was even greater than our *collegia* records reveal, since vicinal occupational organization was perhaps more difficult in Rome than in other urbs. Here are some of the specialities that were found in the imperial era: unskilled laborers of all kinds, physicians, goldsmiths, pastry makers, castanet players, checkerboard makers, perfumers, barbers, hay dealers, sculptors, bridesmaids, actors, dancers, jugglers, gladiators, students, and veterans. *Collegia* were allowed at times in the army, but were banned when they seemed likely to become an independent military force. Veterans could become politically important through their *collegia*.

At the height of Rome's economic success, there were *collegia* that resembled, in name at least, the purely social and licentious social clubs of the Athenians. Waltzing called them *"cercles d'amusement."*[65] He records the Ball Players, the Late Drinkers, and the Sluggards among others. It seems likely that these too were, at least partially, lower-class organizations, making a display of mocking the indulgences of the wealthy—available information is not very adequate as to the identities of members. Timbs notes Cicero's participation in a social club—Cicero was a noted man but he was an *ignobilis*, not upper class.[66] The extent of purely social clubs, like those of the Greeks, is hard to determine. Indulgence and sybaritic luxury were so well established as part of the competitive informal Roman life that it seems unlikely that they would take corporate egalitarian form. Cultic practices and Dionysian rituals are another matter—they were common, and this religious character of revelry may be the source of some confusion. It is quite possible that the practice of meals at commemorative meetings degenerated into drinking bouts and their religious purposes were lost sight of, particularly as the Empire drew to a close, but they were still religious gatherings.

Youth *collegia* were modeled after the adult ones. They often had an adult curator, and an adult *quaestor* for financial management. Thus instigation was intentionally formalized among youth.

Many statements made about *collegia* are true of *sodalitas* as well. Several sources treat them as synonyms. They were probably more distinct in the earliest periods. In the beginning, the *sodalicium* was apparently a cultic organization of the *gens* or family association (to be discussed later). Public cultic worship was devoted to gods worshiped by all Romans; families might be oriented to worship of unique family deities, and associations emerged to better provide the essentials of cultic practice, particularly sacrifices and burial rites.

In time, sodalities became more independent as the *gens* became more numerous and adapted to change. Under the Republic, the sodalities were also understood to be political organizations, a claim made regarding *collegia* at the same time. This was undoubtedly true, since any association aligned with a *gens* in some way was a source of solidarity of people having a common identity and frequently a common interest deriving therefrom.

Both *collegia* and *sodalitas* served at times as the basis of mobilization of mobs, organizing rabble-rousers and troublemakers and the like. But it seems unlikely that they ever became consistently as conspiratorial or corrupt as the Athenian *hetairiai*—the Romans had closer control over organizations than that.

The early emperors encouraged emperor worship, though some apparently had a few mental reservations. Julius Caesar encouraged a *sodalicium* devoted to worship of Julian family deities, and other emperors routinely followed similar practices. After imperial suppression, when *collegia* were again allowed, other *sodalitas* developed also, devoted to acceptable deities.

The Roman idea of small religious organizations devoted to single deities was well established, and thus later monotheistic religions, devoted to sweeping claims to univeral obedience, had little difficulty fitting the pattern by stressing the collegial fellowship aspect of their religion rather than the Roman imperial form. Patronage in a family system was consistent with a patron-client attitude of family deities, expressed through small organizations. Jewish religion also fitted this paternal pattern, and it had little difficulty adjusting to the Roman provision of small *collegia* for family communities; even though the Jewish god was claimed to be all powerful, to Romans he was the god of the Jews themselves and not of others. Hence Jewish communities worshipped Yahweh with little interference. Nor was Mithraism, a Persian religion, treated differently at the outset, for though it put Mithra forward as a ubiquitous deity, the other natural elements of the Mithraic formula seemed familiar. Mithraic *collegia* were spread widely by traveling Romans, particularly soldiers. Mithraism (one author calls it "almost monotheism") might well have become the state religion of the Roman Empire instead of Christianity—but Constantine made his choice and speculation can't change it. Voluntary associations were the vehicle of both. Christianity's radical pacifism made it unacceptable to the military, and thus Mithra had a more effective missionary organization. Contrast: Mithra astride the wild bull, knife to its throat; Jesus the meek, astride an ass. Both took their initial hold in the lower classes, but in the long run Christianity also proved adaptable to the Roman elites.

It is doubtful if Christianity would ever have been more than an obscure Jewish cult had it not been for the Roman historical provision for freedom of association, and its embodiment in the *collegia*. Again, the stress on both civil rights and civil liberties in the model proves crucial.

Christianity easily adapted its idea of fellowship to the *collegium*. When Christian ideas became subversive of Caesarian absolutism, it was possible for the fellowships to continue to meet as *collegia* for burial, under the general indulgence of burial associations.

The letters of Paul to the Romans indicate that the Roman Christians may have been considered as *collegia*; 1 Corinthians 11:22-34 is interpreted by Brown as evidence that early Christians met in *schola* (clubhouses of *collegia*).[67] Brown's calendar of Christian development places the nascent church as a Jewish sect from A.D. 30 to 100; an illegal association from 100 to 250 with allowed burial organizations; systematic persecution from 250 to 260; relative freedom and prosperity, 260 to 300; renewed persecution under Diocletian from 300 to 313; toleration under Constantine after the Edict of Milan, 313 to 337.[68]

What were the *collegium* and *sodalicium* like as organizations? The records that have been preserved are much better than those of any other ancient society. In addition to documents such as the *lex collegia*, and comments of writers of all sorts, we have the unusual source of inscriptions in stone. Since most *collegia* and *sodalitas* had funerary purposes, and since Roman burial was ideally in a crypt or tomb with a commemorative stone tablet, a study of tomb inscriptions becomes a mine of information about voluntary associations. An enormous amount of effort was put into the recording and analysis of such material in the nineteenth century, particularly by German scholars, among whom Theodore Mommsen was a leader.[69]

One *collegium* (133 A.D.) went so far as to carve its rules on the walls of its *schola*; perhaps this is the oldest record of voluntary association operating procedures known to history. Here are the main points (paraphrased from Dill).[70]

The members shall be energetic in contributing to the interment of the dead. Members shall make regular payments to the fund. The entrance fee will be 100 *sesterces*, plus one flagon of wine (though wine was drunk at meetings, it was also used to sprinkle over graves). There will be a monthly subscription (stipulated). Slaves may be members, with their masters' permission. A funeral grant equal to the sum of three months' subscriptions will be made to one designated heir of the deceased member. From the funeral grant, one-sixth may be distributed among members present at the funeral. There will be provision for burial of the intestate. The corpse of the deceased member is to be transported up to twenty miles to the place of burial by a committee of three members who must submit an expense account. Fraud by the corpse committee is punishable by stipulated fines. Members who die more than twenty miles away may still be buried at the site, at the expense of the legatee.[71]

Other *collegia* had detailed rules about decorum. Fines for misbehavior were specified. Dates of meetings were usually set on anniversaries of certain deities or on a certain day of each month.

Many organizations specified the maximum membership. At times this was fixed by law. Actually, stipulation by law of numbers and meetings was a typical Roman device to prevent growth of political opposition.

A person of wealth might organize a *collegium* for his own commemoration, and endow it with sufficient funds so that the interest would provide perpetual services, a practice that reemerged in medieval Europe. Some bequests, however, were more simple, as in this epitaph: "He bequeathed to his guild, the rag dealers, a thousand *sesterces*, from the income of which each year, on the Festival of Parentalia, not less than twelve men shall dine at his tomb."[72]

The government of the *collegia* was developed under principles set down in the laws. These changed with time. Freedom of association prevailed until near the end of the Republic. Though suppression occurred in 64 B.C., the *collegia* were liberated by Clodius in 58 B.C. and then suppressed again under Julius and Augustus. The final resolution was a restoration by Augustus but with a permit from the government, under the proviso that meetings could be held monthly and then only for payment of fees. Paradoxically, it was under this restriction that the organizations grew to their greatest prosperity, in the period from about 100 A.D. to 300 A.D.

The structure that developed in the *collegia* was, perhaps intentionally, modeled after the structure of the city itself. There were obviously an excess of offices. Rolls had to be updated every five years, and some that were preserved show that there was strict attention to gradations of rank. One *collegium* of smiths had fifteen patrons at the top of the list, followed by twelve decurions, three honorary members, twenty-eight plebians, and several mothers and daughters of the organization.

The naming of offices seems similarly concerned with fine distinctions. The affairs of the organizations probably required relatively few functions, but the offices or statuses established might include *ordo, plebes, decuriones, quinquennales, curatores honorati, patroni, quaestores, magistri, prefecti, praesides,* and almost any other public official name. Not all of these were found in each one, but it is clear that there was an extreme concern for elaboration of statuses and fine gradations of ranks. The distribution of food or other valuable assets within the organization was sometimes related to rank—the typical Roman voluntary association was not an organization of equals. It is hard to tell from records whether the rank titles

were make-believe or whether they were actual municipal authorities who had a responsibility of regulation. Apparently both practices occurred. But in either case, inequality prevailed. It is hard to
see how the association could become a pressure group or civil
instrumental association in either case.

This practice seems even more ironic when we note that the rules
stipulated democratic procedures—one member, one vote. Most
voluntary associations as we know them now are organizations of
equals, particularly the smaller ones. This equality is not so much the
result of intention, ordinarily, as it is the result of the fact that
voluntary associations are formed in pursuit of common goals or
interests, which means that the membership is composed of people
having a common class position or a specific community involvement
that leads to those similar goals and interests. The same principle was
operative among the Romans; the communities, however, were
structured in very different ways, and it is to community structure
then that we must look for the explanation. The issue is similar to that
identified by Gunnar Myrdal in *An American Dilemma*.[73] Myrdal
observed the extreme but encapsulated and ineffective participation
of American Negroes (*ca.* 1940) in voluntary associations as a sub-
stitute for healthy participation that got results. Myrdal called it
"pathological." Negroes organized voluntary associations like those
of whites, with similar offices and functionaries, instead of pursuing
their own unique interests in their own unique ways.

A preliminary explanation about inequality in Roman
organizations may be given before we take up in detail the description of the features of Roman society that make a fuller answer
possible. Roman society was highly stratified economically and politically, but so far as religion was concerned, there was equality.
Appropriate burial was a prominent part of Roman religion. Romans
were united in an intense desire for appropriate burial. They were
frequently in social contact across economic barriers for purposes of
patron-client relations—status pretenses, flattery, and ingratiation
were often a more decisive bond in Roman society than formal
interest-oriented collectivities of equals. It was not inconsistent
then for voluntary associations to be assemblies of unequals
whose relations were those of the "vertical" dimension of social

inequality. They were merely doing collectively what they otherwise did individually. It is hard not to adopt Myrdal's attitude—Roman voluntary associations were mostly pathological, though, as in Myrdal's case, the value judgment is facile if you are an outsider.

There were voluntary associations throughout Roman history and they always had these limitations, even as the society changed from a kin to a social class structure under a powerful emperor. An explanation must be sought in terms of the organization of these relevant enduring elements of society as these changes occurred.

The fuller explanation of the nature of Roman voluntary associations may conveniently be started with the family system. Its features bear comparison with those of Athens and also of China and, in particular, with the family associations that were prominent in each case.

As in Athens and China, the family system had two main components: a household, which was the basis of procreation, religion, economic production, ownership, property inheritance; and a clan association, which was a religious-political unit. Perhaps the key sociological distinction in each society was that the death of the family head altered or destroyed the family, while the family association was perpetual and in fact increased in stature by a death. The family association is a holding company of spirits in perpetuity.

The Roman family association was called the *gens*. Authorities generally agree that little is known of the organization and control of the *gens*. Abbott says that there is no record of any *gens* under control of a single individual.[74] Councils of *gens* elders are heard of under the kings (i.e., prior to 509 B.C.) because the *gens* leaders then formed the Senate and elected the kings. The *gens* seems to have had similar functions to those of the Athenian *genos*; the similarity of names suggests some interrelation, and both are typically traced as sources of the biological term "genus."

Johnson says the activities of the early *gens* were the making of binding resolutions, guardianship of minors, care for the insane and for spendthrifts, receipt of property of the childless, religious services and sacrifices, the holding of common property, and ownership of a burial ground.[75] Such a statement is subject to misinterpretation

because the *gens* was steadily replaced by other forms of organization
as time went on and some of the functions were abandoned. The
religious functions of the *gens* were carried out through *collegia* and
*sodalitas*. Carcopino says that by the second century A.D. "the
ancient law of the *gens* had fallen into disuse."[76] Other changes
accompanied this, including decreased *potestas* of the *pater* and
increase of significance of cognatic kin and affines. This change
coincided with numerical increase of *collegia* for other purposes, and
so their relation with collectivities other than *gens* though a casual
connection is hard to identify.

One very significant social institution had its origin and matrix in
the *gens*: the patronage system. *Clientes* were hereditary dependents
with some of the privileges of the *gens*.[77] They owed specified
services to the *patronus*. The later abstraction of these terms from
the family institution to more diffuse use between nonkin status
unequals does not diminish the fatherly quality of the relationship.
Patronage was a fatherly role activity, giving money and support for
deference. This diffusion of patronage to the entire society was a
gradual affair, and as the *gens* lost its significance, public patronage
increased.

The contrast of the Roman, Athenian, and Chinese ethics of role
relationships is marked, and crucial for the understanding of the
social context of association formation in each case. Briefly, the ideal
typical Chinese role relationship was filial piety and specified formal
obligations; the Athenian, friendship; the Roman, patronage. The
Roman model is more like the Chinese than the Athenian in that it
was oriented to relations between unequals. This is not to say that
Romans thought friendship unimportant, but only that patronage
was the axis bout which all relationships revolved, and the result was
that friendship had a special and limited quality.

The Roman patronage system was thoroughly institutionalized—
so much so that it has to be described in detail to be believed by
modern readers. During the Empire it was customary in Rome for
each client to visit his patron at dawn. The patron would receive him
while remaining in bed, with servants hovering around to make his
arising as pleasant as possible. It was complicated by the fact that
every patron was also a client in his own fashion, to a patron higher in

rank to himself—every one, that is, except the emperor himself, for whom only the gods were *patroni.* In addition to the payment system to clients, which at one time was fixed at 6 1/4 *sesterces* a day (probably this held only at the middle levels), there were other privileges that expanded and informalized the system. At least some *clientes* were expected at any meal, and places were usually set for a certain number of them. Economically, this worked out fairly well, since it was prestigious to have an excess of food, and the *clientes* served to cut down the waste. It was also routine to give one's used clothing to *clientes*, and hence there was a diffusion downward of clothing. It is merely guesswork, since data on details are never quite above suspicion, but maybe that is why we have records of *collegia* of rag dealers but none of used clothing salesmen in Rome![78]

It was in the traditions of antiquity that a patron might adopt sons and daughters into his *familia*, and thus bestow on them the rights of inheritance. This was the ultimate success of a client. Toward the end of the Empire, perhaps in times when the morale of Romans was suffering from military defeats and domestic overindulgence, biological heirs were not preferred to adopted ones. One did not wish a woman many sons at her wedding. Marriage even became undesirable for some, and rich bachelors at least had the advantage of a larger retinue of clients who were particularly flattering and attentive. Some patrons are said to have cultivated a sickly look and certain preparations were known which bestowed a morbid pallor on the user. There is even record of one club of sycophants (perhaps a *collegium opificum*) that specialized in poisoning rich bachelors if the price was right. How much of this is practice and how much is illustrative exaggeration it is hard to say—nevertheless, it is hard to exaggerate the ubiquity and significance of the highly organized vertical principle in Roman society, and it is patent that it defined the scope of voluntary associations and perhaps also limited their development as instrumental associations.

It was mentioned that the *gens* gradually gave way to other forms of organization. Among these changes were the emergence of the *tribus* and the *curia* as more significant institutions in the urbanization of Rome. The *tribus* was an official region of the city; everyone belonged to one, and membership was hereditary. The *curia* "had

common religious rites, common festivals, and a common hearth."[79]
It is hard to know what Abbott, otherwise a very lucid scholar, meant
by "common hearth." It could not be taken literally, since so many
people were involved. It will be assumed that the term is meant
figuratively as a common loyalty. Thirty *curiae* were organized into a
*comitia curiata*, which was a popular assembly in the Royal era. New
*gens* could be added to a *curia* by vote of the *comitia*, and a device
was thus created for absorption of new family units, and significantly,
for inclusion of new religious elements (organized by *collegia*) of such
families, into the populace.

This device, and other means of synthesis that followed, are vital to
understanding the voluntary associations of Rome and its empire
because they provided a means of integration of the large lower-class
population who were qualified for membership in religious voluntary
associations. Rome expanded by conquest as well as by natural
growth, but conquest was always the more important. Therefore
some means of integration of captured slaves and ethnic groups was
necessary if unity was to be kept. Unlike Athens, which had no viable
method of absorption of metics (guest people) into citizenship, Rome
was always tolerant. It successfully institutionalized synoecism (integration of foreigners) as a principle of growth at an early date.
Slaves were frequently manumitted—so much so that at times laws
were enacted to slow the process. Freedmen formed a large stratum
and were welcomed into many areas of Roman civic life.

In earliest times a man became a part of Roman society by
establishing a client relation to a patron in a *gens*, or directly to the
king. In the fourth century B.C. a number of legal changes took place
that gave representation to the propertyless strata and accelerated
their political and civic assimilation. Under Appius Claudius Caecus,
censor in 312, landless freemen and freedmen might join any tribe
they wished. The change was not admitted without challenge, but in
general, the way was paved for assimilation of the lowest classes into
citizenship. Rome recruited personnel by conquest and provided
institutional arrangements for making their offspring into Romans.
One of the most important of these institutions was the cultic *collegium* or *sodalicium*.

Assimilation policies were not without limits. The aristocracy preserved its powers with zeal and often did so by restrictions on selection to offices, manipulation of entrance qualifications, and so on. Wealth alone was not a qualification. In addition, there was a general consensus over centuries that the rural life should be preserved, and land ownership laws were often manipulated to control land wealth and this had numerous diffuse and specific effects that limited the rapidity of integration of farmers into city life.

Freedmen were used by Roman leaders in a fashion similar to the Chinese use of eunuchs and medieval monarchs' use of Jews. They were useful because of the wealth they had or the special services they could perform, but above all, they were desired specifically because they could not hold certain categories of offices. Their condition limited their ambition. Wealthy freedmen in Rome were political eunuchs at court.

Each of the groupings tended to have its own *collegia* and *sodalitas* for religious purposes, particularly burial. Integration of class or ethnic groups meant integration of its voluntary associations. As long as the public cults were observed, private cults were not challenged, and hence *collegia* could grow at any level of the class system, though the rich tended to enter *collegia* as patrons, and I found no record of *collegia* of equally ranked upper-class members.

The articulation of the voluntary associations with the patronage system was decisive in determining their character, but it did not eliminate them or greatly diminish their numbers. One other feature of Roman life, that of the purpose and structure of government, did have the consequence of limiting the scope and effectiveness of voluntary associations. The voluntary associations were secondary institutions, tied to the *gens, tribus,* and other units, and their vitality was related to these more than to that of government itself.

Experimentation and variations in the structure of government were common in Rome. The struggles between *gens,* tribes, patricians, and plebs, and other categories were continual, and the structure of government reflected the status of the struggle. Nevertheless, throughout the 1,200 years with which we are concerned here, Romans always seemed to possess a pride, a central idealism that held them together while the most drastic changes in the structure of government went on. One of the sources of this deep pride was the continual Roman involvement in military ventures and empire building. This military aspect has been taken here as the identifying feature of most importance for analysis of Rome, because of its priority in Roman life. This, and not maintenance of free institutions, including voluntary associations, seems in retrospect to have been the Romans' basic commitment. Military organization, in its spirit and in its actual structure, always stresses the prepotency of authority in social relationships, and inhibits the growth of pluralistic associations that might provide a challenge. Rome is an excellent example of Randolph Bourne's maxim: war is the health of the state. To take just one example, Roman militarism inhibited the growth of a merchant capitalism that elsewhere has typically generated a profusion of associational forms. Let us trace this issue.

The rational reconstruction of Roman society into a military state was accomplished in several stages, but the most decisive legal change was probably the Servian military reorganization of the late Royal era. What essentially happened was that the old system of the tribal or phratry-based military was replaced by a system that allowed the plebs into the army. This meant that the property test for military service replaced the kin criterion. Sociologically, the change under way was essentially an alteration in the stratification system from a family-patrician to a class system with an oligarchical or aristocratic core of power operating through a massive bureaucracy. Though the reorganization was solely military, its consequences were far-reaching.

Military service was thus made the normal career of a large number of citizens, and since citizenship was opened to a larger number of men, the reorganization effected a vast transformation of society in several generations. It should be added, since it is not obvious to us now, that military service was usually eagerly sought by most men as a career; among other attractions, it offered a chance for booty, land to settle on, or perhaps a change to a career in colonial administration or some other form of preferment.

Military service dominated the careers of young men; ten years was the normal term. As a by-product it prevented full development of a number of careers in trade and manufacturing. For this and other reasons, Rome never developed a full merchant capitalism; booty was always a prior commitment, and even trade was keyed to military conquest. To a considerable extent, the Romans had the reverse of the American colonial formula—the flag follows the dollar. For the Romans, the *talent* followed the flag. Unlike medieval Europe, in which merchant capitalism was the basis of the gild system and the religious fraternities that were related to them, Roman merchants *as a stratum* were neither powerful nor politically significant. There were rich merchants, to be sure, but the wealth, even wealth in trade, was derived from military conquest or political empire building, not on development of the institutions of merchandising. This absense of a merchant stratum meant that one possible source of a competitive pluralistic elite was missing, hence one explanation, though not a complete one, for the relative prominence of voluntary associations in the lower classes.

Further, the military commitment meant that Rome's agriculture was undermanned at times. To support a city the size of Rome, food often had to be imported. The Roman military course, like the Spartan, was one from which there was no turning back.

The military often played a role in politics. In the Empire period, legions in the field often saw that their fortunes lay with their specific commander, and many a field commander returned to the gates of Rome with his legions to claim high office by threat as well as by acclaim and gratitude. However, one of the more significant results of militarism was that political affairs were dominated by the upper classes, who had either completed military service or who avoided it despite the influence of public assemblies like the *comitia curiata*. The Senate became in time the province of either the patricians or (later) an elite from the plebeian and patrician wealthy. The imperial task of the absentee field army thus essentially undergirded the growth of an oligarchy at Rome, for correction of whose abuses the voluntary associations were impotent.

The transformation from a kin-based patrician to wealth-based *nobilitas* elite in government took about five hundred years. But it remained an aristocracy all the while. The aristocracy did not simply drive out pluralism; there is no evidence of anything like the Greek political *hetairia* at *any* stage. And though the lower-class plebs gradually won the right to representation in government, they did not in the process bring the lower-class *collegia* with them.

One way that economic organizations gain power when they are not organized into large-scale units of production is to organize federally or in councils of shops or of gilds. This practice was noted among the Nupe. The late Roman *collegia* were organized into *arte*.[80] The *arte* was a name given to a community or council of gilds. It is difficult to estimate the extent of the movement. Paul-Louis, in his comprehensive economic history of Rome, does not even mention the *arte*.[81] *Arte* later became the generic Italian word for craft gild, and the source of "artisan."

As the Empire approached its last days, several transformations of its voluntary associations were evident. In faraway places, the imperial bureaucracy sometimes attempted to economize or exert control by cooptation of *collegia*. In one cited case, a sort of colonial voluntary fire department was pressed to a compulsory liturgy service. In other places, membership in *collegia* was made compulsory. In the late Empire period, the state applied the doctrine of *origo*, which meant that individuals had to carry out certain responsibilities at the place of birth. The *collegium* served as an instrument of registration for this policy, and even the chlldren of members had to belong to a *collegium* in order to be citizens. The "gilds" at this stage accepted into membership large numbers of people who had no common economic purpose but only a need to be registered in the central municipal *album* as citizens. Whereas gild membership in medieval Europe bestowed citizenship privileges and power, the Roman member was restricted and controlled and put to state purposes. It was the death of a voluntarism that had always been restricted, limited, and impoverished. Many must have escaped the effects of regulation, for there is record of *collegia* that apparently survived for six hundred years as medieval gilds. The Christian voluntary associations were coopted in another sense: they gradually developed into a church, with a Roman bureaucracy like that which once oppressed them. The term *collegia* survived as a cultural reality and took on new vitality as the name for the gild of students who were later so significant in medieval life.

## The Voluntary Associations of Ancient Judaism

Neglect of research on voluntary associations of the Old Testament peoples is strange, considering their historical significance in the development of Christianity and Western civilization. Christian scholars' attention to the problem stems from the significance of the doctrine of the Covenant for the associational form of the Protestant church.[82] Jewish scholarly inattention to voluntary associations, both ancient and modern, is even more surprising, considering the significance of such organizations for charity, mutual aid, and education in modern urban Jewish life and the historical import of the Covenant.[83] The reason is not the obvious lack of salience of the abstract concept of voluntarism, for there is not much print devoted to the best-known Jewish organizations themselves.

The primary sources to be used here include the Old Testament itself; Jewish encyclopedic references that rely on the Old Testament books or the Mishnah; Old Testament scholarship on particular issues; biblical social science, particularly anthropology, archaeology, and sociology. Biblical social science has tended to be tied to or integrated with seminary studies and is little known in the original disciplines. Biblical sociology, which was quite a lively pursuit for a few decades in the youth of sociology, has disappeared; one reason is that the historical sociology of Troeltsch and Weber proved to be more sound and has been accepted into seminary scholarship.[84]

The voluntary associations of ancient Judaism were the gild, possibly some forms of fraternity or burial association, and the synagogue (possibly not as ancient). The main question to which inquiry will be addressed is: What does the Old Testament itself, considered as a historical document, yield about voluntary associations of Jews? This framework of course determines the time period of the inquiry, which falls naturally into the prekingdom era (i.e., before about 1000 B.C.), the kingdom, the Babylonian exile, and the return.

The sources for this first part are the New English Bible (NEB), the Jerusalem Bible (JB), the Revised Standard Version (RSV), and the King James (AV).[85] The New English Bible (the most recent text) will be used as the key, with mention of the others where there are notable contrasts. The dates of first publication: AV, 1611; RSV, 1951; JB, 1966; NEB, 1970.

There are two entries in 1 Chronicles 4 that make references to gilds. "Seraiah was the father of Joab founder of *Ge-harashima*, for they were craftsmen"[86] (NEB, 1 Chron. 4:14). *Ge-harashima* is translated "the Valley of the Craftsmen," which may have reference to the ancient practice of residential neighborhoods of workers of a single craft. This practice will be referred to as "vicinal organization"; the research problem in each society is to determine whether it implies gilds, and if so, what kind and how voluntary they were. AV renders the passage as ". . . Joab, the father of the valley of Charashim."[87] JB and RSV are similar to NEB.

A second reference in 1 Chronicles, is in verse 21: ". . . The sons of Shelah son of Judah . . . Laadah, founder of Mareshah, the clans of the guild of linen-workers of Ashbea."[88] RSV has a distinction similar to that in verse 14, that will be the basis of a later comment: "The sons of Shelah the son of Judah: . . . Laadah, the father of Mareshah, and the families of the house of linen workers at Bath-asheba."[89] Neither "father" nor "founder" is wholly satisfactory, as will be seen. The RSV choice of "house" instead of gild seems to be a more cautious and preferable option because "gild" has unexamined connotations, as mentioned earlier. JB uses "clans of linenworkers," an emphasis that may also be challenged.[90] AV has ". . . the families of the house of them that wrought fine linen, of the house of Ashbea."[91] Significantly, the King James version was written in an era when gilds were in the decline or out of favor.

In Nehemiah 3 there are a number of references to repairs on the walls of Jerusalem. Various occupations took responsibility for their own sections, which again suggests the common pattern of vicinal organizations of crafts into gilds. ". . . Malchiah, a goldsmith, did the repairs as far as the house of the temple-servitors and the merchants, opposite the Mustering gate, as far as the rood chambers at the corner," Neh. 3:31.[92]

AV uses the Jewish "Nethinims" instead of "temple servitors," which seems more useful so far as tracing the *Nethinims* to other contexts is concerned.[93] RSV refers only to "the house of the temple servants and of the merchants."[94] NEB does the same.[95] JB, by transposing verses, produces a more decisive version: ". . . Malchijah, of the goldsmith's guild, repaired as far as the quarters of the oblates and of the merchants, opposite the Watch gate."[96] Significantly, the entire third chapter is titled "The volunteer builders." "Oblate" has two meanings, that of service, and that of a lay brotherhood; here the brotherhood is intended, and perhaps, therefore, a voluntary association.

There is another reference to vicinal craft organization in Jer. 37:21. "Then King Zedekiah gave the order and Jeremiah was committed to the court of the guard-house and was granted a daily ration of one loaf from the Street of the Bakers. . . ."[97] The other versions do not differ significantly.

Reference is made in 1 Kings 20:25 to "the brotherhood of the prophets,"[98] "company of prophets,"[99] "sons of the prophets."[100] Similar terms are used in 2 Kings 4:1, 2 Kings 4:8. Weber identifies these as gilds (discussed later).

In the King James version, the Psalms have dedications or credits to a supposed composer or author. The names that appear may be traced to other sources in relevant OT books. Many of these are apparently eponyms for actual gilds of musicians, the name being merely a conventional way of designating a gild by its traditional, perhaps mythical, founder. This naming device has a long history and is found again in medieval Europe, where gilds sometimes assumed the literal foundation of their organization by the saint to whom the gild was dedicated. Perhaps the neologism "hagonym" is justified in the later case, to characterize the Catholic custom of dedicating churches, fraternities, and gilds to saints. Eponymic customs were noted in the sections on Rome and Greece, and the practice is probably found wherever family associations embrace ancestor worship or cultic practices and give rise to specialized associational cults.

Among the psalmic dedications are the names of Asaph, Korah, Mahal, and Juduthun. Sellin and Fohrer refer to "guilds of temple singers like Asaph and Korah."[101] Asaph, Heman, and Jeduthun are mentioned in 2 Chron. 35:15; Jeduthun in Pss. 39:1, 62:1, and 77:1; Asaph appears alone in numerous Psalms.

Sellin and Fohrer believe that many of the Psalms were actually composed by members of the musicians gilds or were gild prop-

erty.[102] They identify Psalms 42-49 as Korahite, 50 and 73-83 as
Asaphic. Conversely, the Psalms of David are thought to be mostly
dedications, and the tradition that David was a singer may be a later
invention to rationalize the account.

The most significant information about these associations appears
in 1 Chronicles 25, which is a list of singers and their functions. This
section of the work of the Chronicler (*ca.* 250 B.C.) is a narrative about
David (*ca.* 1000 B.C.), and the building of the temple, the orders and
functions of the Levites, the classifications of the priests, the cantors,
the keepers of the gate, and other details.[103] This information, together with citations concerning Levites and these particular names (i.e.,
Asaph, Korah, Heman, Jeduthun) in Ezra 2:41, 70; Ezra 7:7; Neh.
7:43-46, 73; Neh. 11:17, 22; Neh. 12:46; Neh. 13:10, demonstrates
that the Chronicler's construction is a fiction. The decisive fact is the
large inconsistencies in numbers of generations back to David. What
conclusion is to be accepted from this internal criticism?

Pfeiffer's conclusions about this information is radical but seems to
fit the facts.[104] He suggests that the label "Levite" was applied to *all*
who undertook temple service. Once this was done, it was justified
by adopting a lineage suited to the people in power. This interpretation makes sense in light of the revisionist writings of contemporary
anthropologists, who have found that many primitive tribes deal with
problems of social organization by fictive kin constructions. Who is
counted as kin is a matter of the definition of the situation. Therefore
the numerous references to Levites in the Old Testament, except
where the early tribe is intended, may refer to associations of religious workers, some of them voluntary.

With this thesis, we may return to the previously noted problem in
1 Chronicles 4, where there was alternate use of "father of" and
"founder of." The issue for the translator is probably that of confusion
about whether the genealogy was actual or fictional. "Father of"
seems more naive.

If Pfeiffer's fictive kin thesis is true, it also means that some of the
doubts about the voluntarism of the gilds of singers, temple-
servitors, and gatekeepers are removed. A "clan-gild" (NEB, 1
Chron. 4:21) would not so likely be voluntary as to membership.

Probably it was a gild in which ascription was a dominant but not exclusive way of recruitment, as in the medieval European gilds. Such a gild may still sustain a considerable proportion of voluntary action. The gilds of Asaph, Korah, Heman, and Jeduthun were probably not closed or ascriptive clan-gilds, at least in the postexilic period, and may have existed even earlier.

We turn now to the subject of the volunteer army.

In Judges 7 the story of Gideon's war against the Midians is described. Yahweh tells Gideon that he is to excuse anyone of his army who is afraid. Twelve thousand find honesty the best policy and depart to more peaceful pursuits. By a further sign, the remaining ten thousand are reduced to three hundred. Three hundred with Yahweh then easily defeat vast numbers of the enemy.

Weber interprets this as an instance of exemplary charismatic leadership. The leader lacks all power of coercion. "Furthermore, all participation in war expeditions is voluntary, only indirectly compulsory through ridicule and shame."[105] This interpretation leaves doubt about the purely voluntary nature of Gideon's army. It does, however, suggest the need for further investigation into voluntary participation and its sources in social structure. Since the ends are predetermined, "Formal Volunteer Organization" seems to be the appropriate designation.

Weber's interpretation of Deut. 20:1-9 proceeds along similar lines. Yahweh does not demand war service of some categories of people. The passage in 20:8 is interesting. "Is there any man here who is fearful and faint of heart? Let him go home lest he make his fellows lose heart too."[106] This seems to be a counsel of pragmatism rather than voluntarism.

Of the four translations used here, only the Jerusalem Bible prints all of Tobit, Judith, Esther, and 1 and 2 Maccabees. The Maccabees, in particular, give interesting evidence of the impact of Greece and Rome on Israel.[107] JB notes that Maccabees may be seen as the record of the resistance movement against Hellenization. First Maccabees covers 175-134 B.C., and was written before 63 B.C. (JB, p. 569); 2 Maccabees has about the same chronology.

In 2 Macc. 4:7-20, the story of Jason's purchase of the priesthood is told. Jason used his authority to establish a gymnasium at Jerusalem. This undermined Jewish piety and greatly offended the righteous. The gymnasium was not a voluntary association, since control was probably not entirely in the hands of members. In Athens it had an officially appointed board. Perhaps the one at Jerusalem was a Formal Volunteer Organization.[108] No doubt the nakedness characteristic of the Greek gymnasium was abhorrent to Jews, though the issue is not mentioned. Perhaps more to the point, the individualism of Greek voluntary participation would be quite foreign to communally minded Jews.

The armed resistance to Hellenism that fills the pages of both books is voluntaristic. For example, in 2 Macc. 2:42, there is a description of "a community of Hasidaeans, stout fighting men of Israel, each one a volunteer on the side o the Law."[109]

In general, the material in Maccabees is not very decisive so far as voluntarism is concerned. We only learn that an occupied country resists by spontaneous response based on their religious commitment. More knowledge of the social structure of the Maccabees would be necessary before their volunteer army could be compared with the voluntary military force of the Cheyenne, described in Chapter 2.

It is possible that some of the sects that existed before Jesus were voluntary associations or communities controlled by voluntary associations. Baron and Blau make that interpretation of the Essenes.[110] The Essenes were an ascetic organized community with high entrance requirements and strict discipline. They, unfortunately, left little evidence of their way of life. Numerous religious writers have speculated that Jesus was an Essene. Other sects include the Therapeutae, Sadduccees, Pharisees, and Samaritans. In each case, there is no information that would lead to the conclusion that they were voluntary associations or had them in their community life.

It is obvious from the sketchy nature of the foregoing material that an extensive critical analysis of the literature of the Old Testament concerning gilds, sects, and fraternities, supplemented by other sources, would be necessary before a decisive theoretical explanation could be attempted. The Jews left only a tiny legacy of written material, compared to that of Rome and Greece, and it is unlikely that there will ever be enough data. The interpretive comments that follow are, therefore, quite speculative.

Weber stresses that one of the most distinctive things about the Yahweh tribes of ancient Israel was that they undersood themselves in historical terms. They perceived the meaning of their religion in the continuity of the tribes rather than as a response to nature. The Covenant with Yahweh was unique at the time, in social structural terms, in that it united people who were often seasonally mobile and scattered, into a military alliance under one god. Their fanatic subordination to one god created the normative basis of contractual relations with each other that were relatively peaceful, and were consistent with fraternal association formation in a number of ways. Can instances of voluntary organization other than those identified be reasonably surmised? What is the theoretical significance of a central ethical principle such as the Covenant for association formation in other social systems? Comparison with the *tao, maat*, and *mos* comes to mind.

Weber speaks of "synoecism," a term that refers to the practice of integration of foreign elements into the social structure of a city. This issue was encountered in the creation of Athenian *demes* and Roman *tribus*. The Israelites and others who occupied the eastern Mediterranean were constantly faced with invasions and occupations as the millennia-long struggle between Egypt on the south, and Assyria and Babylon to the east, surged and erupted through their land. In addition, the struggle for dominance between pastoral and urban forms of economy resulted in mechanisms of accommodation of foreign people. In this situation, certain occupations were the monopoly of metics who were permitted formal organizations. Besides the occupations specifically mentioned in connection with vicinal occupational patterns, which others were subject to gild organization? Which were reserved to metics and why? Was there meaningful continuity between this practice and the Jewish medieval gilds in which the Jews appear as metics with similarly restricted rights?

Weber suggests that prior to the Babylonian exile, in which Jewish religion underwent transformation, there were "gilds of magicians." The *Nebiim*, ecstatic warriors, were associated with these magician gilds.[111] At the same time, the *Rehabites* were frequently mentioned—a cult that survived in spite of the instability of the tribe of which they were composed. What was the organizational form of these cults and "gilds"? Unfortunately, the term "cult" is often used even more carelessly than "gild." Can textual research or supplementary materials identify the organizational nature of these cults?

The issue of permission in prevalence of voluntary associations has been encountered in every study of states so far. The Israelites experienced yet another variant. The issue here is that while the Jews were drastically restricted as a captive people, they were free within their own walls. The Jewish life during the exile and that which followed in their ancient homeland was lived in virtually complete social closure. It was this drastic restylization of Jewish life into a closed community, concerned in minute detail with purity and protection from contamination, that stimulated growth of the synagogue and made voluntarism possible within the walls. "Permission" again seems too narrow a concept for the many-structured forms that make voluntarism possible.

We turn now to more detailed analysis of Jewish gilds.[112] Throughout the Old Testament there are numerous mentions of occupations, some of which were discussed previously, and those that usually form gilds are plentiful. From such information, an estimate may be made of the possible scope of gild organization in ancient Judaism. In Duckat's list of biblical occupations, there are forty that were probably organized into gilds.[113] Duckat cites C. H. Gordon's claim that during the fourteenth century B.C., there was "a widespread organization of guilds that included the following: herdsmen, fowlers, butchers, bakers, bronze-, copper-, and silversmiths; potters and sculptors; houseboat and chariot builders; local and long-distance traders, priests, musicians, and special classes of warriors."[114] If we follow this reasoning, which indicates that there was a stratum of wealthy consumers who required markets for products of farming and husbandry, the forty is a conservative estimate. As noted regarding early Roman gilds, the list reveals that certain necessary occupations, such as weaving, may have been done in the home, probably by women, and not in special community shops of entrepreneurs. Probably not all were organized into gilds at the same time; but gild organization has everywhere proved to be a durable social device, and once the means of organization is learned and put into practice, it forces others to adopt the same mode in order to acquire the same sanction or mandate for economic privilege.

How is this remarkable early development of Jewish gilds to be accounted for? The location of Israelites on the major land trade routes brought them into frequent contact with travelers to the great cities and undoubtedly led them to emphasize some production for trade, even among herdsmen. Numerous of the early Israelite tribes were village dwellers; some were even herdsmen with no permanent home. Though there were fortified cities in Palestine from very early times, from the later biblical era there is evidence that certain of their crafts and gilds were intentionally relegated to villages, on the basis of their efficient use of raw materials or because it was undesirable to have them in cities. Skinners, for example, were sent to villages or at least outside of cities, because of the unpleasant smell. Other gilds that were characteristic of villages were those of potters, dyers, and weavers.

Later, when we turn to England, it will be seen that gilds were *permitted* there only in cities, and this was generally true throughout Europe. It was shown that gilds were found in villages in India, and it was probably true in the Roman empire as well. Setting aside the issue of permission, which is theoretically spurious, what are the requirements of gild location? At the minimum, the gild requires a large enough settlement for a concentration of workers in one or closely related trades. This was accomplished in India in very small settlements because the caste system led to the desirability of a village of one subcaste, and therefore of one occupation. In ancient Israel there were several forces that led to development of gilds in small settlements. Of greatest significance, after the exile, was the extreme need for ritual purity, which led to legal precision in carrying out the operations of most work. This is best accomplished within a carefully controlled and supervised setting, such as that provided by the gild, or in a foreign city in a ghetto. Second, and related to the above, the cultural unity of Jewish life meant that even the most isolated of settlers were well educated in religion and related cultural affairs, and even a small group of men might form a synagogue, which was a voluntary organization that proved to be well adapted to symbiosis with the gild. The tradition of high-quality craftsmanship was, of course, important. This was ancient. Although Solomon had to import skilled workers to build his lavish temple, the contact that resulted with the foreign workers supported and continued a tradition of craftsmanship. That was only one instance, and cultural exchange with other city craftsmen was not infrequent.

It seems likely that the period of the great Israeli kings, ushered in by David, was responsible for social conditions that were conducive to the growth of rationalism and intentional associations of several kinds, among them gilds. Solomon organized the territory surrounding his palace into administrative districts for tax purposes, as was done later in both the Greek *demes* and Roman *tribus*. This effectively superimposed a rational administrative system over the tribal system and made possible the extension of urbanism to a wide district. Such strategies were typically responsible for eventually breaking the hold of family or tribal associations on political life, and led to a new form of stratification compatible with the growth of a class system. Further, though there is little direct evidence in this case, systematic taxation usually leads to responsive strategies by citizens, one of which is tax farming, which is efficiently done through associations. As in the case of Hindu gilds, the gild leader, or in other cases an oligarchy, may encourage this as an efficient and profitable device that stabilizes the gild.

We have seen previously that gilds vary as to voluntarism. What judgment can be made in this regard about Jewish gilds? Membership was tied to competence in occupations that were hereditary. Members had a number of alternatives, however. Fathers often simply preferred to have their sons follow their own trade, and it was simple to do so, since the child was exposed to the trade in the home-shop from infancy. We have the image, probably much distorted, of Jesus in the carpentry shop of his father. Joseph could, in fact, have been a gild member—but Jesus neglected the trade. Fathers could apprentice their sons to another trade, not the least of the reasons being the imbalance between hereditary recruiting and market conditions. There is biblical mention of children being thought simply unsuited for a certain trade. Widows, who did exist in spite of the ancient custom of the levirate, sought an advantageous placement for sons. Perhaps it was reasons like these that led Duckat to doubt that "Biblical associations were as rigidly exclusive as the medieval craft gilds."[115]

A second reason to suggest that the gilds may have been voluntary is that they frequently acquired supplementary mutual-aid purposes, which were purely voluntary.

The synagogue was a development of the Babylonian exile period, though there is speculation that earlier references to assemblies of elders may have referred to a synagogue of a sort that was separate from the direct influence of the temple. Passages in Ezekiel would establish the date at the sixth century B.C. During the exile, cultural closure was accelerated and protective isolation from host people was developed. The role of rabbi came into existence as a much needed interpreter of the complex web of rules of purity, cleanliness, justice, and decorum. The synagogue, as an institution, became a small community organization that was distinguished from the priest-dominated temple. The temple priesthood was authoritative; the synagogue was a democratic organization of community members and families. The rabbi of the synagogue was not a dominant leader but a skilled teacher and interpreter, a first among equals, whose power stemmed from his wisdom. He was typically an ordinary craftsman who was also qualified in the law through extraordinary intelligence and diligence. There is, then, every evidence that the synagogue was entirely a voluntary association, differentiated from the temple just as the medieval fraternity was from the Roman Catholic church.

There are several things that support the interpretation that the gilds and synagogues had a rather easy accommodation to each other. Many gilds had a specific symbiotic relation with a synagogue. Larger gilds had their own synagogues. Perhaps in such cases there was a tendency to a sharper distinction between voluntary and nonvoluntary aspects of gilds themselves, the ritual affairs of the gild becoming a part of the synagogue.

The synagogue appears to bear more resemblance to the medieval fraternity than to the gild. The fraternity-gild distinction is unfortunately not kept clear in most writing on medieval life, though there is ample reason to do so, as will be explained later in detail.

The *Hevra* (or *Havurah*) *Kaddisha* is a "mutual benefit society whose services were restricted to its members, irrespective of the social, religious or charitable purpose for which it was established."[116] The predecessor type was the *Havurah*, a restricted funerary association of members of a certain profession or craft. This form may have been due to the influence of Hellenism, since earlier the burial would have been a strictly family function. Rabinowitz does not attempt to establish the earliest date of this form, but its specialization makes it seem unlikely in the pre-Christian era.

Ancient Jewish voluntary associations were not highly differentiated by type, and the few distinctions we have mentioned reveal a high degree of community integration. There were no political voluntary associations; though gilds may have been influential, and the synagogue certainly was, they were not politically specialized within the community. As long as Jews were captives or lived in ghettos as guest peoples, they were not citizens and had no basis for political activity. There is no record of purely social fellowship organizations, nor is it conceivable that licentiousness would have any place at all in Jewish culture as an organized or specialized activity, as it did among the Greeks.

A concluding note is appropriate here about the omissions in this account. The most significant lacuna is that of Egypt and the other Mediterranean contributors to Jewish culture. The wide diffusion of small fraternal organizations in the area, however, makes it unnecessary to study every society. The omission of Persia is regrettable. Jewish communities were widespread throughout the Mediterranean as guest people; the Jewish merchants were a vehicle of communication of culture for the first 1,800 years of the Christian era, and their influence has been largely overlooked by scholars. The role of the Jewish gilds was comparable to that of the Arab brotherhoods (and later, the Islamic) as transmitters of culture across the vast chasm of years from the collapse of the Roman Empire to the freshening of civilization that began Christendom's second millennium.

## Notes

1. Wolfram Eberhard, *Conquerors and Rulers: Social Forces in Medieval China*, 2nd rev. ed. (Leiden: E. J. Brill, 1970).

2. I am hampered by lack of language skills here. Bibliographies of Chinese dissertation and other research, however, support the contention that there is a genuine lacuna in the literature itself, regardless of the language of inquiry.

3. Pierre B. Maybon, *Essai sur les Associations en Chine* (Paris: Plon-Hourrit, 1925).

4. Hsien Chin Hu, *The Common Descent Group in China and Its Functions* (New York: The Viking Fund, 1948). The facts I have used on the *tsu* are all from Hu.

5. Ibid., p. 9.

6. Kung-Chuan Hsiao, *Rural China: Imperial Control in the Nineteenth Century* (Seattle: University of Washington Press, 1960), pp. 34-49.

7. Ibid., p. 7.

8. Ibid., p. 37.

9. Sidney D. Gamble, *North China Villages: Social, Political, and Economic Activities Before 1933* (Berkeley and Los Angeles: University of California Press, 1963), pp. 32-34.

10. Ibid., p. 35.

11. Ibid., p. 36.

12. Ibid.

13. Arthur H. Smith, *Village Life in China* (New York: Fleming H. Revell Co., 1899), p. 153.

14. John Stewart Burgess, *The Guilds of Peking* (New York: Columbia University Press, 1928), p. 27.

15. Ibid., passim.

16. Ibid., pp. 16-19.

17. Chung-Li Chang, *The Chinese Gentry: Studies on Their Role in Nineteenth Century Chinese Society* (Seattle: University of Washington Press, 1955), p. 64.

18. Burgess, *The Guilds of Peking*, p. 64.

19. Max Weber, *The Religion of China*, trans. and ed. Hans H. Gerth, (Glencoe, Ill.: The Free Press, 1951), p. 65.

20. Clifford A. Geertz, "The Rotating Credit Association: A 'Middle-Rung' in Development," in Immanuel Wallerstein, ed., *Social Change: The Colonial Situation* (New York: John Wiley and Sons).

21. Sidney D. Gamble, *Ting Hsien: A North China Rural Community* (New York: The Institute of Pacific Relations, 1954), p. 14.

22. Yu Yue Tsu, *The Spirit of Chinese Philanthropy* (New York: AMS Press, 1968), passim. Much of Tsu's work (first published, 1912) is propaganda and poorly documented.

23. Smith, *Village Life in China*, Chapter 14.

24. Ibid., p. 142.

25. Weber, *The Religion of China*, p. 209.

26. Jean Chesneaux, *Popular Movements and Secret Societies in China 1840-1950* (Stanford, Calif.: Stanford University Press, 1972), pp. 1-3.

27. Ibid., p. 3.

28. Ibid., p. 6.

29. In this respect they resemble the African rather than the European type discussed in Chapter 2.

30. The term "state" has been kept in the title here, and this may cause some confusion. India was, during the time under consideration, a unified state for only a short time. It was a series of states or principalities for a longer time. If its cultural unity, particularly under the caste system, is the focus, "nation" would be more appropriate.

31. Don Martindale, *Social Life and Culture Change* (Princeton, N.J.: D. Van Nostrand Co., 1962), pp. 179-85.

32. Arnold M. Rose and Caroline Rose, *Sociology: The Study of Human Relations* (New York: Alfred A. Knopf, 1969), pp. 323-36.

33. Charles Drekmeier, *Kingship and Community in Early India* (Stanford, Calif.: University of Stanford Press, 1962), p. 19.

34. Ibid., p. 278.

35. Ibid., p. 277. Varna is a general term for caste groupings or strata, probably originally a designation for color.

36. Jeannine Auboyer, *Daily Life in Ancient India: From Approximately 200 B.C. to 700 A.D.*, trans. Simon Watson Taylor (New York: The Macmillan Co., 1965), p. 103.

37. Drekmeier, *Kingship and Community in Early India*, p. 277.

38. Where gilds fought in England, it was as mobs rather than as armies. The apprentice boys rebellion in Londonderry (a London gild enterprise) is a famous example of a slightly different kind.

39. Max Weber, *The Religion of India*, trans. and ed. Hans H. Gerth and Don Martindale (Glencoe, Ill.: The Free Press, 1958), p. 36.

40. Max Weber, *The Sociology of Religion*, trans. Ephraim Fischoff (Boston: The Beacon Press, 1964), p. 111. For a fully developed treatment of

*ressentiment*, see Max Scheler, *Ressentiment*, ed. Lewis A. Coser, trans. William Holdheim (New York: The Free Press of Glencoe, 1961).

41. Weber, *The Sociology of Religion*, p. 111.

42. Ibid., p. 97.

43. Ibid., p. 102.

44. Weber, *The Religion of India*, p. 326.

45. Arkon Daraul, *Secret Societies* (London: Tandem, 1965), pp. 159-70.

46. Authorities do not always concur on the convention to be followed in English rendering of the suffixes of these nouns. The one chosen here is consistent with most of them. But also see the text regarding *hetairoi* and *hetairai*.

47. Robert W. Connor, *The New Politicians of Fifth Century Athens* (Princeton, N.J.: Princeton University Press, 1971), p. 11. Connor follows George Grote in this construction.

48. Ibid.

49. Charles Lécrivain, "Thiasos", in Charles Daremberg and Edmund Saglio, eds., *Dictionnaire des Antiquités Grecques et Romaines*, 5 vols. (Graz: Akademische Druck, 1969), pp. 258-60.

50. The text available to me is partially obliterated here.

51. William Smith, *Dictionary of Greek and Roman Antiquities*, 2nd ed. (London: Taylor, Walton, and Moberly, 1848).

52. Ibid.

53. George Miller Calhoun, *Athenian Clubs in Politics and Litigation* (Austin, Texas: University of Texas Press, 1913).

54. Connor, *The New Politicians of Fifth Century Athens*, p. 75.

55. Ibid., p. 29n.

56. Mariano San Nicolò, "Guilds in Antiquity," in Edwin R. A. Seligman, ed., *Encyclopaedia of the Social Sciences*, 15 vols. (London: Macmillan, 1948), Vol. 7, p. 205.

57. Ibid.

58. R. Cagnat, "Sodalicium, Sodalitas," in Daremberg and Saglio, *Dictionnaire des Antiquités Grecques et Romaines*, IV, part 2, p. 1372.

59. Ibid.

60. A. E. R. Boak, "Late Roman and Byzantine Guilds," in Seligman, *Encyclopaedia of the Social Sciences*, Vol. 7, p. 207.

61. San Nicolò, "Guilds in Antiquity," p. 206.

62. Jean Pierre Waltzing, *Etude Historique sur les Corporations Professionelles chez les Romains Depuis les Origines Jusqú á la Chute de l'Empire d'Occident*, 4 vols. (Louvain: Paters, 1895), I, p. 33.

63. San Nicolò, "Guilds in Antiquity," p. 206; Frank Frost Abbott, *The Common People of Ancient Rome* (New York: Bilbo and Tannen, 1965), p. 216.

64. Paul-Louis *(sic)*, *Ancient Rome at Work* (New York: Barnes and Noble, 1965).

65. Waltzing, *Etude Historique*, I. p. 51.

66. John Timbs, *Club Life of London*, 2 vols. (London: Chatto and Windus, 1865), Vol. 1, p. 2.

67. G. Baldwin Brown, *From Schola to Cathedral: A Study of Early Christian Architecture and Its Relation to the Life of the Church* (Edinburgh: David Douglas, 1886).

68. Ibid., p. xvii.

69. Theodore Mommsen, *De Collegiis et Socaliciis Romanorum* (Kiliae: In Libraria Schwersiana, 1843).

70. Samuel Dill, *Roman Society from Nero to Marcus Aurelius* (London: Macmillan and Co., 1904), pp. 260-61.

71. In the next chapter similar practices regarding corpse transportation of English gildsmen will be examined.

72. Abbott, *The Common People of Ancient Rome*, p. 222.

73. Gunnar Myrdal, *An American Dilemma*, 2 vols. (New York: Mc-Graw-Hill Book Co., 1964), pp. 952-55.

74. Abbott, *The Common People of Ancient Rome*, p. 1.

75. Harold Whetstone Johnson, *The Private Life of the Romans* (Chicago: Scott, Foresman and Co., 1932), p. 29.

76. Jérôme Carcopino, *Daily Lifesin Ancient Rome* (New Haven: Yale University Press, 1940), p. 77.

77. Abbott, *The Common People of Ancient Rome*, p. 1.

78. In modern America used clothing is sold through voluntary associations, the main ones being the Salvation Army and Goodwill Industries, plus various periodic rummage sales. These succeed because we reject direct charity to the poor. Patronage and voluntarism are similarly reciprocal in many societies. The voluntary associations may provide a secondary economic system in democratic-industrial societies where the primary one is oriented to high levels of productivity and pride in consumption. The differentiation of used clothing commercial (i.e., for profit) stores involves another set of issues.

79. Abbott, *The Common People of Ancient Rome*, p. 18.

80. C. W. Previté-Orton, "The Italian Cities 'Till c. 1200," in H. M. Gwatkin et al., eds., *The Cambridge Medieval History*, 8 vols. (Cambridge: at the University Press, 1929), Vol. 5, p. 237.

81. Paul-Louis, *Ancient Rome at Work.*

82. For example, the seminal volume on voluntarism in religion, edited by D. B. Robertson, makes only scanty reference to the Old Testament. D. B. Robertson, ed., *Voluntary Associations: A Study of Groups in a Free Society, Essays in Honor of James Luther Adams* (Richmond, Va.; John Knox Press, 1966). The volume has no detailed citation of voluntaristic research on the Old Testament. It is possible that I have missed some items in the vast number of articles on the Old Testament, but the generalization undoubtedly holds.

83. A survey of Jewish encyclopedias in print and Jewish seminary indices reveals little attention to voluntary associations of *any* era.

84. A useful review of biblical sociology research is contained in Herbert Hahn, *The Old Testament in Modern Research* (Philadelphia: Fortress Press, 1966). The works consulted here include W. F. Albright, *From the Stone Age to Christianity,* 2nd ed. (Baltimore: Johns Hopkins Press, 1957); Salo Baron, *A Social and Religious History of the Jews,* 10 vols., rev. (New York: Columbia University Press, 1952-1965); Salo Baron and Joseph L. Blau, *Judaism, Postbiblical and Talmudic Period* (Indianapolis: Bobbs Merrill Co., 1954); Adolphe Lods, *The Prophets of Israel* (New York: Dutton, 1937); Roland de Vaux, *Ancient Israel: Its Life and Institutions* (New York: McGraw-Hill and Co., 1961); Louis Wallis, *The Bible is Human* (New York: Columbia University Press, 1942). There were many German works in the same period, which remain untranslated, and appeared to have dominated the field.

85. No modern Catholic text was consulted, an omission that results in a biased account here. *The Holy Bible, Authorized King James Version* (London: William Collins Sons and Co., 1958); *The Holy Bible, Revised Standard Version* (New York: Thomas Nelson and Sons, 1951); *The Jerusalem Bible, Reader's Edition* (Garden City, N.Y.: Doubleday and Co., 1968); *New English Bible* (Oxford: At the University Press, 1970).

86. NEB, 1 Chron. 4:14, p. 448.

87. AV, 1 Chron. 4:14, p. 380.

88. NEB, 1 Chron. 4:21, p. 448.

89. RSV, 1 Chron. 4:21, p. 423.

90. JB, 1 Chron. 4:21, p. 431.

91. AV, 1 Chron. 4:21, p. 380.

92. NEB, Neh. 3:31, p. 536.

93. AV, Neh. 3:31, p. 451.

94. RSV, Neh. 3:31, p. 502.

95. NEB, Neh. 3:31, p. 536.

96. JB, Neh. 3:31, p. 508.

97. NEB, Jer. 37:21, p. 965.

98. JB, 1 Kings 20:35, p. 389.

99. NEB, 1 Kings 20:35, p. 404.

100. RSV, 1 Kings 20:35, p. 381.

101. Ernst Sellin and George Fohrer, *Introduction to the Old Testament*, trans. David E. Green (Nashville: Abingdon Press, 1968), p. 262.

102. Ibid., p. 283.

103. These phrases are chapter titles in JB.

104. Robert H. Pfeiffer, *Introduction to the Old Testament* (New York: Harper & Row, 1948), p. 799.

105. Max Weber, *Ancient Judaism*, trans. and ed. Hans H. Gerth and Don Martindale (Glencoe, Ill.: The Free Press, 1953), p. 11.

106. JB, Deut. 20:8, p. 209.

107. The use of Maccabees for analysis of foreign impact on Israel was suggested by Weber, *Ancient Judaism*.

108. David H. Smith, Richard D. Reddy, and Burt R. Baldwin, eds., *Voluntary Action Research: 1972* (Lexington, Mass.: Lexington Books, 1972), pp. 176-77.

109. JB, 1 Macc. 2:42, p. 573.

110. Baron and Blau, *Judaism, Postbiblical and Talmudic Period*, pp. 75-80.

111. Weber, *Ancient Judaism*, p. 97.

112. In this section I have drawn heavily on Mark Wischnizer, *A History of Jewish Crafts and Guilds* (New York: Jonathan David, 1965).

113. Walter Duckat, *Beggar to King: All the Occupations of Biblical Times* (Garden City, N.Y.: Doubleday and Co., 1968).

114. Ibid., p. 321.

115. Ibid., p. 322.

116. Louis Isaac Rabinowitz, "Hevra," in Cecil Roth and Geoffrey Wigoder, eds., *Encyclopedia Judaica*, 16 vols. (Jerusalem: The Macmillan Co., 1972), Vol. 8, p. 442.

# 4 *English voluntary associations: from religious fraternity to secular club and religious sect*

**Part I: Comparative Study of Major Types**

INTRODUCTION

T he voluntary associations of England before Queen Elizabeth I were all some form of religious fraternity. Even before her reign was over, secularism was emerging rapidly, fraternities and their economic or political form, the gilds, were diminishing rapidly in significance, new forms of voluntary association were emerging everywhere, and voluntaristic Protestant sects were vexing the established church. Seldom does history show *organizational* changes as striking as this. Yet through it all there was continuity: Some gilds continued almost unchanged and corporations emerged from others; and Catholicism developed new forms of outreach based on ancient values. In addition, the vigorous new clubs had minor precedents even in the medieval years.

It seems strange that this change has not been the subject of more concentrated sociological analysis, for it offers so many chances for insight into social process and change. In this chapter, the ideal-typical method will be used to encompass the vast amount of data into parsimonious form as a basis for comparative analysis of the voluntary associations of the two periods regarding the topics outlined in Chapter 1.

The time covered may be divided into two parts for analytical purposes. The first era begins as the religious fraternity emerged from its origins in feudalism before the second Christian millennium. "The year 1,000 may be taken as a turning point," says Bishop.[2] It was indeed about that time that accelerated changes began to take place in England. Whatever the origins of the new forms may have been, the Norman conquest (1066) crystallized the nascent movement, and records of many fraternities are found as early as the late eleventh century. The dividing point of the two eras can be set at about the middle of the sixteenth century, the most significant event being the Act of Conveyance of Henry VIII and associated destructive actions of about two decades during which gilds and fraternities were emasculated and the monasteries almost totally destroyed. The destruction was not followed at once by new institutions. The partial restoration of the gilds under Elizabeth was a sort of null period in which the gilds did not really flourish, nor was thorough secularism encouraged. The end of the second era is, like the beginning of the first, somewhat indefinite. In this case, the reason is not obscurity of data but academic convenience. The analysis is carried forward selectively into the eighteenth century solely to trace the emergence of some of the types of organization that succeeded the clubs of the gentlemen hedonists: the workingmen's organizations, the Friendly Societies, the residential club, the unions, and the Methodist phase of the Christian sects. The period between eras was not devoid of activity; some *groups* will be identified that crystallized into associations toward the end of Elizabeth's reign. Schematically, the eight centuries may be crudely represented by the sequence: voluntary associations, groups, then voluntary associations again.

The conventional way to approach the problems of eras in European history is to use "medieval" and "renaissance" plus finer divisions and modifiers. These will not be used, at least in the conventional sense, though "medieval" will sometimes be used to generally designate "ancient" or "earlier." Both terms have acquired meanings that I wish to avoid. In particular, "renaissance" is used as an independent variable too often, to prove why something had a certain character. That is an error of sequences. The object here is to establish the nature of certain kinds of organizations, not to assume something about them because of when they existed. Medieval, then, refers to a time, not a characteristic and if someone can furnish me with an agreed-upon list of what "renaissance" was a rebirth of, establish the identity of the parents, and prove the validity of its *karma* and *dharma*, I'll then be sympathetic to its use. In addition, the term "renaissance" typically is defined solely in terms of relevant cultural phenomena—and to do so establishes the priority of culture as a causal phenomenon, an assumption I wish to avoid.

The wider range and greater accessibility of data in the later era make feasible a more comprehensive analysis than in previous chapters. Here the list of topics (existence, prevalence, variety, purpose, consequence) that were discussed in Chapter 1 may be more fully explored. This chapter and the next will be treated as an analytical unit. First, some major contrasts between the organizations of the periods will be presented, to set the stage. Second, the thesis of the two chapters, concerning the sources of organizational existence, will be outlined using the ideas developed in Chapter 1 in a new form. Following this, a more complete and detailed analysis of the two types will be made, with coverage of deviant types and their meaning. Before presentation of the major contrasts, however, some comments on the methods of research are in order, because the historical-sociological method used is more exact than in the previous chapters and the data present issues not covered in the general comments in Chapter 1.

METHODS OF RESEARCH

The need for a new account of the field is evident to any scholar, no matter what his discipline, who pays serious attention to the sources.

Since the original documents are inaccessible, most writers have had to rely on secondary sources that are ideologically biased. English medieval documents are not centralized, because most of the medieval municipal governments are still operating units that treat gild records as local government documents. Most of the London gilds have had at least one historian, typically a member with little technical training who, like one whom I shall forebear to name, stated his purpose as identification of the "curious things" in his gild's records. Gilds outside of London, especially in the smaller towns, are studied less often but more systematically and in fuller context, since the scope of the studies of the local historians demands it. Many such writers, however, tend to perpetuate the errors of those who have gone before, and it seems evident that writing a gild history has become little more than a status ritual; every gild has to have one to qualify as an historically significant organization. It's like tracing your ancestors back to beheaded nobility, ignoring the hanged horse thieves encountered along the way.

European gilds were, and still are, formally ranked in ordinal sequence and seem bound to make their histories a part of their display of ceremonial standing in that ranking. This makes objectivity difficult in some cases, though the histories are often voluminous, full of data, even if not interpreted adequately, and one can draw one's own conclusions. Charles Gross, one of the best of the outside gild analysts, caught the essence of the matter when he said that "the little that has been written on the subject is . . . replete with errors, whose wide prevalence renders it doubly difficult to give a lucid exposition of the nature and growth of the institution."[3] The eight decades that have passed since his statement do not give cause to alter the verdict very much. Mention, therefore, should be made of the few sources that seem to be exceptions and on which I have relied extensively, though the debt is often not stated: Kramer, Unwin, Kahl, and Gross.[4]

The materials regarding the early (about 1000-1500) and late (about 1550-1800) eras differ somewhat in reliability. The fraternities and gilds that existed prior to the eighteenth century encountered severe ordeals. One of these was the London fire of 1666, which destroyed many gild halls and with them their records. When

Henry VIII perpetrated the infamous Act of Conveyance of 1545, he destroyed many monasteries and gilds directly, and others simply sensed the changing times and quit. Henry granted reprieves to a number of gilds or fraternities that had reputations for service and charity; others were skilled at pleading their own cause and managed to survive. Even a change (from Edward to Mary or Mary to Elizabeth) of official religion did not faze some: one year their records stated that the company went to the church and heard mass, the next year the record said that they went to the church and heard a goodly sermon. But it is likely that the lesser gilds were hit harder, and therefore, we may understate their earlier prevalence and significance. Henry's son, Edward, was somewhat more prudent than his father, though restrictions continued through his brief and supervised reign; Henry's daughter Mary restored many gilds because she was pious and Catholic; Henry's daughter Elizabeth restored selected others because she was shrewd and needed their money. But the records were jeopardized in all cases, either as to existence or content, and those made and kept were often cautious, as if those who had experienced the terror of religious persecution were keeping in mind that it could happen again. Another source of record attrition was the neglect of public records by careless officials. Many valuable scrolls were decayed, nibbled by rodents, lost, or destroyed by various means. Many borough records are kept carelessly in present-day municipal vaults, on the same shelf where they were put by some clerk five hundred years ago; they are often not made available to scholars for reasons that seem obscure to outsiders.[5] The final problem occurred during the blitz bombings of World War II that destroyed many London gild halls, and the property that could not be sequestered in time.

The data on the secular clubs, besides simply being more recent and more frequently available in printed form, come from sources subjected to different kinds of problems. From the start of Cromwell's rule until the revolution of 1688, the clubs were particularly controversial in politics, and information on their meetings is subject to partisan reporting. What we know about the regular life of the clubs tends to come from private journals and from commentators cited in the newspapers of the times. These papers tended to cite only the more interesting or scandalous affairs. Club minutes are scanty; gild minutes are numerous. The seventeenth century created a new level of documentary material quite suited to catching more subtle themes than in the case of the earlier gild. ith adequate caution, comparative statements can be made that meet the minimum criteria of ideal-types, even if they do not always prove them to our complete satisfaction.

In addition to biases among amateur gild historians, there were numerous publications that attempted to use the gild as a basis for economic or political reform. Among these are found the Guild Socialists, and conservative Catholic writers such as Clune (1943) and Gasquet (1907).[6] A bias in another direction was found in nineteenth-century Liberal economists (following Adam Smith) who accused the gild of economic tyranny and restrictiveness, which held back the growth of capitalism. Among these groups there are frequent citations and numerous petty polemics that did little to promote objectivity.

The following citation from a seventeenth-century scholar, who was concerned, like the present writer, to determine the truth from documents of the distant past, seems to sum up the whole problem nicely. The source is Robert Brady, a remarkably astute commentator on historical methodology who deserves better publicity.

'Tis all I could find worth notice, amongst the many Volumes of the ancient Monks, they being nothing Almost but vast heaps of Legends, Tales, and vulgar Reports which passed for current in those ignorant and credulous times; nor is any more methodical or authentic Story to be expected for some, and those not a few years yet to come; yet out of these Clouds of darkness, out of these voluminous, idle, vain, inconsistent discourses, a man may pick out matter sufficient for strange admiration. . . .[7]

THE MAJOR CONTRASTS BETWEEN FRATERNITY AND CLUB

The ideal-typical voluntary association of the seventeenth and eighteenth centuries was the club. It was a small, simple, urban organization of people who gathered frequently for entertainment or enjoyment, including various creative activities such as poetry, music, debate, political argument, and scientific analysis. This entertainment or enjoyment was so prominent a theme that the club will be called a single-purpose organization. It was not affiliated with other organizations, nor did it have sponsors other than its members. It did not own real property. Common religion was not a basis of membership, and religious dispute was normal. In this regard, the clubs were *intentionally* different from the gilds that still existed. Many clubs had a "one of a trade" rule to ensure variety.[8]

The ideal-typical voluntary association before the Act of Conveyance was the religious fraternity, alternately known as a gild (or guild), brotherhood, confraternity, sodality, or just fraternity. The term "confraternity" was also used to refer to persons enrolled in an album to receive special prayers during mass, particularly by monks in an abbey. The persons so enrolled were not related to each other in a group and hence did not form an association. Of the terminology of the ancient world, "sodality" and "fraternity," of Roman origin, were the survivors; "college" had acquired a more limited application in education; and the Greek and Jewish words did not find their way into English. In this account, the term "fraternity" will be used to designate the noneconomic religious organization, and the term "gild" will be reserved for the fraternity with economic, political, or governmental or other purposes, which sometimes set in motion a process that eliminated voluntarism in the entire organization. This does not imply that in individual cases a fraternity always preceded each gild, but only that the idea of organizing small religious fraternities was the basic process in the entire society as had been the case in Rome. The fraternity was usually a small organization, found in all nonfeudal settlements of all sizes. Under special conditions, in its maturity it could grow quite large. It was usually affiliated with a parish church, chantry, cathedral, or abbey. It was a multiple-purpose organization, in which religious duties were of high priority and the only element that was always present. Other purposes were, variously, mutual aid, burial and commemoration, fellowship and feasting, drama and ceremonial sponsorship.

It was the successful development of the fraternity as a multiple-purpose organization that made it congenial for medieval man to adapt the religious fellowship to economic and political or governmental purposes and create the organization that we know as the gild. Like any social form that becomes widely accepted, the fraternity was put to a variety of uses, the most prominent of them being the gild, and in these some variation of organizational form eventually emerged. The variations typically involved some internal oligarchy and other forms of internal stratification. English gilds are, therefore, typically quasi-voluntary associations. Where works on gilds employ definitions, unfortunately a rarity, the gild is more often than not simply called a voluntary association. Since most such writers are content not to pursue the matter another step and inform us what they think a voluntary association is, this is of little advantage. In addition, it is rarely clear whether the full range of organizations that bear the name of gild (or guild) is intended; whether the companies like the Staplers or Merchant Adventurers are included; or if modern uses are meant that tend to signify a woman's service organization or professional association. The procedure used here, to recapitulate, is to distinguish the fraternity, always a voluntary association, as the analytically and only sometimes historically generic form, and to identify the circumstances under which its applications to other institutions led to deviation from the voluntary association form.

Here are some typical definitions of gild from the literature of the field. "In the broadest sense guilds [*sic*] are voluntary and permanent associations for the promotion of common interests."[9] And a definition in context from one of the better amateur gild historians: ". . . The voluntary association of the Gild and municipal government began to influence one another and to coalesce."[10] Gross, who concentrated on only the early *gild merchant*, says that "gilds may be briefly defined as voluntary associations for mutual support."[11] Obviously, the weight of evidence among those who define it at all, is to identify the gild as a voluntary association, but as noted above, this is by no means decisive.

COMPARATIVE MEMBERSHIP MOTIVES, ETHICS, AND ORGANIZATIONS

The psychological sources of organizational existence may be examined by means of a method suggested by Max Weber's classic analysis of the *Protestant Ethic and the Spirit of Capitalism.*[12] Uncertainty about election by God but conviction of predestination led the individual Calvinist to unrelieved and comprehensive personal disciplined endeavor and accumulation of capital. The fraternal ethic, in extreme contrast, was a consequence of the certainty of purgatory. The medieval Roman Catholic's conviction that purgatory was real was coupled with an uncertainty of the fate of his soul in traversing it. This uncertainty led to intense religious work directed primarily through the agency of the church, work for which his income could become instrumental. The fraternity was a specialized community voluntary association to better accomplish this result, and it was precisely because it was a work organization that it was so easily turned later to purposes for which work, in the more conventional economic sense of the term, was appropriate. The concept of liturgy, though since modified by diverse usage, indicates what is intended here. Liturgy is religious work, in which men seek religious rewards through human endeavor. If the idea of the gilds and fraternities as work organizations is kept in the forefront, a great deal of the confusion about these organizations can be dispelled.

In the later era, there are two main kinds of voluntary organization to account for: the club and the Protestant sect. The club will have priority in this study, not because it was more important, but simply because the sects have been better accounted for in sociological and religious research. In addition, the sects vary greatly as to degree of voluntarism, which, in fact, was one of the main sources of conflict and ultimately organizational differentiation among them; only the club was clearly a voluntary association in all of its aspects.

The motive of the club member was hedonism, the search for pleasure expressed variously in sensual, erotic, intellectual, or aesthetic modes of action. The club brought together people with congenial interests and created new interests in those it brought together. Like the fraternity, success led to new applications, and many clubs abandoned their voluntarism to accomplish a purpose to which their debate oriented them.

MEMBER IDENTITY AND ORGANIZATION: EXISTENCE OF THE FRATERNITY

We may now proceed to examination of the sources of existence and prevalence of the voluntary associations of the medieval era. The first inquiry will concern those aspects of the model that have to do with the collective action orientation. In Chapter 1 this was divided into four aspects: permission, instigation, resources, and rewards. We begin with the relationships among instigation, resources, and rewards.

The wealthy medieval noble provided for the perpetual welfare of his soul by religious work of a qualified functionary, if possible in the family chantry or chapel. The Roman patrician had done the same thing a thousand years before. A wealthy man could buy or build a chapel in a church, and this carried the right to select his own clergyman. Wills often designated trustees for managing the organization of the activity and its perpetuation. Some wealthy men provided alternate sets of trustees to watch the first, and still more wealthy, or perhaps just more anxious, ones provided a third set to watch the second. The ordinary burgess (or burgher), of lesser social standing, took purgatory just as seriously, but his means differed. The burgess was the ideal-typical fraternity man—the civically qualified owner of property, having tenement in a borough. To be a burgess, one passed a means test; was of good character, which included establishing that he was of "lawful blood"; was capable of earning a living (i.e., paying taxes); and took a sacred oath of political loyalty. A man often became a burgess through an economic gild, and perhaps also through a fraternity, though this is not always clear in documents. The returns from the parliamentary demands to gilds for information in 1388 show that at that time many did not distinguish clearly between the names of fraternity and gild, but were probably clear about what they were doing, and it is this that concerns us. The burgess accomplished through the gild, and other free men through the fraternity, what the noble did with personal wealth. Through the organization he developed solidarity with others to provide systematically for the unfortunate each day, and thus for his own soul in purgatory. This "payoff" was the ultimate motive for collective action, and from it stems the collective action orientation of medieval man.

The reliability of the organization was of great concern to the burgess. He committed much of his time and resources to it, and had to rely on it to function in perpetuity. It was, therefore, natural that the fraternity had a number of agreements to ensure organizational performance. The fraternity member took a solemn religious oath to carry out obligations for the welfare of others, the bargain implicit in the act being that they would do the same for him if he was in need. This was not a contract with men in the full sense, but a contract with God. The benefits were not calculated on an actuarial basis, and members frequently voted assessments for special cases. Identification as a member qualified the person to receive benefits; it obligated him in turn to give to those in need. The two acts were each contingent on both the individual's economic fortune and on his moral qualifications. This uncertainty about contingencies provided a strong force of organizational solidarity, and a practical reason for organizations. The nature of the organization thus created becomes more clear if it is viewed in contrast to the rotating credit societies described in discussions of Africa and China, where the financial rewards were calculable by rational means leading to performance guarantees and mutual aid on condition of contractual fulfillment. The fraternity and gild were obviously based on very different motives. The rotating credit society paid off in a certain time; the fraternity paid off in heaven.

Much of the solidarity of the organization, once it was formed, lay in the meaning of the oath of obligation, which had the long tradition of feudalism and related laws behind it. In addition, there was in principle little general authority per se for the medieval man, but only a series of personal relationships, defined in law and enforced by known and predictable penalties. Disrespect to the superior person in such a relationship was a sin, and thus there were both religious and civil penalties for breaking an obligation. Organizations seemed to endure well—the social forces which bound them were strong and multilinked. Thrupp speaks of these relationships as "authority," which is not a typical sociological usage.[13] It was contractual, and in such a situation the imbalance or one-directional flow of influence that is characteristic of authority was lacking. The obligations were to persons, and not to the offices of the persons. The similarity with the attitudes of the Athenian citizen is remarkable.

Compared to Weber's Calvinist *ephors*, who were never quite sure of their election, the fraternity brother was never quite sure of his soul's future. He did not know how much effort was needed, and since the religious demand was open ended, he hoped to give it all he could. Robertson puts it bluntly: "Medieval Catholicism . . . stressed the duty of gaining sufficient property and of refraining from squandering it through excessive generosity."[14] The fraternity helped deal with the individual's anxiety about the frighteningly real but incalculable world of life after death. And death was an ever present reality to the medieval man in whose world the birth rate and the death rate were both very high. Unwin stresses this death theme in his analysis of the importance of the afterlife as a motivation of the medieval man.[15]

The fraternity helped solve the problem of life after death on a day-by-day basis, as well as providing assurance that there would be a suitable effort on behalf of a soul after death when a man himself could do nothing on earth. It was an amazingly effective source of organizational solidarity. But of perhaps as great a significance and more easily overlooked, the fraternity helped to establish for a man what a suitable effort should consist of, just as gilds helped establish standards about the quality of craftsmanship in making a pair of shoes. In any work organization, workers need such a definition, no matter whether the work is done by a person on his own behalf or on the behalf of others. The noble met the problem of purgatory with a human contractual relationship of his own making following the feudal manner; the fraternity man and the gild member made arrangements through their organization. Through the organization, the fraternity member met the church's demands on a practical basis. For six hundred years or more, the fraternity stipulated how many candles or how much wax for certain obligations, the number of obits, the personnel of the funeral procession, and so on.

The fraternity and gild relationship to a church may be described in one sense as a kind of business relationship. Clergy commonly charged for the work they did. Getting people through life and through purgatory involved an immense amount of activity, and taking fees was the way it was paid for. The gild brought all of its religious business to a church, and in many cases, these collective arrangements were both more efficient and more effective than individually hiring a priest. It was the kind of a deal no businessman could refuse.

The gild and fraternity solved another perplexing problem for medieval man, that of usury. Usury was a matter that vexed all Christians and was the subject of an immense amount of theological hair-splitting. The mutual-aid organization provided a solution in that it regulated loans and set the condition of joint ventures, particularly involving the capitalization of shipping. It was also useful in a practical sense in that it established a private milieu for transactions and it limited scrutiny. Because of the social bonds of the organization, other forms of security were less necessary and interest not so much of a temptation. Weber's work on usury and gilds is of considerable interest in relation to gild formation.[16] For Weber, the gild is a "regulatory group."[17]

The handling of charity was a perplexing problem for medieval man, and the gild was crucial in solving the problem. There were increasing numbers of unfortunate and poor cast into the cities and onto the highways by the breakdown of feudalism, changes in land ownership and use, plague and famine, and by the continual wars that weakened all of Europe. Government was never able to adequately cope with the issues, and in many ways the fraternities and gilds stepped into the breech. The problem may be viewed as consisting of internal and external aspects. Internally, the fraternity provided for care of its own unfortunate members through a mutual fund or insurance, and as objects of charity. Externally, alms for nonmembers were a continual problem and until much later when systematic endowment policies were established, the major one. The association usually provided for a limited amount of alms in its plans (or sometimes in its charter), but *always with the provision that the recipients be worthy*. The fraternity thus provided for both a minimum and a maximum amount of brotherhood and so solved a lot of problems for the members. There must have been some medieval Latin equivalent of the phrase any modern door-to-door canvasser hears too often: "I gave at the office." There were, particularly in the later centuries of gild life, planned provision for endowment of hospitals and schools in the charters and budgets of the organizations. In this case, even the gild that had ceased to be active in control of the economy was significant because it provided a workable way to dispose of one's estate to worthy causes through known and predictable organizations that would carry out the burgess's wishes. Such gilds often controlled large estates and were in effect the equivalent of the modern nonprofit corporation or foundation. In the nineteenth century the English gilds came under severe criticism for the handling of their properties, particularly regarding taxation.

In the early epoch, the fraternity was often concerned with the care of lepers ("lazars"). Some special fraternities came into existence for that purpose. Some occupational fraternities or gilds, because of their unique skills, were given care of lepers by the governments, and among these the barber-surgeons were prominent, particularly as city gatekeepers or inspectors on call, in which posts they served as much to keep out lepers as to attempt to cure them. In sum, the record of the fraternities in alms and charity was of only modest proportions: the organization regulated charity as well as providing it. The fraternity did not love the unlovable.

The fraternities, particularly in the early years, did not have edifices of their own for meetings or religious services. However, there are records of fraternities in parish churches in which the organization met in the church house or mansion, but not the church itself. In some cases, the fraternity used the premises so frequently that it became theirs in practice. The fraternity might also endow the construction of a private chapel in or near the church.

From the fourteenth century, there are a number of records of fraternities that had begun to take on the functions of an economic gild but which did not have a royal or municipal charter and, therefore, maintained a blissful ambiguity about their legal status. Such organizations may have had some wealth and a hall of their own, or in towns of relatively small scale, they might share a gild hall with some other organization. For the most part, the fraternity was not the owner of a clear title to real property, its major expenditure being for a pall tapestry, which, however, might be very elegant. The prominence of the tapestry in property inventories is a material reminder of the religious values of the fraternities and gilds.

The fraternity member acquired an added identification with his community through the affiliation of his association with a particular church or religious body, and a more specific religious role identity by the fraternity's routine practice of taking a patron saint. In some cases the patron was that which gave a name to the church. In other cases the patron had a special significance because of the residence of the members in a certain parish, which in turn was sometimes due to the vicinal concentration. It is difficult to find information that would lead to a decision about which of these factors was cause and which was effect. At any rate, the medieval burgess never lived very far from a church (in London usually not more than a quarter-mile), visited it frequently, and legally belonged to it. With the addition of membership in his fraternity, the sense of belonging was strengthened by another strand.

As the economic gilds began to emerge from the fraternities, or developed independently, the gilds began to range beyond the bounds of the local parish and its church in their attempt to contol the trade in which they were engaged. As gilds became established and stable, they took on visual symbols of their trade, the most significant of which was the livery. The livery is special clothing for ceremonial purposes, unique in design for each organization. As the gild system settled into a fixed stratification pattern, the livery became a matter of the social standing of the gild in the ranking system. Most workers' shops were identified by a unique sign or object that designated the trade practiced within, a necessity in a time when the majority of passers-by did not read. This practice is now confined mostly to taverns, and to little plastic decals on shop windows of the many tradesmen who help keep traditions alive in the modern ways; signs were once very competitive, and since shops were small and close together, size and height above the street had to be set by law. The gildsman was personally recognizable by his work clothing, which was not only functional but emblematic of his social condition.

The barber-surgeon, for example, in addition to his ordinary formal work clothing and apron, wore spurs while at work cutting hair and bleeding patients, the spurs signifying readiness to ride to a patient without delay.[18] It was this work clothing that was probably the gildsman's emblem of identity in the gild itself, though records of the era are rather obscure on the matter. Since gild members tended to be from a given locality, and a rather narrowly defined one at that, it is quite likely that they were similar in wealth and social standing, and the livery was not likely a major competitive issue at home.

In spite of male dominance in many areas of life, the fraternity had female members, and not simply token ones either. Membership in economic gilds came through apprenticeship or qualification, which was almost routinely expected of males, but it also occurred as a right of inheritance or patrimony, and in such cases widows or female progeny acquired membership. Purchase of gild membership was legitimate but seems rarely to have resulted in female membership. Thus the fraternity was more completely egalitarian in membership, and in its practices simply reflected the universal membership of the church itself. Nevertheless, a review of hundreds of charters of fraternities and gilds (sometimes indistinguishable) does not reveal women among the leaders of the associations. Coote systematically compiled data on a number of kinds of facts for more than five hundred gilds, but does not mention women as *prominent* members.[19] There do not seem to be sororities anywhere in English records that I can find; since there were special fraternities among monks and priests, we might expect to find them among females in nunneries but apparently there were none, nor were the Beguines, a lay order and a voluntary association, prominent as they were in Belgium.

In England there were a few gilds composed solely of female workers, but fewer than on the continent. The issue was that concentrations of women workers, such as the spinners (i.e., spinsters), arose in England at a time when the craft was being transformed into an industrial shop that was under a male master who would himself be a member of a gild and whose workers might be classed as servants rather than journeymen.

The fraternity member was a Christian and was expected to be an exemplary one. In fact, early charters indicate that behavior control was viewed as a major reason for the existence of the fraternity. The associations seem to have found it necessary to have a great many rules about behavior. In addition to the rules about payments of alms and religious obligations mentioned above, the fraternity seems, like the gild from which it is indistinguishable on this point, to have provision for adding from time to time specific items to deal with orderliness within and without the organization. The member was expected to do nothing that "wolde turne the craft to schame," and to "respect the chastity of the master's wife" and "hys felows con-cubyne."[20]

Things mentioned most often are ordinary matters that bother anybody in a meeting. To deal with problems of procedure, the fraternity had a beadle who called members to order and helped to enforce rules. Members were not to argue, curse one another, fight, or take one another to an outside court. The fraternity had its own enforcement mechanisms and recourse to the clergy; the gild had formal courts that wee upheld by municipal law, which was often strongly influenced or actually run by gild members acting as aldermen or mayor. For less serious issues, there were a variety of exhortations: members were not to enter the ale chamber without permission, nor to drink too much when they did. Members were not to sleep during meetings or to interrupt speakers. Jangling was prohibited in a number of charters. Specific penalties were usually mentioned for each offense, more often in wax, candles, or ale than in money.

One of the reasons for the stability of the gild and the fraternity is that they were both able to call on religious authorities to assist in enforcing rules and meeting obligations. This was, however, mostly a reserve power and was not usually utilized in day-to-day affairs. To do so would make the relation with the church too close and threaten the autonomy of the association. This autonomy was jealously guarded. Gilds sometimes hired chaplains and paid priests for service, and thus kept them under control and at a distance.

It was common in the nineteenth century to write of the gild as a form of social organization that displaced the kin so far as mutual aid was concerned. This was only true, if it is accepted that the *frith* (tenth century or earlier) was a gild as is sometimes the case in historical treatises, because the *frith* provided security in situations where kin was not adequate. It is too facile, however, to conclude therefore that the fourteenth-century gild displaced the kin as the Anglo-Saxon *frith* had done. In part, the error is simply a confusion between comparative and historical methods. But there is a sense in which the fraternity, and the fraternal aspect of the gild, did displace kin. That concerns the funerary and mutual-aid functions. The fraternities definitely dominated funerals, a function provided by kin or through feudal bonds in rural areas. It is problematic whether the fraternity displaced kin in mutual aid. The rules of gilds and fraternities were often written to provide that the organization supplement rather than replace the family.

Obviously, a large number of the foregoing observations about the fraternity have to do with the stratification system of English society. So much so, in fact, that this will be the subject of added comment later when the gilds themselves are analyzed further. We now turn to a comparative description of the club, attending the same kinds of topics as those just considered on the fraternity.

MEMBER IDENTITY AND ORGANIZATION:
EXISTENCE OF THE CLUB

The ideal-typical club member was the gentleman, a prodigy of hedonism. The gentleman had a secure income without an enacted work role. In terms of honor (Weber's concept for the purely social realm of stratitication, as distinct from class and party) the gentleman claimed and was given respect, typically because of his lineage, accomplishment, or preferment. He was not concerned about work to assure his election to heavenly standing, since he already had earthly nomination. For him work gave no religious call, and the ideal-typical religion of the gentleman, if he had any at all, was deism, which created a rational god that was much more accessible to men and made little fuss about the hereafter. The very source of the gentleman's immersion in the pleasures of the present arose from the fact that the past and the future were relatively secure, even if not ideal. Neither work nor religion (nor the religious universities) was a central life interest leading to recreation or leisure as alternatives. Politics sometimes caught the gentleman's attention, and later the drama and arts became sufficiently institutionalized to become preoccupations. The gentleman's problem was ennui—not purgatory or election. His subjective world was present-time (though later intellectuals were concerned with history and with ideal states of the future). The country gentleman, with whom we are not concerned here although he fits some of the analysis, had the pleasures of his estate: management of land, hunting and shooting, and the fine arts of social life. The city gentleman was a person in search of a life of the present, and the club provided its nucleus for him. It should be noted that men with landed wealth frequently kept residence in the city as well; one of the more significant attractions of the city was its social life, and the club was frequently one of the most significant of these. The very intensity of club life was thus partially provided by the fact that it was a seasonal or periodic specialty for a significant proportion of its members.

Many of the clubs of which we have record had members who were well-established, older citizens. This may be something of a distortion so far as actual proportions are concerned, since it was also true that much participation was by youth whose affairs were not so noteworthy. Jones speaks of participation as "a passing stage of late adolescence" for many club members.[21]

The gentleman and musicians, dramatists, actors, and authors typically showed a symbiotic relationship throughout the seventeenth and eighteenth centuries that was quite enduring. The gentleman frequently dabbled in these areas as an amateur, and the companionship of talented professionals stimulated him and enhanced his ego. All had a certain flexibility in role demands and had established control over their lives that made club life possible. More significantly, they seemed to complement values and interests in a way that was mutually desirable. We shall return to this matter later.

Since neither the future nor the past provided club members with a basis for commitment to an organization, what produced organizational solidarity? One answer is that in the long run there was less solidarity. The life of the club was typically much shorter than that of the gild, and where it did endure, it was because a particular combination of persons developed further goals from their interaction, which proved satisfying to achieve. The members themselves were the major resources that led to organizational growth, and when the original members died or lost interest, the club was imperiled. A second answer is that many of the clubs of which we have record seemed to center around a charismatic leader. Ben Jonson was the leader of one of which Shakespeare was a member. Raleigh was another leader. In the eighteenth century, Samuel Johnson was the charismatic leader of several clubs, and perhaps the prototype clubman of all times.[22] Many Whig leaders were also vital forces in coffeehouse clubs. The role of the charismatic leader is most evident at the start of the era; both James I and Charles I were kings who supported the merry life, and the charismatic leaders of the early clubs were favorites of courts and the nobles themselves whose patronage was vital in growth of the arts, particularly music and drama. As club life became more widespread, it diffused down the stratification system and perhaps the charismatic leader became less significant. Third, the club led to creativity or it failed; there were no formal pluralistic religious goals or implied alternate activities to sustain its life as was the case with the fraternity or gild. Its pluralism lay in its members, not in its goals.

By membership pluralism, as contrasted with goal pluralism, is meant that clubs that succeeded seem to show a salubrious combination of types of people who served as sources of diversity and tolerable conflict. The theme was "a lord among wits and wit among lords."[23] Members were selected by those already enrolled, and those were picked who seemed acceptable both because they were gentlemen, and interesting companions of an evening of "fine discourse," as Pepys has it. The model of Chapter 1 stipulated that existence and prevalence of voluntary associations required sufficient diversity of goals in a society. This condition was realized, and in fact even more than in the earlier era. Here we add the further interpretation of singular (or fewer) goals in the association provided that the personnel are sufficiently diverse. Further dimensions of this issue include the distinction between religious and nonreligious goals, which here involves the transformation in England from monolithic Roman Catholicism to monolithic Anglicanism and gradually to a pluralistic Protestant-dominated secular society.

Early clubs were apparently quite casual about membership rules or followed the Apollo's merry ordinances, but later ones, perhaps when charismatic leaders became less prominent, had sets of procedures that became more and more explicit. Most clubs had an upper limit of membership, set by the size of quarters they used and some idea about how many members were needed for a pleasant evening, and as vacancies occurred they prepared lists of candidates for replacement. There was some procedure for blackballing, though the clubs differed as to the number of negations that were allowed. One prolonged dispute centered around the merits of allowing one negative vote or none, and the arguments showed considerable consciousness of a kind of nascent theory of group structure. With such procedures, the club with attractive members kept some if its attractiveness simply because it managed a nice balance between exclusiveness and qualified accessibility. This moderate exclusiveness, plus the publicity given to prominent clubs, led to copying by other clubs. In the seventeenth century the success of clubs of prominent men was a significant aspect in instigation of clubs of the entire middle class.

The setting of the club also bespoke its orientation to the present. Early clubs met in rented quarters in taverns. In the decade of 1650, coffeehouses developed in similar buildings, and clubs rented rooms in them for a particular day of the week or fortnight. The English residential club is a much later phenomenon, largely nineteenth-century, and will not concern us here.[24]

The temporary nature of early clubs is also revealed by their lack of property. Some of the established clubs, in which feasting was prominent, acquired fine dishes and silver plates or cups. Some clubs that used the same premises for a considerable time, acquired paintings of merit, and those that were fortunate to have artists as members often became the recipients of their works. The club of which Sir Joshua Reynolds was a member acquired some fine portraits by the master himself. By contrast, the more prestigious gilds (but rarely the fraternities) often had portraits of members or masters, and a loving cup or communal ritual drinking vessel, which might be lavish.

Compared to that of the fraternity members, the clothing of the clubman was not a matter of much concern as long as it suited a gentleman. It is rarely mentioned, except in the more extreme later clubs in which foppery was notorious. Members were simply stylish and individual in their taste.

In contrast to the highly specific financial system of the fraternity with its payments and fines, the club had very simple financial arrangements. Most clubs had a simple bookkeeping system and an officer in charge of accounts. His principal duties were to see that the bill for dinner and drink was paid and the fees collected. This sometimes was a thankless task, and the club records are replete with mention of unpaid debts. Perhaps the reason the problem existed is that a gentleman's word was his surety, and since the status of gentleman was eagerly sought, many people passed as gentlemen whose income would not allow the style of life they followed. The same issue existed regarding gambling debts, which arose from club activities and resulted in club involvement in settlements. The clubs did not have rules to deal with such affairs and handled them on an interpersonal basis.

The club was a male establishment. Clubs occasionally admitted female guests but normally had no female members with full status. As one early club put it, "ladies of spotless character" were admitted on special nights to its social and musical entertainments.[25] This claim of virtue was perhaps more characteristic of the early than the later clubs, and may even in its time have been more of prudential public relations than prudery. Some of the more extreme clubs seemed to acquire courtesans who were visitors at the clubs when needed; the French clubs of the same era established such women (*filles de joie*) in separate houses owned by the club. Of the two types of organizations, the fraternity was the more egalitarian. Certainly there was no linear progress toward female liberation. If anything, the sixteenth through nineteenth centuries marked a retrograde movement so far as equality in voluntary associations was concerned.

MEMBER IDENTITY AND ORGANIZATION:
EXISTENCE OF THE SECT

Max Weber's investigation of the relation of the Protestant ethic
and the spirit of capitalism was in a sense concerned with a side issue,
a derivative of the more significant problem for most Protestants of
the relation of a man to his god and his church. It was also, at various
times, a matter of subsidiary importance for the religious man whose
pressing interest during the time with which we are concerned was as
much with politics and government as economics. From the start of
the later period until after the Act of Toleration, a dominant concern
was civil liberties, which was a matter having political and religious
facets but the same ultimate source of oppression: the British
sovereign who was head of both church and state. The short period of
the Protectorate was, of course, unique.

While taking cognizance of the criticisms of Weber's thesis, it shall
be accepted here as a sufficient general explanation of the
phenomenon of that individual motivation to economic activity that
Weber called modern capitalism.[26] Anxiety about election by God
derived from a more general conviction in Calvinist theology that
there was a covenant with God that preexisted the life of any man. It
was this idea of the covenant that formed the basis for organizational
solidarity: a group of individuals united for disciplined worship and
regulation of behavior in the congregation.

The idea of a covenant was an ancient one. It was the core idea of
ancient Hebrew solidarity as well, and significant in early Christianity. The thing that made it prominent in Calvinism was that it was
assumed to be preexistent. It became significant in Calvinism
because it was an assumption, an *idée fixe*, the idea from which the
rest of the reasoning radiated.

Protestantism was progressive in general. Eisenstadt says this was
due to three things.[27] First, there was an attitude of "this-
worldliness" and transcendentalism. Second, there was individual
activism and responsibility. Third was belief in unmediated direct
relation of man and God, leading to the possibility of a direct personal
definition of action and a reshaping of institutions as a result. In
Catholicism the relation of man to God is mediated by the church, to

which end the fraternity and gild were effective instruments. In Protestantism the sect figuratively merges the functions of gild and church, and acts directly. This third reason seemed to become more significant and more radical with the religious movements that did not take on the responsibility of national rule as the Puritans did.

The era of Puritan ascendancy in England was the time of birth of the next wave of creativity of voluntaristic churches. Among others that emerged in the search for alternatives to Anglicanism and Catholicism were the Ranters, the Levellers, the Fifth Monarchy Men, and the Quakers. Of these, only the Quakers achieved a combination of individual and group ethics that allowed organizational survival. The Quakers had much in common with the Ranters, with whom they shared the intense concern for a direct experience of God, a movement in the soul of the sensitized individual of a spark of divinity to which the person hoped to respond. Unlike the Ranters, the Quakers provided a practical means of collective human judgment over the waywardness of human perception of what was and what was not divine action. It was this formula of interaction between the personal and group religious experience that led Quakers to an organizational form that remained voluntary at each organizational level. Between 1650 and 1688, George Fox and his followers led a precarious existence under constant persecution; thereafter they experienced some systematic discrimination but did not find too much effective interference with their practices.

The Methodist movement in the eighteenth century was the next dynamic voluntarist religious force on the English scene. The Methodists represent the end of our period of analysis and will not concern us further. Methodism was not only a voluntary church, but its values led to support and development of numerous other voluntary associations.

The comparison of the medieval fraternity (and gild) and the later club is the most significant pairing for explanatory purposes. Nevertheless, it is obvious by the data presented above on Protestantism that the picture is not complete by a simple one-to-one comparison. Those organizations have been selected that best represent the spirit of their ages, and the fraternity and the club are the obvious choices. What actually happened, depicted heuristically, is that the fraternities and gilds continued, in emasculated form, and the emergence of Protestantism as a particularistic, nonuniversal church, left open the choice of nonmembership; and secularism and the vast new range of values that it made possible led to a period of inventiveness in nonreligious organizations. In the early era there was a church of sinners, the monastic organizations of religious purists and the fraternal and gild organizations of Catholicism in liturgical, economic, political, and community welfare activities; afterward there were religious purists in various sects, and there was secularism. Protestantism created purer churches and liberated sinners. In terms of individual religious vocation, the extremely religious man of the Protestant era found his niche in the sect and not in the monastery. Bendix cites a very trenchant passage from Weber that summarizes the issue well. "Puritan sects had been a special case of voluntary association among persons who shared a common style of life and who wanted to exclude non-believers from the social intercourse of their group."[28]

Before pursuing the historical emergence of the fraternities in detail, a more careful description of the monasteries is in order, since it proves to raise some points about voluntarism that we have not yet encountered.

## Part II: Religious Organizations in Social Change

### THE MONASTERY: QUASI-VOLUNTARY ASSOCIATION

Most modern analysts of voluntary associations, and even of religious organizations, tend to ignore monastic life. The monasteries are cloistered and easily overlooked. This was not the case in medieval England, where they were powerful and very much involved in rural life and even in cities. At their peak, there were 600 to 700 monasteries, friaries, and nunneries in England.[29] They were economically and politically powerful, provided hospital care and one of the major sources of education, were major landlords, and proved influential in molding the character of the times. The concern here is with their voluntarism, which decreases the space allotted to them considerably.

In a seminal article for the development of voluntary association theory, Gordon and Babchuck selected difficulty of access as one of the three most important classificatory characteristics of voluntary associations.[30] The monastery is an organization with difficult access. It may or may not involve a high opportunity cost; that is, it is not certain whether the novice foregoes other important benefits to join that might in many cases provide a test of whether the activity is voluntaristic.[31] Gordon and Babchuck, however, do not deal at any length with the issue of difficulty of leaving membership. It is usually assumed, and certainly consistent with our modern understanding, that the option of membership is bidirectional. The person who may voluntarily enter may voluntarily leave. The novice to the monastery committed himself to a rule that led to extremely rigorous discipline and compliance with great austerity. Monasteries were not typically democratic. And yet, even though we moderns cannot understand how anyone could voluntarily do such a thing, for the most part the monk's poverty and asceticism were a self-creation, and a voluntary product of his own right to self-assignment. It was not so much brainwashing in the modern sense as volunteering to do one's own cerebral laundry.

The term "quasi-voluntary association," defined in Chapter 1, is similar to the usage derived by Scherer from Joachim Wach.[32] To review: this term is used for organizations that, in their mature phases, consistently exhibit only one of the many definitional features of the voluntary association; here the issues in questions are voluntary membership and voluntary action of members in member roles. The monastery, because of its extreme demands on individual members and associated involuntary actions, deserves this modified label. There are exceptions, however, to be discussed.

Wach identifies the monastery as a protest organization within the ecclesiastical body.[33] The monasteries arose when the Christian church, after the early centuries of struggle, adopted a policy of universal ascriptive membership and accommodation with the world, which could not provide through normal church membership the radical purity of religion which is one possible interpretation of the Christian scriptures. In this sense the monasteries certainly *originated* as voluntary associations. The fate of most of them was eventually to become involved in economics, politics, and even military life, which necessitated growth of power to ensure survival. The monasteries suffered an erosion of original voluntarism both from accommodation to the world and to the church. The struggles led to continual search for new disciplines or rules, reforms of organization and administration, which recurred continually over the earlier period of the study.

The Benedictine rule, which dominated Christian monasticism for six hundred years, was a simple and flexible set of principles that utilized liturgical prayer, private reading or prayer, and manual labor in a combination that led to each phase providing meaning to the other. The resulting culture involved specific norms as to simplicity, community, enclosure, silence, stability, regularity, obedience.[34] Pope Gregory the Great was an advocate of the Benedictine rule and sent monks to England. Under Dunstan (tenth century) English monasticism was revived, and under the sympathetic guidance of King Edgar, the monasteries gained freedom from some demands of feudalism. The voluntarism of the monasteries was limited by their need for an income, which led to numerous feudal relationships, vast problems of property management, and use of hired labor and servants. Another limitation on the freedom of the monasteries was interference by the bishops. In principle, the monasteries were responsible only to their order, either in central administrative authority at the foundation place, or to Rome itself. But they were each located in an ecclesiastical jurisdiction, and in it the bishop claimed certain rights of inspection and control. Many convents record attempts by local bishops to dictate devotional practices and to control financial affairs.

Three types of religious specialist may be identified in the era from 1000 A.D. to suppression in the early sixteenth century: the monasties, the canons (the "canons regular"), and the collegiates. They were increasingly voluntaristic, in the order named. The canons were a clergy group having a common life under direct rule of the bishops. The collegiate groups were a corporate association under local democratic governance, often following the rule of St. Augustine.

The friars were strong in England, from their origin in the thirteenth century. The Friars Minor, the Franciscans, were originally exemplary prophets, converting the populace by living the radical simplicity of Christian poverty. They were, however, eventually to come under rather severe rule. The Friars Preachers, the Dominicans, were essentially a democratic body of volunteers, emissary prophets, who led by teaching. Their dominant role in Oxford and Cambridge reproduced much of the organizational form that Dominic had learned in the collegiate gild of students at Bologna.

Many members joined monasteries for reasons consistent with the spirit of voluntarism. There are, however, frequent mentions of more devious cases. Parents sent some children for education or for discipline; some came as an escape from worse conditions elsewhere. Girls of upper-class families were sent to nunneries, often against their will. Some old men entered to atone for an earlier career that was less than holy.

The Cluniac monasteries were noted for their administrative reforms and their flexibility. This must not be construed as a move toward voluntarism, however. The Cluniac rejection of extreme asceticism led to popularity and wealth, but not more to voluntarism than the others. Thompson believes that, by contrast, the Cistercians gave their members considerable autonomy to form their individual and corporate life, and from his description it seems reasonable to identify Cistercian monasteries as true voluntary associations.[35]

The wealth of the monasteries was not uniform. Many tried to keep to ideals of poverty, and others were forced to. But their wealth, on the average, was considerable. That, in fact, was a significant reason why Henry VIII expropriated them, and by that time, very few of them were more than quasi-voluntary associations.

From 1050, Cistercian monasteries employed nonmonks. The obedientiaries frequently hired these *conversi* or lay brothers, who served as cooks, barbers, and butlers and were sufficiently numerous to have their own gilds within the walls.[36] This fact testifies to the scale of the monasteries and shows that they were not simple homogeneous units of people leading a devout life: many kinds of auxiliary voluntary association were necessary to carry out the religious life for the community of which the monastery was the center. In this sense, the monastery may be seen as a kind of occupational community united under common religious values and rule.

This concludes analysis of the voluntarism of the monasteries. A brief analytical restatement, therefore, may be made before continuing with other issues. The most prominent feature of monastic life from about 900 to 1550 A.D. was the continual process or organizational change in search of an ideal. The monasteries existed because the church allowed and encouraged organizational differentiation as a way of dealing with potential failure of the church's mission to the world. The ideal was voluntaristic asceticism. The reality was that the monastery needed to survive in a feudal world that required the development of power, and within its walls it required the reserve power to compel ascetic behavior. Every attempt at monastic innovation eventually led to organizational maturity in which voluntary asceticism was undermined and defiled by power. The instigation of new monastic forms was realized by constant striving for ascetic perfection that the Bible and the historic church always held in highest esteem. The permission, and indeed the demand, of the church for this ideal was relatively unchanging. The heroic religious lives of such men as Francis of Assisi were examples of the voluntaristic ideal, and many such leaders emerged to stimulate new voluntaristic endeavors in each generation.

THE EMERGENCE OF FRATERNITY AND GILD

Attention now returns to the emergence of the fraternal organization, a topic that was introduced at the start of the chapter.

The gild emerged (or reemerged) in almost every country in Europe at about the same time, around the year 1000 A.D., developed into an essential and vital part of the social organization of the time, and then after many centuries was transformed into a ceremonial organization or charitable trust serving the function in Europe that the foundation or welfare organization serves now in the United

States. The career of the gild is from voluntary association to corporation and back to voluntary association, a turnabout in a thousand years.

Some dates may be suggested to mark the several eras of gild history. Kahl says that the economic function of gilds had surpassed their religious and social practices by the fifteenth century, which is as good a date as any to mark the plateau in voluntaristic practices.[37] Kahl sees the nineteenth century as the start of a last phase in which there was a return to fraternal structure for purposes of charity, using income from property, which was usually obtained from endowments. The career of the gild was not uniform in all of its divisions. The *gild merchant* (an Anglicized form of *gilda mercatoria*) died out in the fourteenth or fifteenth century; some merchant gilds gave away to corporations in the sixteenth and seventeenth centuries; some craft gilds are still operative, particularly those in the service trades that did not undergo industrialization. Kahl's summary is accurate, however, so far as the economic leadership of the gilds is concerned.

This remarkable history establishes it as a form of human organization worthy of closer attention than it has had in the past. In this section, the available historical materials have been given a social interpretation and elaboration, to set the context for later systematic analysis.

There is scattered evidence that some Roman gilds survived from the fall of the Empire until the start of the second Christian millennium. Gregory I (590-604) lists gilds in Rome and Naples.[38] In addition, there were gilds or similar organizations in places often ignored by Western scholars, such as Islamic Asia Minor and pagan Scandinavia. Lambert notes the influence of Syrian merchant gilds in the time of Augustus.[39] They constructed gild buildings in many ports in which they had trade relations. The Jewish gilds depicted in Chapter 3 were found everywhere that there were Jewish communities in Europe and, in fact, kept gild traditions with greater continuity than the Romans and their successors.

There were some specific barriers to direct survival of gilds. Charlemagne (d. 814), in his attempt to establish an empire, suppressed gilds, which were potential sources of opposition. His main objection seems to have been that the gild was competing loyalty. He decreed "that no one shall presume to bind himself by mutual oaths in a gild (*geldonia*)."[40] The emperor himself, however, was a member of a satyrical club in the palace. "The palace scholars and members of the court formed a club, in which everyone took more or less funny false names. Alcuin was Flaccus; Charlemagne, King David."[41] One can imaginatively reconstruct the scenario: when you play party games with an emperor who had a custom of executing people rather casually, it's a very good idea to have some labels for play-identities so you can know when people are kidding. It's not too different from the touchy problem of the English court gentlemen who risked beating Henry VIII at tennis.

Gilds at the time must have been sufficiently established to draw Charlemagne's attention. In addition, they must have had some staying power, since some of them seem to have survived the suppression, or began again soon after.

"In 825, Emperor Lothair issued his *Constitutiones Olenensus*, wherein eight cities of northern Italy were named as suitable centres of population for the establishment of new *collegia*. . . ."[42] Lacroix makes reference to French *collegia* of locksmiths in the fifth century, of bakers in the 630 laws of Dagobert, fishermen in 943, and bakers again in 1001.[43] Seven gilds of artisans served a palace in Lombardy in the tenth century.[44] Orozo has traced the history of a twentieth-century Spanish fisherman's gild that claims continuity with Roman times.[45]

Roman gild continuity in England is only speculative. Unwin believes that London porters and watermen's gilds may be the same that the Romans developed, or found, when they first settled on the banks of the Thames.[46] These cases are not based on firm evidence, nor are there reasons to believe there was much continuity of influence. Lambert, however, has evidence of a *collegium fabrorum* of smiths in Britain, during the "reign of Claudius."[47] Since the Romans established *collegia* in many of their conquered territories, there is no reason to doubt this, nor that there were many more.

There is a tendency among English gild historians, who are frequently members of the gild, to try to extend claims to the earliest possible antiquity, and they seem to be quite willing to accept oral tradition in their own gilds as adequate evidence. However, there is reason to go along with them here, since there was a fixed resource niche involved in each case, to exploit continually by forms of manual labor that have changed but little in two thousand years. It seems plausible too that Roman influence could have been exerted. Coote supports a germane continuity thesis by listing a large number of similarities between the structure and functions of Roman *collegia* in Britain and later gilds.[48] There are two objections to this. First, and most obviously, small voluntary associations are similar everywhere, and correlation is not necessarily causation. Second, and more cogent here, Roman ways of life infused the Roman Catholic church and the church was the bearer of culture everywhere across the centuries from the fall of the Empire to the year 1000. The cultural part of the Roman Empire did not fall. It may be the continuity of the church and not the Empire that Coote discovered.

There may have been gild or fraternity continuity transmitted through the Eastern establishment of Christianity, particularly along inland trade routes through the Danube Valley and the Byzantine. Around 750 A.D. there were gilds as well as secular clubs of gentlemen in Constantinople.[49] The tenth-century *Book of the Prefect* of Constantinople lists twenty-one ordinances of Byzantine gilds.[50]

We do know that gilds were strong in the Mediterranean Islamic countries for at least two centuries before they became prominent in medieval Christian Europe. Islamic domination of commerce and shipping in the Mediterranean was favorable to growth of both craft and merchant gilds. Massignon notes the existence of gilds of "shepherds and boatmen from the canals of lower Mesopotamia side by side with small artisans of Aramaean, Iranian and Coptic origin."[51] Gilds of husbandmen are rare; a later English one was the parish fraternity of shepherds of Holbeach.[52]

The Karmathian fraternal movement of Islam is significant for our examination of European gilds. It functioned as sort of a Masonic brotherhood, cutting across all social strata and even including some Christians who lived in Islamic countries, often as trade agents. The Karmathians and the Islamic merchant gilds were points of contact with Italian Christian traders when they ventured forth on the seas again before the year 1000.

Early Florentine merchants were accustomed to build a gild chapel in any port where they had steady trade. This was necessary, since early trading voyages involved much longer stays in foreign ports for trading and loading than those with which we are now familiar. This building custom was probably reciprocal. We know that several north European Atlantic countries established such outposts (Hansa) in London. The extent of influence of these contacts is hard to trace, but we do know that in London the organizations had similar form, which was necessary to facilitate trade.

If the Islamic brotherhoods influenced England, that influence may have been strongest through contacts between Italian, French, or Spanish traders and not directly. Staley finds the *first* formal record of Florentine commercial trade with England as late as 1154.[53] By that time, Roman and Florentine gilds are known to have been developed (or redeveloped) and flourishing, and probably others as well. English gilds were also in existence, though not as successful at that time in economic regulation.

Mutual-security organizations were very prevalent at the time that cities began to emerge in England after centuries of political turmoil under a succession of rules. The *friths* were mentioned above. These must be counted as the most direct antecedent of the neighborhood or parish fraternities and also of the economic organizations. The multiplicity of similar names of variants of the security organization is testimony both to the widespread insecurity of the feudal era and to the increased communication between the countries. *Guild* is the rendering in most later English accounts. Some attempts have been made to trace the organization names to the Germanic *geld*, since monetary payment for injury (*wergeld*) was a part of such organizations. Many authorities now believe that the similarity of the names does not imply that there was a direct connection between the organizations. Other related names were *gield, gyle* (Welsh), *goel* and *gouil* (Breton), *feill, feil, feighal* (Gaelic), *gulde* (Dutch). One who paid geld was a *gegylde*, or in Norse a *bauggildi.* Some verb forms include *gylden, gildan,* and *geldan.*[54]

As noted above, the Germanic fraternity has sometimes been held to be the origin of the gild. It served as an intermediate organization that supplemented or replaced kin bonds. Feasting and drinking seemed to play a major part, probably based on traditional pagan meanings. Brentano thinks that the social organization had a separate origin from the religious organizations that were later Christianized.[55] Bloch describes the Germanic gilds succinctly. "Their common characteristics were the oath, periodic drinking bouts, accompanied in pagan times by religious libations, occasionally a common fund, and above all an obligation of mutual aid. . . ."[56]

Fraternal organization within Christianity was well established before parish fraternities were common. In France and Germany, as well as in England, priests occasionally formed their own gilds. The gild of Kalendars was a priestly gild for observation of special days of the church calendar. The name stems from the Roman *kalends*, the first of the month. Both burgesses and priests were organized in gilds, as we see from the Capitularies of Archbishop Hincmar of Rheims, in 858. "They shall unite for offerings (especially of candles), for mutual assistance, for funeral services for the dead, for alms, and other deeds of piety."[57] The principles set down by Hincmar were to be echoed over and over, nearly identical exhortations are found in England eight hundred years later. This seems to underscore the case made earlier for the independent origin of the religious fraternity.

Hincmar went on to give stern warnings that the pagan side of things was not to be allowed the upper hand. Members were to stick to the religious purposes of the club and not turn it into a *diabolicum*. He was specific about the number of ritual drinks a priest might take in carrying out his religious duties.

The English *frith* more clearly shows a governmental role. There is no reliable evidence that it originated in a religious fraternity, but it did have an oath of mutual obligation. Brentano uses (erroneously, I believe) the copula *Frith-gild*, suggesting their close relationship. The *frith* was a territorial organization, in which membership was compulsory for all persons above the age of sixteen, and therefore it was not a voluntary association. Bloch cites an early English gild ordinance that certainly shows similarity to the purposes of the Germanic clubs: ". . . For friendship as well as for vengance we shall remain united, come what may. . . ."[58] L. Smith makes it clear that the *frith* originated in a community need for security. It was an association of men together for common objects of private and individual benefit, in which each man gave his *wed* to abide by their internal by-laws, while *Frith-bohr* was the banding of men together, within the limits of a boundary, in which each joined in the *borh* or pledge for the keeping of the peace, and the performance of public duties, by all others.[59]

The aspect of mutual liability traces to much earlier times, and is mentioned in the laws of King Ine (688-725).[60] It should be pointed out, however, that King Ine is sometimes put to use as a sort of convenient fountainhead of historical first causes, as was King Numa (or Romulus and Remus) for Rome. Where associations, such as the *frith*, must seek compliance by force or strong authority, they cannot long maintain a voluntary character. Their effectiveness is threatened unless everyone joins.

The English *frith* was paralleled by other varieties of peace associations on the continent, which are very similar as to function but usually bear another kind of name. Most good records occur on the occasions when peace associations were successfully coopted or captured by ecclesiastical authorities. Adams says that "some of them, like the London guilds organized in 940, resembled the vigilante committees of the 19th century American frontier; and like them, they disturbed civil and ecclesiastical authorities almost as much as the brigandage they set out to attack."[61] Adams also notes religious peace associations in western France in 989, Auvergne in 990, and ones under secular domination later in Flanders and Normandy. In many cases, both church and nobility tried to control these mutual organizations that presented the dilemma of useful but potentially subversive action. The ubiquitous church had the better of things, perhaps because it was under common (though distant) administration. The church acted to regularize the peace associations through two actions, the Peace of God and the Truce of God— efforts, essentially, to ensure religiously sanctioned peace for, respectively, all of the people some of the time, and some of the people all of the time. The idea is intriguing. If there were enough sacred reference points to which we could appeal, there might be no time left to fight at all. The least we could do would be to stop all wars every afternoon for tea.

Perhaps the clearest example of origin of the gild from the fraternity when it was put to use as a work organization, is that of the university. The early medieval university was a gild or gilds of scholars in Bologna (perhaps before 1000 A.D.) and a gild of masters in Paris and at Oxford.[62] The very name "scholar" stems from the Roman *schola*. The role of the scholar was recognized as an occupation; hence the university was an occupational gild (not simply a fraternity) of a religious character and as such clearly preceded many occupational gilds. "The univeristy, in its scholastic sense, was simply a particular kind of trade gild—an association of persons following a common occupation for the regulation of their craft and the protection of their rights against the outside world."[63] The transition from a peripatetic gild to a residential university of colleges in the hands of career officers was a matter of several centuries. Perhaps the end of the voluntary aspect of university gild organization can be marked sociologically at the time that new fraternities of students began to emerge as protest groups to oppose the stabilized rule of gild masters and officials, leading to conflicts in which voluntarism gave way to the need to compel utilization of resources in an authoritative manner.

The London Inns of Chancery and Inns of Court constitute a set of colleges that kept their collegial character. Stow says this of their organization:

> These Societies are no corporations, nor have any judicial power over their members, but have certain orders among themselves, which by Council have the Force of Laws. For slight offences they are only excommoned, that is, put out of Commons; which is, not to eat with the rest of their Halls. . . .[64]

The Inns have four ranks: benchers, utter barristers, inner barristers, and students. Stow speaks of them as similar to the French hostels. From these comments, this would appear to be a gild on the older collegial form that kept its voluntarism because of the extreme traditional character of the British legal profession (to which they also contributed).

From the cases cited above, there is ample reason to assume origins of organizations having most of the ideal-typical features of either fraternities or gilds, in many places in Europe at about the same time, and, most important, there is no reason to assume a clear precedence of one or the other. They were, in fact, basically similar in the role played by religion, whether or not they were wholly voluntary associations or independent work organizations. England, perhaps because of its remoteness from Rome and its frequent change of rule, developed gilds more slowly than France and Italy, and perhaps even Germany. But it developed the *frith*, a religious security organization, more strongly. England's role in the wool trade and its favorable location to dominate shipping were perhaps the most important issues in the growth of economic gilds in the long run.

The case of London may be cited to illustrate the relationship between the Anglo-Saxon *frith* and later forms of organization, both fraternity and gild. Attendance at a *folkmoot* was a duty of all Anglo-Saxon men. It was a yearly occasion for the assembly of all men to hear proclamations, to settle disputes or to have justice proclaimed, and to pay tolls. The *folkmoot* in London met three times a year, supplemented by weekly meetings of the Hustings. The *folkmoot* was analogous to Scandinavian institutions of the same era. In time, the *hallmoot*, an executive court, met frequently to accomplish the same ends more efficiently. The king's side of the duties of *hallmoot* administration was allotted to bailiffs (representatives of the king's sheriff). The occupations once represented at the *folkmoot* that required the most attention were soon represented by permanent agents at the *hallmoot*. They became organized in order to bargain collectively with the bailiffs, and soon did so routinely. The assizes of bread and the assizes of ale were the first to take this sort of legal-economic state-regulated market form. The reason was that the bakers were frequently involved in trouble over the quality of bread, the main item on the urban table. Ale and beer were important household drinks, and their quality was crucial. The bakers made several kinds of loaves from different qualities of ingredients, and each named variety of bread came in a different-weight loaf for the same price. The currency of the time was not very flexible, there being only the silver penny for regular trade. The disputes, therefore, turned on the weight and quality of bread, issues that were much harder to settle than variations of price for a certain quantity of a standard quality. Victualers whose items of trade were not readily controlled in size, such as the poulters, had bargaining problems of an even greater difficulty. In addition, these conditions gave quite an advantage to a baker who had the initiative in driving the bargain. The regulation of a number of the victualling trades was seen as essential, as well as some trades related to clothing. By the time of Henry I, the practice of monopolies to these trades was established in London. In 1179 the king's exchequer registered fines to eighteen "adulterine" gilds that had been in operation and apparently practiced monopoly without royal consent, which had been granted to bakers, fishmongers, weavers, and perhaps others.

Eventually the business of tolls to individual workers became so complex that they sought and were given the right to collectively farm their own taxes. At the same time, some gilds such as the bakers proceeded more directly in the tradition of the *hallmoot*. In the long run, the difference was slight: both the *hallmoot* and the *ferme* (or farm) were grants of power, the difference being the distribution of tasks between gild and municipal officers. The word "farm" is used now without much consciousness of its origins in the Norman *fermer*, to rent or lease, to fix or contract. To have the *ferme* meant, essentially, that the gilds paid a fixed amount to the king for the right to collect their own taxes, and by derivation, to develop an organization by means of which to do so. The *ferme* was a social mechanism at the interface of politics and economics. It was first tried in London under Henry I, in 1130. Richard used the *ferme* more frequently, to raise money for the Crusades.

Sufficient historical facts have now been stated to allow an analytical sociological frame of reference for explanation of the emergence of gild and fraternity. The basis of analysis is the idea of social mechanism. By mechanism is meant a highly specific orderly means of solving exactly defined and frequently encountered problems. The gild will be analyzed as an organizational mechanism at the interface of enterprises. The word "enterprise" is used to signify an integrated set of institutions.[65] The gild is a secondary organization, in the sense that the vital enterprises of economics, religion, and government are not owned by gilds (as organizations) nor wholly controlled by them.[66] The fraternity related some of the community and the church to the economy and the government. Examples in modern communities are not hard to find: lobbying organizations relate communities or interests to government, consumers' groups relate government to the economic enterprise, and so on in a very complex maze. Not all voluntary associations are medial in this sense, but this was one of their most significant functions in the medieval world. In fact, one of the identifying features of the medieval world was the absence of groups that were merely autonomous and unrelated to the church or other enterprises. The *ferme* was a mechanism from the feudal era that was applied widely by monarchs to deal with the problems of relationships with the sets of people. The *ferme* was, in one aspect, a way that organizations were related to each other through the similarity of their relation to the sovereign.

Stenton gives a succinct description of germane mechanisms which operated on similar assumptions.

> The lands held by a great baron or an important church were collectively and indifferently known as a barony, a "fee" or an "honor." Fee means simply those lands with which the tenant, lay or ecclesiastical, is "enfeoffed" by the king to hold freely by definite service.[67]

The concept of honor also referred to a collectivity of estates and then, after time, the regard that property bestowed on the estate holder. Fee and *ferme* were often coupled into one term. The principle of the *ferme* was derived from the basic idea of feudal obligation, a contractual arrangement under law, sanctioned by a religious oath. When the Duke of Normandy conquered England in 1066, he quickly moved on to its subjection by a series of such grants of power to territorial rulers, in exchange for their obligations to him. This grant of seignory was an established idea, necessary before the fraternity could become a fully functioning gild. Here we see the idea of permission made into a general principle of law, coupled with an effective institutional procedure that brought rewards for compliance. Nowhere else in our study of many kinds of societies was there such an effective coupling of permission and rewards for organizational development.

A related mechanism was that of the *soke*. The *soke* is a grant of independent legal jurisdiction. By means of the *soke*, a lord or sometimes a bishop had the right of certain aspects of the king's justice over people who were obligated to him. The *soke*, then, parallels the *ferme* as a social mechanism. Like the *ferme*, its eventual significance was vast. When the *soke* was granted to formal organizations, self-government was possible without the inconvenience or subservience of going to public law officers for judgments and decisions. The *ferme* and the *soke*, in the hands of the feudal lord, meant enormous power over his lieges; in the hands of the gilds, it meant efficient private control over those portions of economic and political life that were designated. The gild was essentially a feudal-derivative institution in an urban setting. The idea of a grant of private justice also had a long history in family life, in which the head of the family traditionally had defined powers over family members, these powers being capable of execution on the initiative of the family head without consultation with the king's officers. The *soke*, then, was a mechanism that made specific application to organizational affairs of a general principle in law that was widely known and accepted. A similar analysis was made in the preceding chapter regarding the Roman *potestas*.

The third social mechanism is necessary to complete the analysis of the gild. The concept of "freedom" was essentially the individual person's side of the *ferme* and *soke*. To have freedom of the city meant to be identified as possessing its rights, within its bounds and out of it, having met the formal requirements of loyalty, tenement, and property. The usual phrase was "free of the city" or "free of the gild." "Freedom" is the medieval equivalent of "citizenship," although the latter term has connotations that do not necessarily apply. *Ferme* and *soke* established the basis of private associational government, and "freedom" the right of the individual to its rewards. When the gild became established as a part of the municipal structure, freedom of the city was normally acquired by means of freedom of the gild. The idea of freedom in English society provided, in terms of our model, the institutionalization of subjective resources. The individual was granted, by a social mechanism established in law, the right of self-assignment.

Freedom of the gild was never an unlimited right for all people, and it was this selectivity that gave the gilds their place in the stratification system and the ability to provide rewards, financial, social, and religious, to members. In addition, freedom of the gild implied certain duties and relationships that regulated the member. Although the associations had the right to decisions about a large number of acts, their rules were made in consonance with those of the municipality. The interpenetration of the city and the gild was not as much a matter of legal but of customary social mechanisms. The gild had roles that penetrated organizational boundaries. That is, certain individuals held offices in the organization and were at the same time performers of implied responsibilities in the municipality. This was sometimes a matter of design. Importance in the gild was usually accompanied by importance in the government. In some cases, aldermen were chosen from among gild officers or former officers. In cases, to be discussed below, in which a few gilds had economic as well as political power in a small city, the gild was in effect or even legally the government of the municipality in economic affairs. Later we will see that, by contrast, the club rarely had such penetrating roles. It did have boundary roles, that is, individuals designated to typically act for the club in relation to nonmembers, but boundary roles do not imply roles *in* other organizations. Penetrating roles obviously have the potential for a high degree of coordination, and a source of organic unity of interests or, from another perspective, of monism of values and centralization of powers.

## DIFFERENTIATION IN THE MATURE PHASE OF THE GILD AND FRATERNITY

The fraternity was an institutional solution to the problem of application of religion of a community to other enterprises. The major differentiated categories are the parish fraternity, the gild merchant (*gilda mercatoria*), the craft gild, and the merchant gild. Other marginal or miscellaneous applications of the fraternity to repeated problems will be identified and discussed later: they had no generic names in their time, and none has been supplied. In each case, however, the theme was the same: the Christian religion implied that all Christians act responsibly through small fellowships of believers to solve common problems.

The fraternity has been already presented in general terms because it is the analytic ideal-type of the era. Thrupp says that "during the fourteenth century, the inhabitants of most of the city parishes developed sufficient initiative to found and keep alive at least one fraternity organization that had no direct connection with a trade."[68] These were fraternities strictly for religious purposes, which seems to indicate that by this time the gilds had become sufficiently oriented to economic issues that separate fraternities were needed, and also that the complexity of the population was such that the gild did not provide a religious organization for many categories of Christians. Fraternities had, as noted prviously, been established centuries before this time. There is also some evidence that the fraternities and gilds were beginning to undergo a stratification process, as the gild became an organization of the best-qualified and most wealthy people (e.g., of lawful blood, whole of limb, burgesses), and the fraternity a voluntary association for mutual and religious practices among people of the residual strata. Thrupp calculated that only 7 of 218 merchants' wills made a bequest to a parish fraternity, but the rest made grants to gilds.[69] Parish fraternities were, however, the most numerous kind, and the most common means through which all citizens participated in normative religious work. Not much detail need be added here, but perhaps it would be useful to illustrate at this point some of the important features of parish fraternity work with a fraternity charter.

The Gild (i.e., fraternity) of St. Michael on the Hill, Lincoln, was among those that sent in a return to Parliament as required in the act of 1388. The document begins with a statement of the exact number of candles to be lit upon the death of a brother or sister, and about the routing to be followed on such occasions. Then the practices of the organization on the feast of Corpus Christi is described.[70]

> At the close of the feast, four wax candles having been kindeled, and four of the tankards which are called flagons having been filled with ale, a clerk shall read and explain these ordinances, and afterward the flagons shall be given to the poor.

Following this, much of the rest of the text is concerned with conduct of members. There is also a note about membership.

> Whoever seeks to be received into the gild, being of the same rank as the brethern and sisteren who founded it, namely of the rank of common and middling folks, shall be charged to be faithful to the gild, and shall bear his share of the burdens. And whereas this gild ws founded by folks of common and middling rank, it is ordained that no one of the rank of mayor or bailiff shall become a brother of the gild, unless he is found to be of humble, good, and honest conversation. . . .

The Gild of St. Michael on the Hill is somewhat unusual in that it is more specific about membership than most, the membership being taken for granted in most cases to be precisely of common folk of middling rank. And although the word "gild" was used in the title by the members, it was likely from the preoccupation with the feast of Corpus Christi that there was no concern with the regulation of economic affairs, which are not mentioned in the chapter at all.

By 1389 there was a definite distinction in the purposes of the parish fraternity and the gild, and probably well before this. It can be ascertained from the name of the organization whether there was any specific attempt to distinguish the religious from the occupational aspects. Some, like the London drapers, named themselves both fraternity and gild. In addition, where the gilds stated that they were occupational, they began to draw back from the full implications of the religious commitments that were embodied in their ideals. This can be read directly from the way that religious purposes are stressed, but also in a collective sense in that over the entire range of gilds making returns, those that identified economic purposes more often mentioned limits to their commitments to members. Surprisingly, many gild charters even stipulated the distance beyond the city walls that a search would be made for the body of one who had drowned, and a limit to the distance a corpse would be brought to the gild meeting place. The Roman gilds has a similar provision for limiting the distance a body would be sought. Of eighty-eight complete charters in the records presented by T. Smith, significantly more economic gilds mention limits than do the purely fraternal parish organizations (calculated by the chi-square technique, one degree of freedom). Thus, even though the name of gild was used, there were real differences in intended behavior as early as late fourteenth century.

The gild merchant (*gilda mercatoria*), the craft gild, the merchant gild, the Staplers, the Merchant Adventurers, the Hanse, the Eastland Company, the Hudson's Bay Company, the Russia Company, the East India Company, were all organizations designed to accomplish one end: economic advantage for their members. They differ as to rights of members, legal form, and concern with religion. They also differ in the extent to which they kept some aspects of their voluntary nature. They may be arranged chronologically only with considerable imprecision, not only because data are lacking, but because in the early states the types probably were not so distinct. The gild merchant was a phenomenon of the eleventh to fourteenth centuries and was found in many of the English small cities or towns. Most merchant gilds emerged from the craft gilds by a process of differentiation. Some crafts, however, were by their very nature mercantile and readily combined handwork and selling from the first. There were, in addition, some purely mercantile gilds from the start. Of these, the Hanse was the name given to Flemish and other trading companies that date back to very early times, perhaps even preceding the year 1000. In the literature, "the Hanse" is continually subject to misunderstanding because, like "gild" and "club," the word was linguistically confusing. In Germanic languages "to hanse" means to share a payment; the noun, however, also referred to specific organizations. "Club" had a verb form too—as late as Johnson's (1755) dictionary "to club" was given prominence, signifying "to pay a common reckoning." The Staplers (from *Stabile Emporium*, or fixed market) were chartered export specialists. More concretely, "the staple" was given (or perhaps formed) to specific gilds as a monopoly, the first corporate form being "the Mayor, Constables and Fellowship of the Merchants of the Staple of England," in 1314. The Merchant Adventurers were import specialists, and also grew from merchant gilds or were originated in a similar manner about 1500. The Merchant Adventurers were first the Brotherhood of St. Thomas Becket, and when they began to expand operations, the name of the martyr was dropped. The Merchant Adventurers received full corporate status under Elizabeth I. The Merchant Adventurers had imitators, gilds that sought to expand trade abroad, but which did not have the legal charter. The Merchant's Gild of St. George, Kingston Upon Hull, founded in 1499, is an example of such an organization that was more inclusive than gilds of specific products like the weavers, but not involved in local government like the gild merchant of earlier times.[71]

The named companies, above, each had special advantages guaranteed by a monarch, in order to competitively exploit a certain area in the national interest by means already known and developed in normal trade. They emerged at times indicated by their title: the East India Company to exploit India, the Russia Company (1555), and so on. An example of interest to Canadians and Americans is the Hudson's Bay Company, which is still an active organization in the region where it began its operations.

Let us begin more detailed consideration of the several types of gilds by analysis of the gild merchant, which is only analytically prior: it was the most general form of the economic gild. The object of this portion is expansion of the general model of the gild developed above, with concrete detail.

The gild merchant had a trade monopoly in a borough, in which workers in many kinds of local trades were members of a single gild. The gild merchant, by precedence and intent, excluded other forms of gild; it was the emergence of the specialized gilds and other political apparatus that eventually undermined it and terminated its operations everywhere in England. The members of the gild merchant sought to control trade to their own advantage, and to do so they required the permission of the borough authorities, with whom they drew up an agreement in considerable detail.

Many boroughs made their laws by borrowing entire charters from established cities. Some cities (not necessarily large ones) seemed to be models for many others, and in some cases, the influence of these cities can be traced through several stages to a large number of others. The gild merchant emerged at about the same times as this process and was very much involved in it, and some gild merchant charters were borrowed as a whole. This practice was responsible not only for the rapid growth of the gild merchant, but for relative uniformity of municipal regulation of economic life, at a time when controlled administration of a national economy was not feasible. Among the prominent parent boroughs were York, Beverly, and Winchester. Boroughs were not simply larger villages; they were strategically designated by the sovereign for a particular preferred status. The sovereign's choice might have a variety of reasons, including political control on regions where specific nobles or bishops were too powerful, or where economic potential seemed significant. Whatever the reason, the choice was a license to grow, usually, though some that were chosen are now very small.

The gild merchant charters reveal a concern with religion very much like that of the religious fraternity. The gild merchant was not so well known for its charity, however. It did keep the feasting and drinking customs that accompanied all gild affairs at the time. It may have been the case that the gild merchant existed at the same time as parish fraternities in some cities; this differentiation would explain the absence of concern with religious work in some gild merchant charters. The records are not clear on the point. Unlike the fraternity, the gild merchant paid a great deal of attention to rights of members in trade, the right of search for violators, the prices or penalties for numerous acts. The gild merchant, on the whole, was a form of economic government by a private association, which it gradually extended to related issues in other fields, and economic and political affairs were dominant.

The right of the gild merchant was purchased at a considerable price. It involved the privilege of the tax *ferme*, which is a simple way for the king to collect taxes and to be rid of cumbersome administrative and legal detail. The tradesmen sought this because with it they got the right to freedom from vexatious tolls of many sorts and paid a predictable fee in their place. The privilege was named the *firma burgi*. The earliest gild merchant of which there is record was probably in operation shortly after the Norman conquest. Burford probably had a gild merchant by 1087, and Canterbury by 1093. Winchester claims gilds from 856, though this may be a *frith*, but it did have a gild merchant very early. At the time tolls were very numerous, involving fees for bridges, fords, roads, sales of goods, and a great many routine transactions that some writers simply label "bribes." The member of the gild merchant thus purchased not only a financial advantage, but freedom from frustration and chaos. He gained local and private control and local justice in many significant things. And by implication, he left to his former competitors the debilitating frustrations and frictions of doing business the old way.

In order to be a member of the gild merchant, the tradesman had to qualify. In general, this means he was a burgess—he was politically and religiously loyal, owned property of a certain value, and resided on a piece of it. It was articulated by Richard II (reigned 1377-1399), in a form that remained unchanged in law until 1835. "Every person admitted to the freedom of the City shall be of a certain Mystery or Craft, and, if a stranger, shall be admitted by apprenticeship only and not by redemption."[72] Jones dates this practice from 1364.[73] The statement by Richard II was merely a formalization of practices that had existed for some time previously. Gross explains membership in detail. "Women, monks, and heads of religious houses belonged to the Gild but they were excluded from burgess-ship; for they could fulfill the obligations of the one but not the other."[74] A person could be a resident without being a member of the gild merchant. There were foreigners who resided in the borough who could not belong to the gild, being subject to another sovereign or another religion (such as in the case of the Jews, to be discussed below). There were villeins who were manumitted or escaped; particularly there were a large number whose legal status was simply unclear in situations where the administration of law was not adequate to untangle complex ob-

ligations. There were sokemen whose *soke* was within the borough
and who were liege men but having the right of willing their
membership. Membership in a gild merchant, as in any gild, was not
alienable—it was personal, unlike stock in a corporation. It could be
transmitted through primogeniture if apprenticeship qualifications
could be met; younger sons could buy membership, and many gilds
allowed widows the inheritance. Unlike the craft gild, in which the
skill of a master in the same trade was essential for membership and
necessary for the gild, skill in any trade qualified a person to be a
member of the gild merchant. Most craft gilds kept a skill re-
quirement for membership, though at times in another trade. The
multiple sources of membership in the gild merchant led to considerable complexity over time. However, there is no evidence that
control passed out of the hands of the people who participated for the
purpose for which the organization was founded: a trade monopoly.

Members of the gild merchant had monopoly over certain kinds of
goods and could prohibit foreigners ("foreigns") from buying or
selling them. Members also regulated each other through the gild
merchant; they had the right to bid on items presented for sale, often
at designated times, places, and prices, so that no member could
control the market by forestalling or regrating, (aggressive market
control), the two cardinal sins of merchandising in the Middle Ages.
But foreigners were needed, because they had money and desirable
goods. The gild merchants, therefore, developed and encouraged a
safeguard. They allowed continuation of the fairs that had existed in
the towns for centuries, and they permitted foreigners to trade at
them. The foreigners, then, could do business one day a week (for
most products) and the gild merchant traders controlled the rest (as
well as influencing the fairs as much as possible).

The gild merchant was a highly prevalent form of gild control over
economic life. Gross found that one-third of 166 towns in England,
Wales, and Ireland had this form of organization under Edward I
(1272-1307).[75] Within this number, there were numerous variations
in operating principles. Of particular interest is the variation in
closeness of the gild merchant to the municipal government. In some
cases the gild merchant seems to have virtually become the municipal government, while in others, the same people ran things but the

roles were clearly separated. "The two bodies, the burgess of the town and the brethren of the gild merchant, who were after all very largely the same people, came to be identified in thought in most towns."[76] The custom of using the gild hall as the municipal government edifice also led to confusion on the issue (and the custom persists to this day in many places in England). Apparently the two were at least legally separate in most places and became more so as the gild merchant began to die out.

Much of the information on craft gilds and merchant gilds that is cited by authorities comes from London records, which have been the most accessible sources. London, however, did not have the gild merchant, and therefore it is likely that its influence is underestimated.

If the gild merchant was so omnipotent, how did the craft gild emerge? The gild merchant was an effective trade monopoly that served a purpose for many years and forestalled growth of specialized craft gilds, either anew or from religious fraternities. As the boroughs grew, the trade specialities became large enough to justify separate occupational gilds, and places with a gild merchant faced a problem of a jurisdictional dispute between the two gilds. More often, the transition was not problematic, since the gild merchant simply ceased to be effective. Throughout the era, there were either laws or customs that specified that a man should have only one occupation or be admitted to only one "mystery" (from the French for "mastery"). A woman was not so restricted. No man would desire to pay the *firma burgi* twice for the same privilege anyway. One frequent solution was to allow the gild merchant to become solely a ceremonial organization while the true regulatory power passed to municipal officials. Some boroughs kept the gild merchant intact and made it the municipal government of craft gilds only, a complex two-tier gild-of-gilds. By the fifteenth century, the gild merchant was mostly a thing of the past. It had served a function while the task was of small scope, but it had been displaced by other forms of rule.

Two kinds of settlement did not qualify for the gild merchant: the village, and the small town. The villages were too small, and in the early years of the era were essentially agricultural settlements of villeins or sokemen. The village too faced the problem of frustrating tolls that limited growth; selection as a borough meant selection for privileged expansion, and not to be selected meant to be destined to remain small, after Henry III. If a town was larger than a village but not large enough to keep twelve watchmen on the walls, it could be designated as a market town or merchant town.[77] The exchequer preferred to have them enlarged to full boroughs, for tax purposes. Not named as boroughs, the towns of Manchester, Birmingham, and Leeds were not gild merchant cities and were, therefore, quite different kinds of places: slower to grow at first, but more able to adapt and grow later. London had already been mentioned as a special case. Gross also notes that some *mesne* towns, under jurisdiction of a lord, were allowed a gild merchant.[78] This is not typical. The Cinque-ports were another special case: a set of towns on the channel facing France, they gained unique privileges for their traditional provision of sailors for the king.

The gild merchant, as suggested before, did not end precipitously as a certain time. It was displaced or followed by other forms of organization, as the borough faced problems of growth and competition. And the demise of the gild merchant did not involve a challenge to the idea of the gild itself. If anything, it proved the fundamental faith in the idea of the religious way of organization of economics and politics, as the craft gild and the merchant gild, equally religious, took over the tasks of work and government.

Specialization as a craft gild led to certain new options in organization. Prominent among these were the advantages offered by the ancient idea of vicinal concentration, a principle that was almost always followed and which, in retrospect, proved to have been responsible for many of the problems that gilds typically encountered. The religious duties of the craftsman were now directed through an organization of workers with similar problems, similar values, and with residence in a small local area, usually of the same parish. It was, therefore, relatively simple for them to evolve from a parish fraternity, or to become a fraternity for the special purposes that an emerging economic specialization indicated. This similarity of residence is attested by the names that the streets, lanes, and courts have taken in the older sections of all English cities that originated in the era. One repeatedly encounters names like Bread

Street, Milk Street, Poultry Lane, Ironmongers Lane, Paternoster Row, the Shambles, and so on. All recall the names of former residents' occupations. The typical shop of the craftsman was very small and was usually located on the street floor below his residence. The shops tended to be concentrated, in spite of what seems like inefficient marketing arrangements for the public in many cases. Nevertheless, some trades were distributed throughout larger cities to meet customers, where they happen to be, or to have access to things needed in manufacture. Vicinal organization tends in time to lead to its opposite, diffuse production. Trade maps of larger English cities frequently show that there were shops distributed throughout cities. One vexatious problem of concentration was that it led to development of nongild shops, either outside the walls or within encapsulated civic jurisdictions (e.g., an abbey), of which there were many in medieval cities. Gilds were rarely satisfied with their police powers over these adulterine gilds or foreigners; even though they had legal jurisdiction over nongild workers, they lacked the personnel to trace down malefactors and prosecute them. In spite of these exceptions, gild power usually centered in the craft neighborhood, though the gild's aegis was greater. Thus the parish could not be the sole basis of organization for all craft gilds, since their problems extended beyond the parish itself. Some gilds attached themselves to cathedrals or abbeys with their wider jurisdictions. No record was found of a gild that was not attached to some religious unit, although there are some cases that are unclear.

Gilds and fraternities frequently took the patron of the church as their own. If the gild had a special chapel in its church, or a place in the church set aside for its use, it was devoted to the saint. The patron saint's day was the occasion of a special gild meeting, and the day was observed with a processional and a mass in honor of the saint. The nature of the occasion was usually described in some detail in the gild charter. The patron saint was often one who had special significance to the occupation of its votaries: St. Joseph for carpenters or St. Peter for fishmongers. There may have been actual continuity with Roman practice here. The Roman *opificum* selected a god for each organization, and this worked out pretty well, since there seemed to be a god for almost every common purpose. It is, in fact, interesting to speculate whether Roman gods themselves endured better when their organizations were prosperous. The English gilds, however, did not show a tendency to proliferation of affiliations with saints: some saints (e.g., John the Baptist) were chosen by many kinds of craft gilds, which is an important issue for this study. It signifies that the religious purpose was still significant, in spite of the economic specialization of the craft gilds—and, of course, that there were not enough occupations represented among saints to go around.

It was noted above that early craft gilds were sometimes indistinguishable from religious fraternities. Let us now take up the issue from the point of view of one organization that declared itself to be a craft gild. The Parliament of 1388 (Richard II) ordered a survey of all gilds. They addressed "the Masters and Wardens and Overlookers of all the Mysteries and Crafts."[79] The returns extant in 1870 for Toulmin Smith's inspection were only a fraction of probable returns, and these a fraction of actual gilds. The ordinances all showed a concern for religion, and sometimes the craft gilds had no evident concern with regulatory matters of an economic nature. Consider, for example, the Norwich barbers. The charter, which is given in full, is one of the shortest among those preserved.

> And a bretherhode there is ordened of barbres, in the site
> of Norwyche, in the worshep of god and his moder, and
> seynt Johan the Babtis, that alle bretherin and sisterin of
> the same gylde, als longe as xii persones of hem lyven, they
> schulen offeryn a candel and to torches of wax; and this light
> they hoten and a-vowed to kepyn and myntenyn, and thes
> other ordenances that ben under vreton, up-on here power
> and diligence, in worschepe of crist and his moder and seyn
> Johan Babtis; and the to torches shul bien of xl. *lib.* weyght;
> and all the bretherin and sisterin shullen offeryn this candel
> and the to torches everi year a misomere day, and they
> herin hare messe at the heye auter atte Charunel in cristis
> cherge, and everi brother and sistir offeryn an *ob.* wyth
> here candel and here to torches, in honor of god and oure
> lady and seynt Johan the Baptis.

> And the to torches, everi day in the year, shullen ben light and Brennynge at the heye messe at selve auter, from the levacioun of cristis body sacrid, in til that the priest have used.
>
> This bien the names of the men that ben mystris and kepers of the gyld.
>
> Philippus Barbur, Jacobus Barbir, Thomas Barbyr at prechors. And these men han in kepynge for the same light, ii. s. in here box.

From the available evidence, it cannot be concluded whether the barbers had further rules that were not stated. In addition, the charter says nothing about membership, whereas many fraternities were specific (as in the charter of St. Michael on the Hill cited earlier). Municipal ordinances may have settled the matter about apprentices, working conditions, and so on. Nevertheless, one cannot escape the conclusion that in the fourteenth century the religious purpose was prominent and the craft gild was sometimes little more than a fraternity of members of a certin craft, and perhaps a voluntary association in the fullest sense. The gild did not intend perpetuity but would dissolve if less than twelve were living, a common practice among fraternities but not a necessity for a gild regulated closely by a municipality. The charter is also notable for its direct emphasis on religious work. The religion of the fourteenth century always made it clear that there were specific things one could and must do for God and his church; the fraternity *and* the gild were both work organizations in religion, and the gild also in economics, and this was one of the foremost reasons for the amazing durability of this form of organization.

Craft gilds had more occasion to exercise authoritative jurisdiction over their members than did fraternities. If the gild or fraternity member had taken an oath regarding an obligation, he could be brought before the bishop and be forced to discharge the obligation. The bishop, too, had the right to grant the use of the *soke*, and so the gild or fraternity might try the person directly if they had obtained the *soke* from the religious authority. Many chose to use the bishop directly. This example of a penetrating role is illustrated in the following ordinance excerpt from the Glovers' Gild, London, about 1354.

> Also, it is ordeyned that if any brother of the same fraternitie of the crafte of glovers be behynde of paiement of his quarterage by a yere and a day, and his power the same quarterage of paie, and if he that do maliciously refuse, that thenne he be somened tofore the officiall and by the wardens for his trespass and rebelness of such manner, duly for to be chastised or ponyssed, and to paie the fine aforesaid, and her costs of the court, as in here account tofore all other bretheren of the same craft wellen answer.[80]

Further inferences can be made from the 1389 ordinance returns about the concern of the gilds to use their funds responsibly. Each gild was required to make account of funds on hand. It was traditional that English gilds had a strongbox (as did Roman *collegia*) for their precious property, including funds, jewelry, and documents. The box usually had three locks, one for each significant officer. One exceptional case was that of the Drapers of London, who had two boxes after 1414: the *Box de Dieu* and the Temporal Box. The distinction of names did not seem to result in a distinction of functions, however.[81] The box (or boxes) was opened at each meeting, and the officers had to account for the contents and for disbursements. The financial contents of the box were reported in the ordinance returns. The Norwich barbers cited above had two shillings. My calculations show an average of about twenty shillings. The range was from zero to forty-seven pounds. From the amounts it may be concluded that the turnover of funds was fairly high, and that the assessments were put to use rather than accumulated. There were few chattels revealed in the reports, and it is unlikely that at the time very many such organizations owned their halls.

Some craft gilds in time gave way to others, as the gild merchant did before, though, as shown previously, the sequence was not simply chronological. A major thing that distinguished the craft gild and the merchant gild was that a distinction arose between manual craftsmen and retail specialists. Another change distinguished masters from journeymen and apprentices. This led to separate gilds for masters and journeymen, and sometimes to gilds for apprentices as well. The division between the master of the small shop and his workers was likely to be one that was associated with different gild memberships of two different strata within a gild; the distinction between the master of a large shop and his workers was likely to be one between a master and his servants, as workers, and did not necessarily lead to changes in gilds at all.

The merchants generally were more wealthy than the craftsmen, but that is not a reliable distinction between them, nor is ceremonial ranking among the inner circle of livery companies. The goldsmiths ranked very high everywhere, and most of them were master craftsmen whose merchandising did not lead to a separation of manufacturing and selling vocations to any degree. Nor was intellectual accomplishment a basis of high rank. Those gilds that we would now call white-collar were often fairly low in the ranking schemes and definitely were craft gilds: the scriveners, parish clerks, surgeons, musicians. But this is somewhat beside the issue so far as voluntarism is concerned: the craft gilds and the merchant gilds did not differ markedly as to voluntarism during the early era. A more important issue in that regard was the extent to which the roles necessary in the operation of the gild led to development of structures that excluded voluntary action.

These functional roles in gilds may be divided analytically into those concerned with members and with environment. The former involved some purely housekeeping obligations such as record keeping, internal order, and ceremonial affairs. Many of the environmental roles are examples of the penetrating roles mentioned above. Member functional roles were similar in all gilds, and to this extent, all had some voluntaristic features (as distinguished from informal features, which is a separate matter). Gild officers were not paid, and many found the duties onerous. There were, in fact, penalties for refusing office, and most masters simply counted office holding as an expected burden to be born during their work careers, perhaps bringing prestige and sometimes access to desirable rewards through environmental roles or privileges that they led to, such as election as alderman or mayor. Gilds might have employees, such as servants, and some of them hired priests, none of whom were granted membership. Among the environmental roles were those concerned with a wide range of activities, some of which involved administration of royal or municipal precepts, political activity, and far-ranging collateral roles, as well as the active proceedings of search for deficient goods, contraband, forbidden competition, and so on. The type of economic activity obviously dictated very different roles. The leaders of the fishmongers' gilds had daily tasks of inspection, which were onerous and authoritative, while dealers in nonperishable commodities, such as the smiths or the weavers, could carry out their roles more conveniently. In all cases the gild leaders had a defined relationship with the borough government that defined powers of search and seizure and made plain what court powers the *soke* implied. Where the gild had strong court powers, it probably was less voluntaristic overall, and more oligarchical. Gilds, however, varied as to officer components. Typical officers were master, wardens, and deans, plus a "court of assistants" that might vary in number and power.

The organizations with a great deal of business had courts of assistants that met weekly or even daily. Nevertheless, they did not delegate much of their power to staff, and this meant that the possible distinctions between staff under the control of voluntary association members were diminished. When the business of the organization grew large, the gild often acquired a hall in which to carry out its affairs. Some of the halls used the same space for meetings and warehousing or marketing, and the hall could be rearranged with large trestle tables for banqueting purposes. Unlike voluntary associations familiar to us now, the idea of an administrative staff was foreign. The contrast with Roman *collegia* is strong—the English gilds had relatively few officers and overworked them; the Romans had little ork and numerous officers. Thus the frequently heard comment about the lavish ceremonies and ceremonialism of English gilds seems out of proportion; true, they did have many ceremonies, but they were quite functional and integrated with their work, and hardly superfluous. The critique may have some substance regarding the twentieth-century gilds, for whom ceremonialism may become an end in itself.

The livery companies, most of which were merchant gilds, consolidated their power in a number of ways. They were ranked officially, and the twelve companies retained the right to elect the Lord Mayor in London and had similar powers elsewhere. This ranked set existed in most European countries, but varied in number and in constitution. They participated in the annual London Lord Mayor's show, which was the major festive event of the year. They vied with each other for the most spectacular displays, and one of the ways that they proved their right to rank was by the amount of money they could put into the show. The Lord Mayor's show was the occasion for a great deal of voluntaristic activity by all of the gilds and affiliated personages. The output of art and poetry on these occasions was prodigious, and of practically no artistic merit at all.


THE FRATERNITY IDEA: SPECIAL APPLICATIONS

A persistent finding of this examination of voluntary associations in the earlier era has been that the voluntaristic religious association changed when put to use in ways other than purely religious, and that this change often resulted in alteration of its voluntary character. This differentiation theme may be illustrated in considerable variety by tracing some of the minor organizations that began as fraternities. The majority of these associations were concerned with charity or other special religious purposes. Another aspect of differentiation, that involving transformation of gilds into various new types, has already been treated.

The significance of a pilgrimage was apparently established early in the growth of Christianity. A voyage to a holy place in England, however, often involved great dangers from the perils of the wilderness and from robbers who, in the absence of a territorial police force, beset their victims on the highways. It was, therefore, customary to form temporary companies of travelers and of pilgrims, and it is of such a company that Chaucer wrote. There were fraternities of some communities that were formed specifically to enable their members to save for a pilgrimage and to have protection in travel. Vinogradoff writes of a gild of wayfarers, the *hermandades,* in Spain.[82] As certain localities in England became known as holy places, hospices grew up along typical routes to them, manned by fraternities of clergy, often from nearby abbeys. Soon after the martyrdom of Thomas Becket, the pilgrimage to Canterbury was high on the list of hopes of many English Christians (now largely replaced by tourists). The road to Canterbury, therefore, was the scene of much voluntary association activity. In Spain, things were even more systematic. Cluniac monks organized hostels a day's journey apart on the roads to Santiago de Compostella, with complete services at each stop, including cobbler and barber. What motel chain does better?

The idea of pilgrimage acquired the status of a holy cause with the hysteria of the Crusades. Seldom has history seen such immense support for a cause, and seldom has the limitation of voluntarism been so poorly predicted. The thing of greatest interest here is the twelve orders of knights founded in the eleventh or twelfth centuries as a result of the Crusades. Essentially, the naive faith and simpleminded zeal of Christians led to numerous crises and needs for succor, to which the new holy orders were a rigidly organized overcompensatory response. The best known of these are the Templars, and the Hospitallers whose proper name is the Sovereign Military Order of the Hospital of St. John of Jerusalem, of Rhodes and of Malta. Other orders include the Knights of Alcantara, Knights of Dobrin, Knights of Montesa, Knights of the Holy Sepulcher, and Knights of the Sword. Each was formed to accomplish some special service to pilgrims. Membership was entered by holy vows and usually accompanied by surrender of all property. Service was intended to be for life, and though some orders later relaxed this rule, it generally held. The rule of most of the orders was modeled after the monasteries of the time, and some of the orders were actually related administratively to a monastery designated by the Pope. The orders generally may be classed with the monasteries as quasi-voluntary associations, in that they met only one of the criteria of the definition.

Of all of the orders, the Knights of the Holy Sepulcher is the only one that was clearly a voluntary association from the start. The members were knighted at the Holy Sepulcher in Jerusalem, and at first had to be of the knightly class in order to qualify. They were recognized by the Pope and later assigned to the care of the Franciscans in Jerusalem. As noted above, the Franciscans exemplified the ideal of voluntarism. The knights remained a religious fraternity throughout, the only distinction from other fraternities we have considered being that they were not attached to a local church but to a monastic order, and therefore it was simpler for them to keep a fellowship over a wide territory.

The Hospitallers and the Templars illustrate the significance of the variations of the interface mechanism concept as it has been used here. These organizations were military interface associations between the monasteries and the several polities. They acquired their definition of the moral order from the monasteries, which stressed asceticism. When recruitment was from the strata of men with a noble or knightly tradition, the orders became military units with extremely effective discipline. Their success was rewarded by monarchs, and each became wealthy in a short time, followed by controversy and political intrigue. Entrance was difficult and required a high degree of commitment—this alone does not exclude them from the category of voluntary association. Exit, however, was also difficult (except at first among the Templars), and this combination of facts led to the possibilities of rigorous internal discipline. The Templars and Hospitallers in their second phase, after failure of the Crusades, were simply religious mercenary armies of noblemen. The surviving orders are now honorary religious fraternities. The Knights of the Holy Sepulcher is a fraternal order for social service and piety, now in its ninth century.

The orders were never of great political or religious significance in England, as compared to their activities in the Mediterranean area. There were, however, from the twelfth century on, members of many of the orders in England, and they sometimes served as a potential force of some consequence.

In medieval England, burgesses and others assumed many duties that we now consider proper only for government action. Religious houses spoke of the *trinodas necessitas*, the three duties. The churches constantly stressed the duty of repair of roads, bridges, fords, aqueducts, sewers, and other public facilities. It was assumed or even demanded that those who lived near such places would attempt to take responsibility for them. Bishops sometimes gave indulgences for repair work. Some of these duties were undertaken by creation of special fraternities like the *pontife*, or bridge brothers. London Bridge was sometimes under care of such a fraternity. The responsibility was assumed in the same spirit that led to formation of the Orders of Knights after the start of the Crusades. It was a religious duty; it necessarily followed that a voluntary association was formed to do it properly.

The burgess would have liked to conclude that the payment of the *ferme* ended his civic financial responsibility. The king thought otherwise. The assumption that Christians would do their duty led to the matching assumption by the monarch and municipal authorities that the sense of duty could be used to accomplish other ends, which were not so obviously the duty of any certain person. These came to be called "precepts." Precepts were used by mayors in the sixteenth and seventeenth centuries when the traditional payments by the gilds were no longer economically adequate for such purposes. This use for civic purposes was accompanied by precepts from the monarch for funds and soldiers. The military precept was a direct derivation from the ancient practice of knight service to a lord. The Tudors were especially adept at using precepts for royal ends, such as raising money for wars, constructing buildings, and so on. Elizabeth extended the practice to the limit, but also exercised the prerogative of granting monopolies to specific individuals for a price. Perhaps the most notorious of the precepts was that of James II, who persuaded the London livery companies to finance the settlement of the Irish plantations, whence the origin and development of Londonderry— essentially a gild enterprise. It is a long road from the first use of the *ferme* with English gilds, through frequent assignment of duties to gildsmen such as watching on the walls and cleaning the sewers, to colonizing territories and associated grim consequences; but it is all part of the same set of assumptions on which gilds operated for centuries: the privilege of economic action was a bargain, made with the rulers, for which the price was exacted in a constant struggle.

The impression was given earlier that gilds were formed when groups of people living in a certain area having common occupations sought out a church, took a patron saint, and developed suitable rituals. It was also true, however, that once certain Christian holy days became important to a populace, fraternities developed solely for the purpose of more effectively celebrating or commemorating the event, and such fraternities were not usually bound to a certain neighborhood. This was particularly true regarding Corpus Christi day, though other events led to the growth of special fraternities as well. The feast of Corpus Christi was initiated by Pope Urban about 1264; eventually the proportion of Corpus Christi fraternities became as much as one-third of the total.[83] York was noted for the grandeur of its Corpus Christi celebrations, and a special Corpus Christi fraternity was responsible for its organization each year. York had a Corpus Christi drama company for each of twenty-four trading companies or crafts.[84] The Corpus Christi fraternity had an important leadership function in towns that had many gilds and fraternities all pursuing their individual purposes. It was the one fraternity for most of the people, for a short period of time each year, and provided a common basis for unity among an occasionally dissenting and factious people. The Corpus Christi fraternity of Kingston Upon Hull had a cumulative total of 16,850 names on its roster between 1408 and 1546.[85]

Though the Corpus Christi fraternities were focused on the celebration of the most important holy day, the organizations often acquired ancillary functions once the fraternity was established. Many had loan funds. Some took responsibility for some particular charity.

There were several alternate ways of organizing the Corpus Christi day celebrations. In London the Skinners' gild took Corpus Christi as their eponym, and then when the day became more significant to the public, the combination became a way of acquiring honorary members as the gild itself became a force behind organized celebrations of the day. The Fraternity of Our Lady's Assumption similarly acquired many honorary members.[86]

There is no indication that the Corpus Christi fraternities ever developed a national organization, though they could not have ignored the existence of the celebrations of other cities, so widely were they known. Their common relationships to the church made such affiliation superfluous. There were, in fact, no purely secular organizations that would make affiliation necessary. The closest thing to a truly independent organization was the *Feste du Puy*. The *Feste du Puy* (or *Pui*) was probably not a national organization either, but a series of voluntary associations of singers and festive performers in various places in England and France. From the available information it is not always possible to distinguish fraternities of singers and minstrels, which were probably simply gilds of professionals, from festive organizations of amateurs.

The Gild of the Holy Trinity was founded at Kingston Upon Hull in 1369. Gilds by this name were known informally as the Seamens' Gilds, and took responsibility for sailors' unique needs. No evidence of formal national organization can be found. Because of its reputation for service, it was exempted from dissolution by Henry VIII.

This section on the various applications of the fraternity idea to medieval life ends with a theoretical inquiry. Can we learn anything about the phenomenon by asking where it was *not* found, as well as where it was? The inquiry is necessarily cautious, since the fallacies of reasoning from the absence of data are obvious. The significance of religion in the gild can at least be illuminated in this fashion. Only one instance of the application of the fraternity to immoral purposes can be found, and that was probably not in England. I refer to the finding by Painter of a gild of prostitutes.[87] Unfortunately, he does not give details. There is no record of organizations *solely* for the purposes of drinking or for carousal as was the case with the clubs. Likewise, there appear to have been no lower-class or nonburgess organizations that imitated or adulated the fraternities. There is a hint of transitory organizations of beggars, "upright men" and their "doxies" (i.e., organizers of deviant groups and their women) in the Elizabethan era, but there is certainly no suggestion that they had any idea that the gild form of organization had any promise for them. In sum, the fraternity idea seems to have been rigidly held by certain social strata and no other, and penetration of class barriers seems to have been negligible so far as organizational ideas and mechanisms were concerned.

Westlake, in his valuable study of parish fraternities, shows that the fraternity idea of mutual aid was extended to deal with some of the problems of rural life.[88] He gives instances where fraternities became active in sharing bulls for stud. They made mutual-aid payments in kind rather than money. There were organizations of "young men, maidens, webbers, tuckers, archers, and hogglers or field laborers."[89] Unfortunately, the author does not give sufficient information to allow inference about the extent of the practices.

As another kind of untypical group, the cultural minority, the Jews are the major example. This is the subject of the next section.

Finally, some facts should be presented here that suggest a possible inconsistency with the observations made in this chapter about religious gilds and for which no explanation seems adequate. Riley, in his justifiably noted volume, *Memorials of London Life*, cites the existence of organizations from the fourteenth century that do not have religious names of the kind that were found among gilds.[90] He lists the Wyndrawers, the Kings Society, the Newemeyne, and the Society of Shipup. The first is a company of wine carters and may simply be a gild that was incorrectly given a common rather than formal religious name in the documents. The Newemeyne were also called the New Household and could be a servants' gild. The other two seem incomprehensible and do not follow the practice of religious naming or occupational designation.

JEWISH GILDS

The gilds frequently made exceptions to their membership rules by strategic inclusion of honorary members, or for people who could qualify by purchase. The occasional appearance of a bishop or a noble seems to be because of the gain in prestige to be thus acquired. They do not seem to have made any exceptions for non-Christians, though. By comparison, the Islamic Karmathian brotherhoods admitted guest Christians. The most important religious minority in England were the Jews, and examination of their reaction to the Christian gilds is very instructive for our understanding of the English society of the earlier era. The key concept of our model is that of permission, which in this instance took a most extreme and barbarous negative form.

Jewish gilds were present throughout medieval Europe, but there is no record of any in England. Jews were brutally persecuted in England and finally driven out in 1290 by Edward I before gilds came to their peak of development but after almost three hundred years of existence of English Christian fraternities and gilds. Jewish gilds reached their highest European development in Poland and Lithuania, where they emerged rather late, as did the Christian gilds there. Under the competition with medieval Christian craftsmen, Jews were driven out of many crafts in England and so resorted to marginal economic niches and to occupations such as banking that were ethically difficult or prohibited for Christians. The Christian gild was an active causal agent in the prolonged persecution, not so much because gilds were especially prejudiced but because their legitimated monopoly was vigorously applied against all who did not qualify categorically for gild membership, and the Jews did not. Prejudice and discrimination are of course interrelated, in the long run.

The non-English medieval Jewish gilds paralleled the Christian ones as far as rules were concerned, but apprenticeship was shorter. In place of the oath to the Christian sovereign, the Jew signed a paper, the *'igareth kakelaf,* which contained elements of the charter. There were similar rules of conduct and duties to the gild. The *Hebroth* (gild) was run by elders, elected for a year. The chief officer was the *Dayan* (judge) who was the spiritual leader. The *Hebroth* was much concerned with obligations that were incumbent on any Jew: charity, care of widows and orphans, observance of the Sabbath, and education. The Jewish communities also had fraternities, the *Hebrah Kaddisha,* which were analogous to to the Christian religious fraternities. The Jewish organizations give the appearance of greater democracy than the Christian counterparts at the same time, but the data are scanty and the conclusion may be illusory.

Why no Jewish gilds in England before Edward I? In the first place, there appear to have been few or no Jewish fraternities in England, and so a potential source of transition to gilds was not present. There was, however, ancient Talmudic reasoning in favor of gild organization. There were sufficient concentrations of craftsmen, where they were allowed. Tradition was always important for Jews, and there was a history of gild organization having at least as much continuity as that connecting the Romans and the medieval Catholic, stemming from hereditary occupations in pre-Christian periods. There were traditional concessions to engilded craftsmen, such as the rules that permitted barbers to work on the eve of the Passover. In fact, the early history of Jewish gilds reads very much like that of the medieval Christian ones. One issue, no doubt, was that the gild merchant developed first in England, and more strongly than in other countries. In the gild merchant, members were of all occupations, a fact that would seem favorable for Jewish membership. As noted previously, the Jews would be excluded on the basis of their religion, and as a small minority, they would not be able to organize a general gild such as the gild merchant that dominated the political scene and permitted no competitors. Following this reasoning, one might expect Jewish gilds in London, where craft gilds emerged well before the major periods of persecution and where there was no gild merchant. There do not seem to have been any, however. In London there was a generalized fear of foreign competition that dates to the earliest records, and this probably extended to the Jews, who might be perceived as foreign as well as non-Christian. This, coupled with the sporadic persecution, was probably sufficient to account for the absence of Jewish gilds. Stenton points out that there were few Jews in England until after the Crusades, and so the total length of their stay was little more than a century.[91] It is ironic, in this context, that Londoners preserve the memory of Jewish presence with Old Jewry Street, where Jewish merchants or craftsmen undoubtedly once lived and carried on business. More ironic still, the official church of the City of London Guildhall is St. Lawrence Jewry, a beautiful Wren church built after the great fire on the very doorstep of the great hall itself. More than a century after the start of the club period, Jews began to reappear in England, and along with the growth of the first synagogue, a gild of Jewish craftsmen appeared, five hundred years after the English diaspora. A synagogue appeared in London in 1700 or 1701, the Bevis Marks. Pepys records contact in London with Jews even earlier.

## Notes

1. The title of this chapter is similar to that of an article that contains essentially the theoretical outline of this chapter and the next. Jack Ross, "Religious Fraternity to Club and Sect: A Study of Social Change in Voluntary Associations in England, 1000-1800 A.D.," *Journal of Voluntary Action Research* 3, 1 (Winter, 1974): 31-42.

2. Morris Bishop, *The Middle Ages* (New York: American Heritage Press, 1970), p. 36. Robert Anderson uses the phrase "Traditional Europe" to deal with material similar to that covered in this study. In similar fashion he concludes that the starting time is not precise, but that about that time the start of a distinctly new era may be discerned. Robert T. Anderson, *Traditional Europe: A Study in Anthropology and History* (Belmont, Calif.: Wadsworth Publishing Company, 1971).

3. Charles Gross, *The Gild Merchant*, 2 vols. (Oxford: At the Clarendon Press, 1964), I, pp. 1-2. First published, 1890.

4. Gross, *The Gild Merchant*; William Joseph Kahl, *The Development of London Livery Companies* (Boston: Harvard Graduate School of Business Administration, 1960); Stella Kramer, *The English Craft Guilds: Studies in their Progress and Decline* (New York: Columbia University Press, 1927): George Unwin, *The Gilds and Companies of London*, 4th ed. (London: Frank Cass and Co., 1963).

5. Nineteenth-century writers noted this problem and attempted reforms. One of the results was a large-scale effort at record retrieval and publication. It was a surprise to me, therefore, to find that the problem stll existed. In one aged municipal vault I found fraternity scrolls from the reign of Henry V lying in random heaps, exposed to the devastation of nature and of bumblers like me. In fairness, some attempt is being made to prepare photocopies of these precious documents, but the situation is still quite unsatisfactory.

6. George Clune, *The Medieval Guild System* (Dublin: Brown and Nolan, 1943); Abbot Gasquet, *Parish Life in Medieval England*, 2nd ed. (London: Methuen and Co., 1907).

7. Robert Brady, *A Complete History of England, etc.*, 2 vols. (London: Samuel Lowndes, 1685), I, p. 109.

8. John Timbs, *Club Life of London*, 2 vols. (London: Chatto and Windus, 1865), I, p. 5.

9. David Herlihy, ed., *Medieval Culture and Society* (New York: Walker and Co., 1968), p. 845.

10. Arthur Harvey Johnson, *The History of the Worshipfull Company*

*of Drapers*, 5 vols. (Oxford: At the Clarendon Press, 1914-1922), Vol. 4, p. 1.

11. Gross, *The Gild Merchant*, I, p. 175.

12. Max Weber, *The Protestant Ethic and the Spirit of Capitalism*, trans. Talcott Parsons (New York: Charles Scribner's Sons, 1958).

13. Sylvia Thrupp, *The Merchant Class of Medieval London (1300-1500)* (Chicago: University of Chicago Press, 1948), p. 16.

14. H. M. Robertson, *Aspects of the Rise of Economic Individualism* (New York: Kelly and Millman, 1959), p. 24.

15. Unwin, *The Gilds and Companies of London*, p. 203.

16. Max Weber, *Economy and Society*, ed. Guenther Roth and Claus Wittich, trans. Ephraim Fischoff et al., 2 vols. (New York: Bedminster Press, 1968), II, pp. 584-87.

17. Ibid., I, p. 340.

18. A detailed study of the barber-surgeon and his gild is contained in Jack C. Ross and Raoul R. Andersen, "Occupational Pluralism: Expansive Strategies in Barbering," *Sociological Review* 20, 2 (May 1972).

19. Charles H. Coote, "The Ordinances of Some Secular Guilds of London, 1354-1496," *Transactions of the London and Middlesex Archaeological Society* 4, 28, 1875.

20. Edward Conder, Jr., *Records of the Hole Crafts and Fellowship of Masons With A Chronicle of the History of the Worshipful Company of Masons in the City of London* (London: Swan Sonnenschein and Co., 1894), p. 43.

21. Louis C. Jones, *The Clubs of the Georgian Rakes* (New York: Columbia University Press, 1942), p. 2.

22. Attention to the way that clubmen like Johnson worked club life into their patterns of work would be a significant way to study voluntary associations. Boswell gives us many insights into Johnson's club life, and other notables left records as well.

23. Thomas H. S. Escott, *Club Makers and Club Members* (London: T. Fisher Unwin, 1914), p. 35.

24. One of the best studies of English residential clubs has been useful in this work, and was also cited in Chapter 1. Denys Forrest, *The Oriental: Life Story of a West End Club* (London: B. T. Batsford, 1968).

25. Escott, *Club Makers and Club Members*, p. 37.

26. An extensive summary of the criticisms of the Protestant Ethic thesis of Weber is contained in S. N. Eisenstadt, "The Protestant Ethic Thesis," in Roland Robertson, ed., *The Sociology of Religion* (Harmondsworth, Middlesex: Penguin Books, 1969), pp. 297-317.

27. Ibid., p. 306-307.

28. Reinhard Bendix, *Max Weber, an Intellectual Portrait* (Garden City, N.Y.: Anchor Books, 1962), p. 67.

29. A. Abram, *English Life and Manners in the Later Middle Ages* (London: George Routledge and Sons, 1913), p. 62.

30. C. Wayne Gordon and Nicholas Babchuck, "A Typology of Voluntary Associations," *American Sociological Review* 24, 1 (February 1959): 22-29.

31. David H. Smith, Richard D. Reddy, and Burt R. Baldwin, "Types of Voluntary Action: A Definitional Essay," in idem, eds., *Voluntary Action Research: 1972* (Lexington, Mass.: Lexington Books, 1972), pp. 171-72.

32. Joachim Wach in Ross P. Scherer, "The Church as a Formal Voluntary Organization," in Smith, Reddy, and Baldwin, *Voluntary Action Research: 1972*, p. 86.

33. Ibid.

34. David Knowles, *The Religious Orders in England* (Cambridge: Cambridge University Press, 1950), p. 12.

35. Alexander Hamilton Thompson, "The Monastic Orders," in H. M. Gwatkin et al., eds., *The Cambridge Medieval History*, 8 vols. (Cambridge: At the University Press, 1929), Vol. 5, pp. 658-96.

36. Ibid.

37. Kahl, *The Development of London Livery Companies*, pp. 1-9.

38. David Herlihy, "Guilds," in William J. McDonald ed., *The New Catholic Encyclopedia*, 15 vols. (New York: McGraw-Hill, 1967), VI, p. 845.

39. J. M. Lambert, *Two Thousand Years of Guild Life* (Hull: A. Brown and Sons, 1891), p. 34.

40. Unwin, *The Gilds and Companies of London*, p. 16.

41. Bishop, *The Middle Ages*, p. 22.

42. Louis D. Hartson, "A Study of Voluntary Associations, Educational and Social, In Europe During the Period From 1100 to 1700," *Pedagogical Seminary* 18 (1911): 12.

43. Paul Lacroix, *France in the Middle Ages*, republished edition (New York: Frederick Ungar Publishing Co., 1963), p. 270.

44. Herlihy, "Guilds," p. 845.

45. Guillermo Moreda Orozo, "Fisherman's Guilds in Spain," *International Labor Review*, 94, 5, (1966): 465-76. The fragmentary nature of the information in this paragraph is unfortunate. A comprehensive study has yet to be done.

46. Unwin, *The Gilds and Companies of London*, p. 352.

47. Lambert, *Two Thousand Years of Guild Life*, p. 31.

48. Henry Charles Coote, *The Ordinances of Some Secular Guilds of*

*London from 1354 to 1496* (London: Nichols and Sons, 1871), pp. 25-30.

49. Bishop, *The Middle Ages*, p. 22.

50. Herlihy, "Guilds," p. 845.

51. Louis Massignon, "Islamic Gilds," in Edwin R. A. Seligman, ed., *Encyclopaedia of the Social Sciences*, 15 vols. (London: Macmillan, 1948), Vol. 7, p. 214.

52. H. F. Westlake, *The Parish Gilds of Medieval England* (New York: Macmillan, 1919), p. 33.

53. Edgcumbe Staley, *The Gilds of Florence* (New York: Benjamin Blom, 1967), p. 600. First edition 1906.

54. The problem of organizational names is analyzed at greater length in the appendix.

55. Lujo Brentano, "On the History and Development of Gilds," in J. Toulmin Smith, *English Gilds* (London: Trubner, 1870), p. lxxxvi.

56. Marc Bloch, *Feudal Society*, trans. L. A. Manyon, 2nd ed. (London: Routledge and Kegan Paul, 1962), p. 420.

57. Hartson, "A Study of Voluntary Associations," p. 11.

58. Bloch, *Feudal Society*, p. 420.

59. Lucy Smith, "Introduction," in J. Toulmin Smith, *English Gilds*, p. xvi.

60. Ibid.

61. Jeremy duQuesnay Adams, *Patterns of Medieval Society* (Englewood Cliffs, N.J.: Prentice-Hall, 1969), p. 17.

62. Hastings Rashdall, "The Medieval Universities," in H. M. Gwatkin et al., eds., *The Cambridge Medieval History*, 8 vols. (Cambridge: At the University Press, 1964), VI; idem, *The Universities of Europe in the Middle Ages*, 2 vols. (Oxford: At the Clarendon Press, 1895).

63. Rashdall, "The Medieval Universities," p. 561.

64. John Stow, *A Survey of the Cities of London and Westminster and the Borough of Southwark, etc.*, John Strype, ed., 6th ed., 2 vols. (London, 1-54), I, p. 125.

65. The concept was defined in this way by Alan F. Jensen, *Sociology: Concepts and Concerns* (Chicago: Rand McNally and Co., 1971), p. 138.

66. Keith Warner, "Major Conceptual Elements of Voluntary Associations," in Smith, Reddy, and Baldwin, *Voluntary Action Research: 1972*, pp. 71-80. In some African and Indian gilds there was joint ownership of capital equipment, but this is as close to ownership of a business as gilds came. They often accumulated funds and particularly remunerative property, but the gild was not itself a business for profit.

67. Doris Mary Stenton, *English Society in the Early Middle Ages*

*(1066-1307)*, 4th ed. (Harmondsworth, Middlesex: Penguin Books, 1967), pp. 67-68.

68. Thrupp, *The Merchant Class of Medieval London*, p. 34.

69. Ibid., p. 37.

70. J. Toulmin Smith, *English Gilds*, pp. 178-79.

71. Lambert, *Two Thousand Years of Guild Life*, p. 156.

72. Arthur Johnson, *The History of the Worshipfull Company of Drapers*, IV, p. 51.

73. P. E. Jones, *The Worshipfull Company of Poulters of the City of London: A Short History*, 2nd ed. (London: Oxford University Press, 1965), p. 55.

74. Gross, *The Gild Merchant*, I, p. 66.

75. Ibid., I, p. 22.

76. Stenton, *English Society in the Early Middle Ages*, p. 181.

77. Ibid., p. 191.

78. Gross, *The Gild Merchant*, I, p. 91.

79. Lucy Smith, "Introduction," p. xxiv-xxv.

80. Coote, *The Ordinance of Some Secular Guilds of London*, p. 8.

81. Johnson, *The History of the Worshipfull Company of Drapers*, IV, p. 109.

82. Sir Paul Vinogradoff, "Foundations of Society (Origins of Feudalism," in Gwatkin et al. *The Cambridge Medieval History*, II, p. 636.

83. Westlake, *The Parish Gilds of Medieval England*, p. 49.

84. William Hone, *Ancient Mysteries Described, Especially the English Miracle Plays on Apocryphal New Testament Stories, etc.* (London: Published by the author, 1823), p. v.

85. Lambert, *Two Thousand Years of Guild Life*, Chapter 9.

86. Thrupp, *The Merchant Class of Medieval London*, p. 31.

87. Sidney Painter, *Medieval Society* (Ithaca, N.Y.: Cornell University Press, 1951), p. 229.

88. Westlake, *The Parish Gilds of Medieval England*, pp. 60-61.

89. Ibid., p. 61.

90. Henry Thomas Riley, *Memorials of London Life* (London: Longmans, Green and Co., 1868), p. xvi.

91. Stenton, *English Society in the Early Middle Ages*, p. 193.

# 5 English clubs and social change

*Society, Company, conversation, Fellowship: also*
*a Company of several Persons joyn'd together for*
*some common interest.*
John Kerry, 1708

*Association. A joyning together in fellowship.*
Henry Cockeram, 1623

## The Emergence of Clubs

The most significant general features of the club were presented in Chapter 4 in the comparative analysis of the fraternity and club. Attention is now turned to analysis of the emergence of the club, in fashion similar to that followed in analysis of the emergence of the gilds and fraternities. As in the case of the gilds, there are early examples, followed by a mature phase. This is not a mere repetition of a pattern, however, for the clubs were not bound to a universal church that bestowed continuity and imposed norms; they were, in fact, distinguished by their secularism and

205

independence from organized religion. The emergence of the clubs more closely resembles a social movement of the modern type, based on rapid communications and on the inspiration and leadership of men who were free to innovate and to follow their own inclinations. Thus analysis of prevalence of clubs must take account of very different kinds of permission, instigation, resources, and rewards than in the case of the fraternal organizations.

Escott dates the first clubs to the Greeks and claims Themistocles as the first clubman.[1] Undoubtedly, the *hetairia* was meant. He identifies Cimon as an enthusiastic club member. Unlike other analysts of voluntary associations who are enthusiasts for the antediluvian origin of their own club or lodge, Escott is a bit more conservative and seems to know the difference between similarity and causation, which was lost on most gild historians. Clubs, as purely social endeavors, existed among many early civilizations, as was demonstrated, and may have offered ideas or inspiration to any who cared to read—and the gentleman and scholars of the early English clubs may have been just such literate people. But it was little more than inspiration, for the immediate involvement in the life of each contemporary club must have been the most significant thing, and none of them seems to have continuity with the past. This was a fresh start.

The first English club of which there is record (other than during Roman occupation) preceded the dates of our second era by some century and a half. There is then another fifty-year period (the reigns of Edward, Mary, Elizabeth) in which some clubs may have existed but for which there is no certain evidence. The explanation of the time gap from the first club to the second might be either that the records of the following era are faulty, or that the first club occurred under exceptional circumstances that were not repeated. The former seems the more likely. Nevertheless, if this mystery is ever solved, it is doubtful if many clubs would be discovered during the hiatus.

Occleve (or Hoccleve), born 1368 or 1369, is said to be the founder of this first English club, the Court of Good Company, which may have been known then by its French name.[2] Allen says that "the

Court seems to have been a dining club of definite membership, with traditions so firmly established that they may well be called rules."[3] The membership included several titled men, and perhaps other literary figures. Chaucer is said by some authorities to have been a member, but he died in 1400, some thirteen years before the first known record of the club. That record is contained in a ballad that Occleve addressed to another member in 1413. "That the 'styward' has warned him that he is 'for the dyner arraye/ageyne Thursday next and nat is delaye.' "[4] The character of Occleve also seems to ring true to the description of later clubmen. He was a government employee, who was known for his disdain for convention. He seems to have had reasons to overthrow convention. He had intended to become a priest, and took the civil service job to prepare for it. When he failed in his occupational plans, he turned to a dissolute life.[5] The theme of role failure leading to hedonism was probably not an uncommon cause of club life, but may not be taken as a general explanation of the seventeenth-century clubs in which the role of gentleman was not deviant.

Occleve made frequent trips by boat from his offices along the Thames to the location of the tavern where he met with fellow club members. It is recorded that he was a spendthrift, and the boatmen could always count on double pay from him for the trip. The club seemed to thrive on secular amusements and hedonism, in an era when little of such behavior took organizational form. Perhaps the explanation of the club is that Occleve and his companions found in the lusty life of the tavern the stimulation for poetry and creativity that they wanted, and that this could not be tolerated in the closed confines of the court and church areas of the old City of London to the east. This distinction between zones of the city held true to a limited extent for several hundred years, and even today London has pleasure districts not too different from the ones Occleve sought out 560 years ago.

The early start of clubs in London was similar to that in Italy. The Society de la Calza appeared in Venice, *ca.* 1400, followed by *Società delle Cene Poetiche* (Poetical Supper Society), a club in which members were required to read poems to belong.[6] Botticelli (1449-

1510) was a member. Benvenuto Cellini was a member of a supper club in the mid-sixteenth century.

The next English club of which there is record was founded by Raleigh in 1603 and also contained a mixture of literary and political leaders. The club met at the Mermaid Tavern. Ben Jonson was an active member. The club was certainly active in 1616, when it may be verified by events there involving famous members. Ward noted of the time that "Shakespeare, Drayton and Ben Jonson, had a merie meeting, and itt seems drank too hard, for Shakespear [*sic*] died of a feavor there contracted."[7]

Jonson was apparently an enthusiastic club leader. He was better known for his later involvement in the Apollo Club. Jonson's rules for the Apollo give an accentuated picture of the differences between gild and club. The rules, the *leges conviviales*, mentioned the custom of dividing expenses.[8] Excessive silence was frowned upon. There were exhortations to friendliness, sharing work, and not revealing confidences. No one, says Jonson, should be compelled to produce *ex tempore* verse. Women of good character might attend.

The second half of the seventeenth century brought the dawn of a new phase in club life. The cause of the change was the simultaneous emergence of extreme political and religious changes and the arrival of a new drink, coffee, on the British scene.

## Drinks and Voluntary Associations

We suit the liquids we drink to the social occasion when we can. Besides our personal preferences and our bodily needs, we adjust to what is available and to what will create the desired effect in the social situation. Medieval men and seventeenth-century clubmen did the same. What did they drink, and what effect did it have on the nature of the organizations?[9]

The beverages available to people in our earlier era would seem strangely limited to us. There were several brands of cheap beer and ale, often made with the most simple processes possible and readily available as a drink in volume for the family. There were also a few bulk wines made locally. The richest men also drank some imported wines, particularly claret, mostly from France, but these wines were few in number and not known to poor men. Other wines were available from the apothecary, for medicinal purposes. Milk was not sold as a retail product, which is just as well, because under the sanitary conditions then in existence, the results would have been catastrophic. In cities, water was impure too. Alcoholic drinks had the advantage of relative purity.

Sack (a dry wine) and porter (a cheap beer) were some drinks of common medieval men available for sale at taverns and sold retail in the cities. There were several other forms of beer and ale. There were no distilled beverages. Drinking, then, was not centered very often on liquids with a high proportion of alcohol. There were no common nonalcoholic drinks available (except water, which was not piped), though there were some steeped beverages and herb drinks for medicinal purposes.

The records of the gilds show that they drank the same drinks that were common in homes. They had their own supply, and perhaps they gained by buying choice items from their fellow gildsmen, the vintners or the brewers. Feasting was common, and drinking accompanied meals. Drinking was ritualized, and the ordinary gild had a loving cup that it was customary to pass around the table, with each man drinking in turn while his neighbor helped him. The drinking custom involved the use of both hands of the drinker, so the neighbor had to use both hands as well, the reason being, it is said, to keep the drinker from being attacked from behind while tippling. The custom of drinking with eating, and the taking of turns and offering of dedications, all undoubtedly helped to limit inebriation. Nevertheless, an evening at the gild hall probably involved drinking quite a lot, and it is unlikely that under such circumstance, free discussion could proceed at length. Uninhibited drinking leads to loss of control by at least some people in most gatherings. Indeed, there is every evidence that one of the basic concerns of the gild was the regulation of problems of interpersonal relations, caused in part by the drinking customs of the time.

Coffee was known in England long before it was readily available. Francis Bacon (d. 1626) wrote in *Sylva Sylvarum*:

> they have in *Turkey* a *drink* called Coffee, made of a Berry
> of the same name, as Black as *Soot,* and of a *Strong sent* but
> not *Aromatical,* which they take, beaten into Powder, in
> *Water* as Hot as they can *Drink* it; and they take it, and sit
> at it in their *Coffee Houses,* which are like our *Taverns.* The
> *Drink* comforteth the *Brain,* and *Heart,* and helpeth
> *Digestion.*[10]

The idea that coffee was good for the digestion was fairly wide-spread. In this era, before scientific medicine, the search for natural or compounded remedies was widespread and was found as a specialty both among the superstitious and among the somewhat more scientific apothecaries. It is not surprising then to note a tract by Judge Rumsey, 1659, called "Organum Salutis, or an Instrument to clean the Stomach; together with diverse New Experiments on the Virtue of Tobacco and Coffee."[11]

Timbs notes a mention of coffee in England in 1621. But it was apparently in use as much as a thousand years ago in Ethiopia, where it was used as a food by mixing the berries, beans, hulls and all, in crushed form into food balls as a supplement on long journeys.[12] Used in that way, the protein content is kept, all but 15 percent of which is lost when brewed and drunk. Coffee was also used as a drink in the current way beginning about the thirteenth century in Turkey. By the sixteenth century, coffee-making technology was sufficiently advanced to be called modern. All that was necessary in England was for a market to develop and for regular supplies to be available.

The first public use of coffee in England was apparently in Oxford in 1650, though some claim an earlier date. Evelyn's diary mentions it at Balliol College in 1637.[13] In 1652 Daniel Edwards, a merchant, brought supplies of coffee from Turkey. The drink became popular among his friends, so he helped his servant Pasqua Rosee, a Greek,[14] to go into the business in George-yard, Lombard Street.[15] In 1651 a coffeehouse was opened by Thomas (or James) Farr, a barber, who drew opposition from his neighbors because of the odors of roasting coffee and the smoke from the faulty chimney.[16]

Perhaps the neighbors were right. A recipe for coffee preparation, dating to 1662, indicates that the beans were roasted until practically black, then beaten and put through a sieve, and finally a one-ounce portion was boiled in a quart of water until a third of the water was gone. The result must have been pretty potent stuff, and apparently it was made this way wherever it was used. The anticoffee faction labeled the result "syrup and soot and essence of old shoes."[17] Regardless of the opposition, the brew became popular very quickly. Perhaps the preference for potency was influenced by the fact that at first the drink was taxed four pence per gallon.

Part of the success of coffee was due to the fact that it was introduced shortly before the London fire of 1666, following the major plague of 1665. When London was rebuilt, the coffeehouses had an opportunity to compete on an even basis with the older taverns. Many coffee houses in London date from this period. The Cheshire Cheese, eighteenth-century favorite of Samuel Johnson, is still in business at a site just off the Strand that it took after the fire. The new coffeehouses also grouped around the Royal Exchange, the financial center of London, and another set was established in Westminster and adjacent Charing Cross, Covent Garden, and Soho. From another point of view, the coffeehouses went away from the old religious and gild center of the ancient walled city of St. Paul's, though later they were found there too.

The coffeehouse furnished a location where men could gather at their leisure and conduct sporadic business that was suited to informality. Most of the business of the Royal Exchange was conducted in coffeehouses. Lloyds insurance company began in Lloyd's coffeehouse, where shipping men gathered to exchange news of voyages. Other coffeehouses also seem to have had specialized clienteles, some of which eventually led to formation of organizations while others merely remained as favored gathering spots. Bastons in Cornhill was favored by medical men; estate agents went to the London on Ludgate Hill; the George in the Strand was a place for lawyers; the Chapter of Paternoster Row was a gathering place of booksellers.[18]

As the coffeehouses grew more numerous and specialized, there were problems for the proprietor. The atmosphere of conversation and relaxation meant a rather slow turnover of customers. There were two solutions. Some coffeehouses charge admission, usually a penny. In paying admission, the customer agreed to abide by the rules and so a clublike environment grew, but it was a business for profit. The second course was to let the premises in whole or part to a club under its own rule. It is the later kind that is of most interest here, but before going on to its implications, some summary comment on the function of the *open* coffeehouse is in order.

The coffeehouses provided a communication center for certain kinds of people. In terms of our model, they provided the situation for a high per capita volume of communication. The open coffeehouses were characterized by the fact that they involved people in professions or in businesses where sharing of news between proprietorships was significant. A setting was needed that provided comfort and informality, which was foreign to the business house itself. The coffeehouse was a kind of neutral territory, a secondary institution, providing formalized informality, and without it the system as a whole would have been impeded. Second, the coffeehouse was new and represented discard of the old ways and the old commitments of the merchant gilds. Like any fad or social movement, its newness was sufficient reason to justify it, at least for a time.

A third reason was simply that the coffeehouse was like the tavern in that it was a place where men could have the company of other men, without the ties of family life. The tavern, however, was an open facility, and women could attend, though it might affect their reputations to do so. The coffeehouse was distinctly a male institution. Famous men had reserved seats; less famous ones came to listen and bask in their radiance. The coffeehouse also served as a source of informal news and gossip, for male concerns. The newspaper, invented and popularized about the same time, reported coffeehouse news, and in the rapidly growing cities of the time in which a man could not easily get all the information he wanted from the church or the town center, such communications were needed and eagerly sought. As a verse of the time had it, "Go hear it at a coffee house, it cannot but be true."[19] The coffeehouse (probably more than the tavern) was also a male place by odor: smoke from tobacco, also relatively new, the smell of coffee, the wood fires, the scent of the periwig (and later peruke), which was powdered and scented, the smell of lamps and candles—this was a era of strong presence of other people and intensity of sensual stimulation. The woman's world was an altogether different sensual sphere, and both wanted it that way.

The coffeehouse was also found in high concentration in districts with many barbershops. When men were shaved daily by a servant at home or by a barber in a shop, the shops also became centers for communication as men waited their turns. The eighteenth-century maps show the two institutions in close proximity near where men gathered for business in the old walled City of London.

The simultaneous occurrence of several sources of sensuality and the rapid growth of industry and empire is no accident. It would be too bold to say that sensuality caused the growth, but the two phenomena certainly shared the same spirit.

The club in the coffeehouse in the second half of the seventeenth century was perhaps also a reaction to the overuse of the open coffeehouse itself, as well as an establishment of a social setting of a unique kind. Club pictures of the era do not seem to indicate so much crowding as in the commercial coffeehouse. Things were more planned. A formal meal was served, and coffee took its place as the symbolic center. Wine was also served sometimes, but it was not as prominent. Later, clubs tended to develop their own recipes for punch; some of these clubs seem to have abandoned coffee as their favorite drink and tended toward inebriation and carousal in place of discussion.

Why coffee, and not tea, as the center of club life? Tea was sold in London before 1651, but apparently did not become a beverage of group sociability. Tea was not commercially available in reliable quality until much later, and that may explain the issue in part. But it is also true that it was the later demand for the drink that led to the delayed growth of the Asian tea trade, just as the need for coffee assisted in the earlier growth of the African and Turkish coffee trade. There are several interrelated reasons for the popularity of coffee itself as a beverage, having to do with its effect on the body. Bramah cites facts to suggest that though tea has about twice the proportion of caffeine by weight, the stimulant is released more quickly in coffee.[20] Tea, when served with milk in the British fashion, absorbs the tannin and provides a mild and long-lasting stimulant due to the caffeine, and a soothing, relaxing effect due to buffering of stomach acids and by promoting peristalsis. Coffee is more aromatic. Coffee, on the whole, affects people as a more lusty drink, and though the difference is not great, it does not have to be more than perceptible to allow it to be acted upon. It was a man's drink. In addition, in the seventeenth century, coffee making required a considerable effort in preparation, all of which was done on the premises with conspicuous display; tea making was done very simply and quickily. Coffee was made by servants at a male establishment; tea was made at home by women or adapted to parlor service and decorum. At a later date, when both beverages were available for home use, the issue then also became one of social class, as ta was cheap (though taxation varied widely) and coffee, with its associated problems in preparation, was a higher-class drink. In the seventeenth-century coffeehouse, a cup cost two pence, a relatively high price, which set it out clearly as no drink for the poor. With the stimulant properties of coffee, so suitable for an evening of arguing or analysis, the novelty, the need for male institutions, the availability of the setting in the rapidly growing cities, the scene was prepared for the rapid growth of the clubs, and grow they did.

After the first wave of enthusiasm for the coffeehouses had abated somewhat, cocoa and chocolate were introduced in the place of coffee in some establishments. The novelty brought some new clubs into existence. One club, the Cocoa Tree, became very popular. Cocoa and chocolate, like milk, do not serve as a stimulant, and did not prove to be sufficiently exciting or attractive to take a place as the center of club life.

The fact that coffee was something of a fad is evident in the nineteenth-century decrease in the proportion of clubs devoted solely to it, and in the proportionate increase in the use of tea. But it is also true that coffee has remained one of the prominent beverages of voluntary association use to this day, now sharing that prominence with other moderate beverages such as beer and soft drinks, as voluntary associations have become more diffuse and adapted to many kinds of purposes.

In Chapter 1, a general set of orienting topics was proposed for organization purposes: *existence, prevalence, variety, purpose,* and *consequences.* Existence and prevalence were the focus of the proposed explanatory model, and the others have been used unsystematically. In the case of the clubs of the later era there are, for the first time, sufficient date to warrant systematic consideration of *variety.* Accordingly, attention is now directed to sections on political clubs, scientific societies, sports, music, drama, Freemasonry, and a new issue, voluntary associations of deviants. In each case, the historical roots in the early era are traced and a sociological explanation is offered of the nature of the changes.

## Coffeehouses and Political Clubs

Many of the clubs that developed in the second half of the seventeenth century resembled the earlier ones very closely. But the political turmoil that characterized the period saw a proliferation of small clubs for discussion of politics and related issues, and these seemed to have an affinity for the coffeehouses that sprang up at the time.

Many taverns had been identified as Royalist or Roundhead in sympathies. The coffeehouses seemed to follow the pattern. The best-known of these coffeehouse clubs was the Rota. Its unique features were created by James Harrington, author of *Oceana*, a major political document of the times, sometimes included as an example of the utopian genre. The Rota drew its name from its revolving membership plan. A person could serve for only three years, after which time he must be replaced. Meetings began in 1659 at Miles's coffeehouse in Westminster. Topics were formally introduced, debated at length, and results of the debate were voted upon. Pepys notes in his diary on January 17, 1660, apparently in reference to it: ". . . So I went to the Coffee-Club, and heard very good discourse."[21]

The Rota itself did not survive to complete even one cycle of its rotation plan. It dissolved at the Restoration in 1660. New clubs soon began all over England, however, and many of them were copies of the Rota. So numerous and diverse were the clubs that they became effective instruments of policy and propaganda.

In 1675 all London coffeehouses were closed for a time by law, and the clubs with them. Arbitrary withdrawal of permission for voluntary association is a dubious political strategy in most circumstances, and especially when both major political factions find them useful. The ban was extremely unpopular and had to be withdrawn.

Of the two major factions, the clubs were most important to growth and unification of the Whigs. The most significant of the Whig clubs was the Green Ribbon. The Green Ribbon Club was actively involved in politics and went well beyond the bounds of simple discussion. At the point that it stimulated mass demonstrations and burned the Pope in effigy, it was an active and disciplined subversive organization and no longer a voluntary association. The club disbanded in 1683 when several members were arrested for plotting against the king. In this and in many other germane examples, the nature of free speech and its relation to action were being conceptualized in voluntary associations and tried in public events—a process that continues to this day with no end in view. Again, we see permission as a two-way process of voluntary associations and political power.

The political club, as a force in British life, endured for a long time and was a significant aspect of political life throughout the reign of the House of Hanover. In general, the Whigs were more active in clubs than the Tories. One reason was the prominence of churchmen among Tories. Another reason was that a major base of Tory power was always the rural areas, and the club flourished where people were concentrated. Both parties tended in later years to some stratification of clubs, and admission to the hihest-ranking of these was tantamount to an invitation to a policy-making position in a party. The idea that Parliament was Britain's most exclusive club was known in the era, and was based on the reality of a substratum of partisan clubs of party elites.

## Hedonism, Voluntarism, and Scientific Societies

Lewis Feuer has argued the thesis that hedonism was necessary for the growth of science.[22] Feuer claimed that in order for science to grow it was necessary to develop trust or acceptance of the senses, in order to replace traditional bases of perception. Among his many examples is a discussion of the role of the coffeehouse in the growth of the British Royal Society. Hedonism may be defined as willingness to be oriented wholeheartedly toward pleasure. The thesis may be extended beyond the role of the coffeehouse to the consideration of the club itself, as has already been demonstrated. The scientific society of the era will be considered as an aspect of the club form of social organization. Like the political club, the scientific society had ends that involved activities outside the bounds of the organization itself; hence the nature of boundary roles again becomes crucial.

The club institutionalized hedonism and enjoyment of the senses, and freed the mind to inquire and to dare where it had been in fetters. By limiting the membership and encapsulating activities within a private social establishment, old boundaries of social experimentation could be abandoned and new ground broken. This could be accomplished because the club had privileged membership and boundaries to control sharing the news of discussion, both in regard to politics and religion, as well as concerning the nature of the physical universe. Without this right of privacy, the member would not risk exposure as a deviant. Embarrassment about foolish ideas is always a risk in new thought: it must be risked for progress to become possible. One cannot, then, explain the phenomenon of the growth of thought solely on the basis of the coffeehouse with open membership or attendance—the private voluntary association with privileged membership was an absolute necessity.

The early open coffeehouse was the locale for gatherings of all sorts of intellectuals. The scientific club developed from these more general beginnings. Sociologically, the Royal Society was essentially a formal group from 1645 to 1660, a voluntary association (club) from 1660, with a royal charter from 1662. In spite of its charter, it did not become a Formal Volunteer Organization; it remained a voluntary association.

Why was the coffeehouse a source of growth of the new sciences, when the majority of the leading scholars of the time were professors in the universities? The seventeenth-century university was not well suited to the intellectual needs of the changing times, just as the craft gild and merchant gild were not suited to the changing economic scene. Both were at one time purely voluntary associations but had developed into highly traditional and rigid organizations with little remaining semblance of voluntarism. In addition, Oxford and Cambridge were not located in London, the major urban center. The universities were still heavily influenced by the traditional curricula, following the ancient divisions into the Trivium and the Quadrivium. Teaching was usually in Latin. Though philosophy and theology had begun to abandon the rigid orthodoxies of Thomistic scholasticism, thought ways were still formal and philosophy was overshadowed by theology. Though many English scientists were trained at Oxford and at Cambridge, among the leading European centers of learning, it was not until they discovered each other in the coffeehouses that they began to break through to forms of thought that were truly scientific. Gresham College, a new institution, was the locale in which members of the Royal Society eventually carried out many of the experiments to which the coffeehouse debates led.

The distinctions may be made more clear by identification of two ideal-typical roles, the scholar and the intellectual. The scholar is a learner of the accumulated knowledge of the past; the intellectual is a person of controversial ideas. Universities usually experience strain in accommodating both kinds of roles. The accommodation is worked out in a variety of ways. The medieval university had few real intellectuals; the later university did and experienced numerous kinds of differentiation to accommodate the strain. The coffeehouse was one such growth. Another was the patronage of intellectuals by the wealthy, often in such statuses as private secretary or tutor.

The experience of Isaac Newton illustrates the importance of the form of organization for development and encouragement of creativity. When Newton joined the Royal Society a few years after its formation, his ideas on light, gravitation, and mathematics were immediately controversial and hotly debated. He told a member, however, that he had taught similar material at Cambridge for many years, but no one there had noticed it.

The Royal Society presented no panacea to solve all intellectual problems. The members' arguments were often futile, and there were continual struggles, jealousies, and intrigues, especially among leaders who saw the society as an avenue to recognition and to funding of projects. Hooke and Boyle were especially involved in such affairs. Some members found that old thought ways were not easily abandoned either, and perhaps the members did not understand how new freedoms could lead to abuses for which wise strategies were needed. The attempt of the society to get support from Charles II is also instructive, for it was both a success in financial terms, and a source of a struggle for control that somewhat limited purely voluntary action.

Charles II was a symbol of the new age of sensual enjoyment. His love of pleasure was widely discussed. It is thoroughly consistent with the hedonism thesis that he saw the need for an organization like the Royal Society and gave it the support it needed.

The course of development of scientific societies in countries other than England illustrates the relation between social context and the orgazational form of innovations. The Italian *Accademia del Cimento* was an organization that bears comparison to the Royal Society. It was a group research academy of paid workers, whereas the Royal Society was a conferring body that stimulated individual research, some of which was amateur and some professional. Some literary societies with an interest in scientific matters preceded the *Accademia*, among them the *Otiosi* (or literary club) of della Porta (1538-1615), which was named the *Accademia dei Lincei* of Rome (1601-1630), of which Galileo was a member.

French scientific societies, like the Italian, were less individualistic than the English. In France, however, the *Académie Royale des Sciences* was directly financed by the government and functioned as a research institute that included some amateurs. The Royal Society had only a paid curator (Hooke).

In Germany, scientific societies were slow to develop. Ornstein, a German, accepts this as a fact and inquires why it occurred. She found the slow development of a national language to be one important cause. Germany developed vernacular-speech voluntary associations, the *Sprachgesellschaften*, which were forces in promoting national culture.[23]

Leibniz was a leader among German scientists in urging the formation of scientific societies. He was a prolific source of ideas for utilization of associations as vehicles for social change, and an effective propagandist and promoter. Through his leadership, Germany became part of the growing scientific community of the seventeenth century.

If the focus here was on the growth of science rather than the growth of voluntary associations of scientists, a more important approach would be to analyze the several ways that the role of scientist developed, among which were the facilitative parts played by groups and associations of intellectuals. It would be a mistake to assume that science could grow only through the instrumentality of voluntary associations. Support of science was a costly affair. Scientists needed incomes, and experiments were often expensive. One commentator speaks of seeing telescope tubes protruding from roofs and upper-story windows all over Paris—each of them constructed at considerable cost and paid for by someone wealthy enough to do so. Workers, therefore, had to seek support of governments and the patronage of the wealthy. In Italy especially, innumerable nobles and merchants invited philosophers to their salons, and the sponsors sometimes became experimenters and, occasionally, thinkers of some consequence. In royal France, Louis XIII, under the urging of Colbert, saw the wisdom of supporting and regulating science for reasons of state. But under the shadow of the sponsored academies there were hundreds of voluntary associations of amateur philosophers and scientists, shaping the thought of the new world, displacing magicians and alchemists, who eventually faded into oblivion with the gilds.[24]

It should be reiterated that the gilds were religious fraternities mediating religion and other enterprises. The scientific society began on another basis. Its members were refugees from the religious domination of universities whose values and norms opposed creativity, supported tradition, and held traditional reference groups and reference others to be valid juries of all ideas. The coffeehouse, club, and scientific society gradually replaced the ancient reference groups. The secular rulers saw their value and supported the scientific societies in their own ways. It was a new game. The church could never again wholly suppress progress. The change was not immediate and total. Careers had to be lived through their cycles. Many thinkers continued to be immersed in both traditional and modern cultures. Perhaps the most ironic of all was Newton, whose mathematics was an enormous accomplishment about which he cared so little that he did not even bother to publicize it until others urged him. He ended his years in vain attempts to develop a mathematical proof of the biblical story of creation while lesser minds were balked at scientific tasks he could easily have solved.

## Voluntary Associations in Sports, Music, and Drama

Nothing so clearly distinguishes the two eras as the use the people made of their leisure. Our primary interest here is in the new forms that emerged in the club period. Brief descriptions of the leisure of the medieval period show how great this change was.

Sports, music, and drama involve learning of skills culminating in a performance, thus possibly involving an audience. They are inherently social. The roles that might be formed into voluntary associations include composers, scholars or organizers, performers, audiences, and critics. Painting, sculpture, poetry, and other writing are also social endeavors in unique ways. We have already encountered writers, artists, and dramatists in the clubs; there is no instance of formation of voluntary associations specifically and wholly of these roles in England at the time, and they will not be considered further.

Crewdson divides the musicians of medieval England into three categories on an economic basis: the sponsored musicians of church, court, and city; the itinerant entertainers who moved from village to village and were legally vagabonds; musicians in other trades who sometimes performed for money.[25] In addition, there was amateur or folk music that was mostly vocal or which used simple unstandard-

ized instruments such as pipes. The sponsored musicians were usually organized into gilds; the others less often.

The dominant medieval music was that of the church. It was
standardized and very limited as to construction. The plainsong, an
integral part of the service, was sung by an official. Congregational
singing was unimportant. Musical instruments were used in services,
and quite a variety were found. The pipe organ was used in England
as early as the tenth century. Choirs were widespread in
monasteries, among the canons regular, and in collegiate churches.

Music schools were attached to cathedrals and abbeys. The training of boys (never girls) for service to the church was the main
purpose of the schools, and instruction in Latin and other subjects
was intended mostly to facilitate that service. When the pubescent
boy's voice changed, his education was completed, though in some
cases a sponsor might send him on to Oxford or Cambridge. Some of
the boys made careers in music directly from music school.

Music was performed in gild meetings for the purpose of
entertainment or for religious observance. The gilds contributed no
unique body of music of their own, except that which they sponsored
as part of a festival. There were, however, gilds of professional
musicians in many places in England. The most interesting of these
were the waits.

The waits (or waytes) were employed by cities as watchmen and
musicians. Except in the largest cities, they always had these multiple functions. Here is an early description. "A Wayte, that nyghtly,
from Mighelmasse til Sjere Thursday, pipeth the wache within this
course iiij tymes, and in the somer nyghtes iij tymes; and he to make
bon gayte, and every chambre dore and office, as well for fyre as for
other pikers or perelliz."[26]

The waits in the early years were not known for the quality of their
music, and many of them knew little more than to blow an alarm. But
apparently they put in their time constructively, for in the fifteenth
and sixteenth centuries they are mentioned as acceptable performers
in major receptions and festivals. In spite of their functions as watchmen, they did not use brass or other metal instruments to sound the
alarm; the trumpet was reserved usually for announcing royalty, and

the waits specialized in woodwinds and stringed instruments. In spite of their increased skill, the term "wait" remained one of derision for a long time—it indicated someone you would pay well to stop playing. The waits are an instance of G. K. Chesterton's dictum that anything worth doing is worth doing badly.

English royal courts had musicians, perhaps since the Plantagenets, and the nobles followed the practice whenever they could afford it. The Chapel Royal was an institution found all over Europe. It was a group of professional musicians in the pay of the king to perform on certain kinds of occasions, mostly religious but sometimes secular (though the distinction) was not clear-cut). Most of England's best-known musicians were gentlemen of the Chapel Royal, a practice that did not stop with the medieval era. Among them were Byrd, Gibbons, Bull, and Blow. The Chapel Royal was not a voluntary association, and in fact it was constantly at odds with the City of London Musician's Gild over rights and privileges. The musicians of the Chapel Royal were responsible for musical teaching duties of all sorts, including usually the royal family. They standardized and controlled music tastes more than any other single force. Although their music was of a high quality, on the whole it was not very innovative, and many of the changes in English music came from outside, especially Italy and the Netherlands.

Itinerant musicians would sometimes try to form themselves into fraternities. But since they were not free of a specific city, they could not gain a mandate for a monopoly. In some cases, groups of troubadors or minstrels succeeded in acquiring gild status.

The *Feste du Puy*, groups of religious singers originating in France, had fraternity status. There was no exact parallel in England of the German Minnesingers, which were voluntary associations. The Meistersingers, which followed their tradition, were not voluntary associations.

Parish clerk's gilds sometimes acquired musical skills while carrying out parish duties. They ended up in numerous jurisdictional squabbles with the musician gilds.

One feature of the gilds of musicians and the waits is not obvious to us and bears stressing. The gilds could be and were sometimes formed with a very small membership. In some cities, there were as few as four persons as waits; yet they always formed themselves into a gild.

Little is known of medieval folk music, if we arbitrarily exclude minstrels from that group. Certainly village performers were not organized into voluntary associations. Early folk carols from Provençal included the *Farandole* and the *Branle*. From the rhythm of their words, it may be concluded that they were meant to be used for group dancing, but apparently not through associations.[27] The Morris dance was popular in the early era, but probably did not take voluntary association form.

The change from our early to late era was not marked by immediate increase in voluntary association formation nor by hasty demise of the old gilds. Music associations lagged rather than led in the progress of music, and as we shall see, this same kind of conservatism prevailed in drama as well. There are several factors involved. The first is that the musician gilds, like all professional gilds, kept some control because they did not experience the transforming impact of economic forces of the sixteenth century as did the merchants. Growth of new colonies, competition of other nations, new forms of organization, war, piracy, and so on, did not challenge these craftsmen whose product was locally consumed as it was produced. The increase in consumption of music was accompanied by an increase of professional musicians, most of whom found employment in royal or noble households, and municipal bands, which kept the gild form of organization alive, though it was probably less effective than before as a monopoly. Elizabeth gave the monopoly of music printing to individuals (Byrd and Tallis), not to the gild of musicians, and this act symbolized nicely the elitism of the era. Although religious controversy affected individual musicians, music was even more in demand and the music gilds survived the demands of the Tudors as well as any. The market for secular music was increased, and as long as music was written on demand of patrons, as it was until the nineteenth century, the need for professional musicians was high. There was, however, no concurrent growth of voluntary associations, neither in the form of unions to replace the gilds, nor of amateur performers.

The madrigal and ayre became popular during the reign of Elizabeth. This was a group musical form, suitable for amateurs without professional levels of skill. It was not until the middle of the eighteenth century, however, that it became the object of voluntary association formation to a marked degree. The reason was that the madrigal required ability to read and money to purchase printed music, and sometimes purchase of accompanying instruments, which meant that it was adapted best to upper-class people. In addition, the madrigal required either a female soprano or a castrato, both of which were unlikely to be acceptable in the all-male clubs; in contrast, the salon or the parlor was a locale where this combination of voices was possible. The madrigal then remained an elite form until further development of the requisites in lesser strata. In addition, as time went on, the music of the madrigal became more complex, particularly with the acceptance of Monteverdi's "second practice" (*ca.* 1600), which revolutionized part music.

The era of Puritan domination produced a change in English music, though not exactly what one might expect from people with a reputation as old fuddy-duddies. As one author of an earlier time, N. Wright (*ca.* 1562), put it, Puritans were those "Whose haughtie, proud, disdainful myndes/much fault agaynst poore music findes."[28] Cromwell, in fact, took up something of the old royal attitude in patronage of music and was himself a keen listener. The tastes of the Puritans in church music was the crucial matter, and perhaps their most regrettable aesthetic excess was the destruction of organs in churches and dismissal of the church musicians. The consequence, however, was that a large group of church musicians were thereby turned to other musical outlets, and made new advances in secular modes. Some of the church organs were even installed in taverns. While religious music was certainly given a new direction, Puritanism did not set secular music back, and probably contributed to its growth.

The Restoration, while signaling new freedom of expression, did so at the expense of the masses. Courtly music was indulged, but music and indeed all forms of recreation continued the elitist course of the earlier Stuarts. Neither the Puritans nor the Court of the Restoration stimulated association growth directly.

Under James II and later monarchs, true voluntary associations for music began to emerge. Nettel says that the Commonwealth had the effect of bringing musical education to poorer people and led to their inclusion in madrigal clubs.[29] He does not give the data that led to this conclusion. Pepys mentioned a music club in his journal in 1667. Thomas Britton, a small coal merchant, was a commoner who had many intellectual interests. He formed a music club in 1678 in his own cramped quarters. When the young Handel played there many years later, the voluntary association had become a concert club that, in the mode of the times, served coffee and charged an admission to the public. In the eighteenth century there were numerous music clubs throughout England for the purpose of singing and playing music. By then, printed music was more easily available and there were a variety of forms of music to use. Some of these clubs were concert societies of amateurs and professional players. The Three Choirs Festival, still in existence, began in 1729. Provincial choir festivals were noted about 1760 in Salisbury, Derby, Leicester, and Sheffield.[30] The Academy of Ancient Music was founded about 1720. With the Madrigal Society, *ca.* 1741, the voluntary association for music reached its ideal-typical stable state—music was performed as a matter of permanent interest in historical musical forms for the recreational enjoyment of members.

The restricted development of voluntary associations for drama and for sport each illustrates a further unique way that the values of seventeenth-century England were expressed in leisure activity.

To the medieval man, physical health was not admirable. The ascetic ideal suffused medieval culture and greatly affected all recreation and physical activity. Physical strength and skill were desirable for war or work, but not for their own sake. It was not until the sixteenth century that contrary ideas began to enter England, and again, a substantial number of them from Italy. Elyot (d. 1530) wrote cautiously and apologetically on the benefits of exercise and began formal academic consideration of the topic.[31] There was, before this time, certainly no leadership from the monarchy or court that would support physical development and associated sports for the benefit of individuals.

The actions of monarchs are a useful way to illustrate these values.

Henry VIII promoted an archers' gild, and this encouragement of archery had many pecedents. His act of 1541 prohibited playing bowls (except among lords). Kings had discouraged or prohibited football as early as 1314. The sports were then "vain games of no value." The other reasons for the prohibition were that sport incited to riot and public disorder, and was not useful for military training. Kings, on the other hand, supported jousting tournaments, hunting, and related skills by strata suited to use them in war.

Under Elizabeth, these traditional activities were encouraged even more than before, and at first glance would seem not to be changed from previous times. But whether intentionally or not, there was a change under way, for the activities that were stressed were no longer specifically geared to war. Archery was diminishing as a serious competitor to firearms, and jousting was becoming irrelevant as well. The distinction between military preparation and personal competence for its own sake was under way, led, significantly, by a woman who knew the difference between personal and military fitness. Elizabeth's successors to the throne continued the trend, and until the Commonwealth era, sport and games were uninterrupted for a century.

The religious leaders of the day had their influence on the changes that were taking place. Luther was in favor of mild bodily training and a healthy body in the service of God. Calvin, more medieval, was suspicious of anything that might be fun. He allowed himself the activity of walking, and had gone only so far as to play a game of quoits. Whatever the effect of this kind of morality on the church community (which isn't well adapted in a practical sense to sports anyway), it left a strong distinction between religious people and nonreligious people, and more significantly, among the religious, between occasions for indulgence in the sport and occasions for restrictions.

The Catholic medieval approach to control of sports and games was to allow periodic indulgence and to make provision for a tactful religious recovery. It was indulgence, catharsis, and forgiveness, plus some time for recovery from injuries. Medieval Englishmen had a series of traditional games for religious holidays. Shrove Tuesday was the occasion of football games of the most violent and extreme sort. A football made of a stuffed skin or bladder was thrown onto a field, and a battle between the sides began, which sometimes carried over onto the streets. Most significantly, the sides were usually neighboring villages, and not teams of specific numbers calculated to represent equality in competition. This was not a voluntary association, operating in a competition under rules agreed on by both sides, but an episode that resulted in mayhem because there was no other way to stop it. The participants did not join in games under agreed rules as a matter of their daily lives and, therefore, were not socialized to team participation in games in any way. The football game involved a clash between cleavages in society for which there was no appropriate superordinate organization. Competitors were identified with villages or parishes. Sometimes apprentices or journeymen of rival gilds participated, but never as teams chosen for specialization in the sport. It was an occasional event tied in some way to the religious calendar or the seasons, as in the case of the Morris dances mentioned earlier. In general, team competition in leagues requires the widely shared cultural knowledge and acceptance of a two-tier form of organization: the organized team itself, and the organization of teams into a superordinate association. The only available models were the church and government, and neither of these was a participant-controlled organization. The gilds themselves, as noted previously, were never federated or formally affiliated with each other, but related only through the civil authorities to which all were subordinate.

Shrove Tuesday was also the occasion for girls' games, which did not necessarily have such an extreme outcome. They played hoops, ball, kit cat, whip and top, and other games.

Easter Monday saw gentler games among the men. Wrestling and other personal competitions were common. Running races were traditional on Ascension Day.

The schools and colleges were as restricted as the rest of the public in the medieval era, and were scarcely more genteel than the commoners. In the seventeenth century, however, the universities began to have teams of various kinds, and to place a positive value on physical development. In 1590 Harrow restricted activity to whip and top, handball, and archery.[32] A Guildford school permitted "run

and play crockett and other plays." Oxford and Cambridge forbade
football until the end of the sixteenth century.

A more organized game of football began to emerge in rural areas
at about this time. But it was still not a league of voluntary
associations. Here is a description of the Haxey Hood game. The
hood was a ball, thrown into the playing area by the Chief of the
Boggans. The players then scrambled after the hood. The Fool
announced the rules: "Hoose agen Hoose, toone agen toone, If tho'
meets a man, knock 'im doon."[33]

The teams were limited to eleven men. The rules seem at least to
have been explicit, even though limited in scope, and the sides were
even in number. Formal organization was emerging, and norms were
specified that the formal organizations could use.

James I, a famous sportsman, attempted to continue and extend
the Elizabethan trend. He tried to introduce golf to England from
Scotland, but with little success. In 1618 he issued his *Declaration of
Sports*, an assertion of rural communities' rights to their ancient
customs regarding sports, particularly sports after church on Sunday.
The Puritans, by that time becoming more vocal, were outraged and
continued to fight the issues under Charles I.

James I instituted many games that only the well-to-do could
afford and which were adapted to display of wealth but not to
voluntary association formation. One of these was Pall Mall, a golf-
croquet game that called for a very long, expensive enclosure. Tennis
continued to be popular among the rich. Bowls was probably the
most popular game, both indoors and out.

A rural game called stoolball began as early as the sixteenth
century. This involved defense of a stump, later a wicket, and gradually emerged into the modern game of cricket. In the nineteenth
century the rules were refined and seasonal team competition between counties became the bulwark of the game.

Cricket became a professional sport at an early stage, and this may
have been responsible for the slow growth of its voluntary
associations. Rural gentry began to hire servants and workers on their
merits as cricket players. There was a great deal of betting. The
betting among the rural gentry had the result of accelerating the
formation of rules and the formalization of practices. Cricket was a

game of leisure and well suited to their needs. Perhaps for these
reasons, it did not quickly become a purely amateur sport. There was
a cricket club at St. Albans by 1666, though its associational status
cannot be ascertained.

A comment may be inserted here that results from these data about
cricket but is also relevant to music and drama. There seems to be an
assumption by many analysts of medieval life, and sometimes modern as well, that the normal course of development of participation is
that amateurism always comes first and then professionalism
corrupts it. The fact that this may be true in such things as American
football is no reason to assume that it is a law of nature. This modern
phenomenon. when used as a mental model to fill in the gaps in the
literature of ancient times, is probably contrary to fact a great deal of
the time, and there is no reason for it. The dichotomy amateur/pro-
fessional does not deal with the facts very well, either regarding
aesthetics or in most other areas of participation in civic life, and it
should be avoided. The simplest and most decisive single structural
variable for explanatory purposes is social class, though this by no
means exhausts the possibilities.

One can dismiss women's sports and related activities in the later
era without much comment. Some followed Elizabeth's lead. But as
time went on, the physical education of the lady was confined to
dancing and the salon arts. Women were mostly spectators and little
more.

Around 1600, horses began to be selected for special purposes,
particularly hunting, war, and racing. Breeding for these qualities
emerged later. Horse racing was mostly a matter for the individual,
not for sharing in voluntary associations.

The foregoing observations about voluntary associations for leisure
in the later era and (generally) the lack of them in the early era, may
be more precisely analyzed if some new concepts are introduced.

It has been assumed that the voluntary associations analyzed up to
this point were continual in nature. Even though they may have only
periodic gatherings of the membership of the associations, such
organizations make provision for their long-term existence or
perpetuity. In order to do this, there must be some arrangements to
assure this perpetuity, such as formally designated offices and

associated responsibilities, records, agreements for officer succession or replacement, and relationships with other organizations that support such provisions, like rental contracts, bond payments for treasurers, and the like. The normal nonvoluntary formal organization is also continual. The business firm, for example, has employees who are enacting its vital roles almost continually. Most of the voluntary associations we have considered are continual in existence, but had much longer quiescent phases. The main difference, then, so far as continuity is concerned, is one of degree and the means by which continuity is provided.

At the other end of the continuum of activity continuity is the phenomenon of intermittent organization. By this is meant that activities emerge that are formally organized but which leave no social expectations for continuity. Intermittent organizations may be either voluntary or involuntary associations. Intermittent organizations are often voluntary associations. Etzioni states this the other way around, which I believe is not as adequate a formulation.[34]

Intermittent associations are easier to originate and less frustrating to work with if they are integrated with a better-established collectivity that can furnish stability and practical resources such as a meeting place, equipment, and the like. A more important issue, though often more subtle, is that the related collectivity furnishes the voluntary association with moral status, legitimacy, and placement in relevant schemes of social ranking. Without this, the organization must start from the bottom to estabish its own legitimacy and ranking, both of which take a considerable commitment of resources that may not be consistent with the objectives that it seeks. The relevant supporting collectivity may have associated personnel who, because they were selected to it on the basis of suitability, are likely to have common interests, skills, and perhaps similar motivations. Intermittent voluntary associations are often sycophants, in a sense, like mosses that live off the tree in which they reside. Their welfare and very life are often dependent on the body to which they are related. At least their success is much more probable if they have such a dependency relationship.[35] In modern communities there are numerous examples of this dependency or secondary phenomenon: scout troops are frequently sponsored by schools or churches, businesses support athletic teams, settlement houses (themselves voluntary associations) support more intermittent neighborhood organizations.

The concept of intermittency has not been precisely operationalized here; though this would be desirable, it would be a lengthy process. Most of our examples will be quite obviously intermittent or regular—the gilds are among the latter, and the seasonal festivals the former.

Now let us apply the concept of intermittent voluntary association to some of the examples given earlier.

Haxey Hood, so far as can be ascertained, was a game that was played each year without any sustaining organization between events. The rules, few in number, were traditional and local. Each year the game was begun anew and died out until the next. Undoubtedly, it could not have come into existence in the same way each year unless the villages provided for it to happen. The same thing could be said of numerous other events of the time, such as the tournaments, the Lord Mayor's Show, coronation events, and so on. These vary as to the extent of rationality in their instigation. The universities either permitted or encouraged intermittent voluntary associations or, what is a different matter, ran them directly under supervision of university personnel. Where tradition is strong and there are sources of culture continuity, intermittent voluntary associations are feasible and frequently successful. The strongest source of instigation was the sacred calendar of the church year, which was contingent on all Christians.

By contrast, the later era of our analysis does not lack examples of regular nonintermittent voluntary associations in music and sports. The glee clubs and catch clubs were apparently of this sort; expected to be in existence constantly, meeting frequently, and either autonomous or related to other organizations for support but not having their existence solely through them. Thomas Britton's music society was a continual voluntary association, albeit somewhat dominated by this charismatic leader. The early era does not entirely lack such regular organizations in leisure activities—the *Feste du Puy* may have been one.

We return now to analysis of music and drama, which, as might be expected, had courses of development that were interrelated. So far as voluntary associations are concerned, however, there were some marked differences, which reveal some interesting things about the social conditions necessary for the existence and prevalence of this form of organization. The drama was better supported in the earlier era than the later one by voluntary associations, though in neither era were there signs of the drama as their sole purpose. Nicoll notes that though there had been amateur companies "from medieval times, . . . only in the twentieth century did they come to take their work seriously and aided in the encouragement of young playwrights."[36] To be amateur is not the same as founding a voluntary association, of course, but the issues are quite similar in this instance. Perhaps the medieval organizations referred to are those intermittent voluntary associations that performed at religious festivals each year. This section, then, like some previous ones, is an attempt to explain the absence of a certain phenomenon, and in similar vein, the potential fallacies of reasoning from the absence of data are noted and accounted for. Following the pattern used in analysis of music and sports, attention will be directed to the kinds of drama in the two eras, and to the collectivities in which they were performed.

Drama will be defined as action including at least a story and impersonation.[37] In the Christian medieval era the drama, following this definition, can be dated to the tenth-century Easter performance of the trope called *quem quaeritis* ("whom seek ye?"). This performance featured the three Marys and consisted of four simple lines. The trope was later expanded and developed for about four centuries without becoming independent of the liturgy to which it was originally related. During this time the clergy acted the parts, and there was no associational development.

About 1200 there were short plays on religious themes, centered on the several seasonal religious holy days. The dramas were interpretations of the dramatic events that the Bible provided: the Resurrection, the Annunciation, the Advent, the Assumption, and the Nativity. Gradually, as the plays became popular, they became separate from the liturgy, though the majority of them were performed in the church edifice, using parts of the building as a series of localities that created meaning by use of associated symbolism.

In the fourteenth century, when the Corpus Christi celebrations became widespread, a cycle of plays was written to celebrate the day. The first of these plays was that at Cambridge, about 1350.[38] The play cycles of the Corpus Christi celebration were integrated sequences of short dramas on very narrowly defined biblical themes. Perhaps the greatest changes, for purposes of this analysis, were that the control of the plays changed from the clergy to the gilds and fraternities, and because of the popularity of the plays, they were shifted out of the church to the streets and squares. It has already been pointed out that one of the functions of the fraternities was to accomplish religious work that the church could not, and this is an excellent example of the success that attended this effort.

Each gild had a play assigned to it by municipal authorities, and the Corpus Christi gild, which existed in most cities that had the plays, took an influential part. The topic of the play was often related symbolically to the meaning of the work of the gild. The York Shipwrights, for example, were responsible for a play on the building of the ark, while the Fishers and Mariners took on the flood itself. Some gilds did not symbolize any germane biblical theme, and one can surmise that their prestige may have suffered from it. Some plays were assigned to a consort of several gilds that were too small to manage a whole play themselves.

The Corpus Christi plays appealed to a large audience, and not a small part of this appeal was due to the use of the vernacular. Latin was being abandoned in everyday use, and English or Anglo-French were found in its place.

Though the gilds thus became very involved in production of drama, there is no indication that the acting was performed by members. Numberous gild accounts list payments to nonmembers for performances and for costumes.

The success of the Corpus Christi cycles was partly responsible for the growth of other forms of drama. Playing companies developed pageant wagons, complete with scenery and dressing compartments, for putting the show on the road. The companies were known to perform their plays many times in each city, stopping on request of a wealthy man to perform at his doorstep. In time, these skilled actors developed a repertoire and toured widely.

In the fifteenth century a play called the *Castle of Perseverance* was widely performed, perhaps by an amateur company.[39] This early form of the morality play followed theological themes, though they did not utilize biblical texts. In the morality plays, single moral ideas were represented by single characters, each realizing its fate in creative role interaction. They were, in a sense, a manifestation of Thomistic philosophy in its most reified form. The famous *Everyman* was a highly developed example of this genre. The simplicity of the morality plays and the bold relevance of their themes to everyday life made them extremely popular. They presented little difficulty of a technical nature, and requirements for scenery and costumes were within the means of all.

By the end of the fifteenth century, small traveling professional companies developed to play the "interlude." This was a compact play that could be performed before a small audience, usually of wealthy men or nobles. At the same time, there were the king's players and similar permanent companies in the palaces of lesser lords.

The universities of Oxford and Cambridge and the London Inns of Court supported groups of players. These may have been amateur, and perhaps they were intermittent voluntary associations.

Around the start of the sixteenth century, for the first time, plays began to appear that had single authors whose names have been preserved. Individuality in all forms of English aesthetics dates from the same era; in this respect it lagged well behind Italy. The anonymous authorship of the past came to an end when the Corpus Christi cycle died out in midcentury with the attacks on the monasteries and the gilds. A brief resurrection under Elizabeth did not endure.

The growth of drama under Elizabeth was a major feature of the later era. As in music and sports, the queen herself was a participant and a leader. She translated one Greek play for English performance and supported the growth of English original drama in many practical ways. The result was rather uneven, however. The municipalities still had great power over their jurisdictions, and even in London the authorities could defiantly prohibit the establishment of a permanent theater. *The Theatre* was established in Shoreditch in 1576. Other theaters followed on the South Bank, and by 1600 the Rose, the Swan, the Globe, and the Fortune were flourishing and there were permanent companies of professional actors. There is, however, no mention in histories of drama of voluntary associations for dramatic production at this time. The actors and writers of the period are, of course, frequently identified in the clubs.

The reign of James I was as supportive of drama as it had been of music and sport. There were changes in the kinds of drama, but not in its organizational form. Charles I continued similar policies. Drama almost came to a halt during the Commonwealth. During the Restoration, however, there were some new directions and a new kind of social context. Charles II, an elitist in all forms of aesthetics, permitted only two theaters in London, and for a time only one actually operated. The policies that Charles II followed made the theater an entertainment for the upper classes and the nobility. The consequence was that the new dramas were written for its elite audience and the mass theater essentially vanished. Charles I supported extravagant spectacles of all sorts, including the masque— a forerunner of opera—for which Inigo Jones's Banquetting Hall (1622) had been especially equipped. The public no longer knew the intense competition of the vigorous companies and writers, and the theater grew less significant in the public consciousness. Throughout the era under scrutiny it never regained its former prominent place in English social life, and existing dramatic forms did not filter downward to become a part of lower-class life.

The significant question for analysis here then would seem to be why drama failed to take voluntary association form, when there was general civil freedom for it to do so (except limitations in London noted above), there was a plentiful supply of material, and apparently a populace with a tradition of interest in theater. None of the previous causes of withdrawal of state permission seems to be involved.

The following reasons seem to be among the most significant. First, when the gild-sponsored drama was destroyed, and with it the entire voluntaristic dramatic endeavor, there was a professional drama already in existence that had emancipated itself from the gilds.

Any new voluntary associations would have to start afresh. The new strata of gentlemen and nobles found the professional drama and the fellowship of the dramatists to their liking. However, their own new form of organization, the club, was admirably adapted to discussing and enjoying individual aesthetic endeavor but maladapted to the intense discipline that drama itself required in playing and producing. Drama would have to start afresh on some other basis than affiliation with the clubs.

The Elizabethan theater was a theater of the masses. Performances were in daylight and usually in tavern courtyards. Admission was cheap. Theaters were accessible and popular. Perhaps the very success of the professional theater, coupled with the difficulties of production by amateur voluntary associations, is the kind of composite but realistic explanation that we seek.

This leads to the third reason for lack of development of voluntary associations devoted entirely to drama. Plays were not available in cheap printed form in the Elizabethan era. It was not thought to be important or desirable to create printed editions of plays, and most professional companies had only one copy. It was not until James I that the first printed plays were available, and then not in volume. This is not decisive, however, for it could be argued as in the case of music that a demand would create the literature as has been the case with other popular ideas.

A more significant reason for the lack of development of drama lies in the articulation of religious values with the social structure of England in the seventeenth and eighteenth centuries. It has been shown that when mass drama diminished in importance, higher-class drama became oriented toward the courts and selected groups. The remaining middle- and lower-class elements were more and more willing to accept a strict Protestant morality in which drama was suspect. Music encountered fewer restrictions, and is distinguished from the drama in this regard.

## Deviants and Extremists in Clubs

The club has a social wall around it. It can keep certain people in or out at will, and control or indulge virtually any behavior it wishes within. So it is not surprising that the club produced its wild men and weird people in its heyday. Here are some of them and what they did.

Young men's voluntary associations of rakes and roués existed in England as early as 1604. They took distinctive names that did not hide their purposes, and which are certainly very different from the sacred orientations of the previous century. There were the Roaring Boys, the Bravadoes, the Roysters.[40] The Nickers earned their name by throwing halfpence against windows. In 1628, note was made of the Buglers, the Mums, the Tityre-Tus, followed at about midcentury by the Hectors and the Scourers. "To hector" means to intimidate or to bully. The name of the club is most apt, since its principal activity, like that of some others, was to "scour" a tavern, that is, to clear the place of its inhabitants by violence, then to proceed through the streets with the same end in view. Some of these were sufficiently organized to become a kind of crime syndicate.

They endured because there was no domestic constabulary to cope with them. They began because a stratum had evolved that had freedom, and an income from sources that required neither a work role nor its restraints. This was a class phenomenon: there were at the same time lower-class deviants, but they could be dealt with by existing legal means. There were the poorhouse, the stocks, prison, and even hanging for relatively minor crimes. The chronicles do not mention them together: lower-class life was not remarkable. It was more than two centuries before the legal institutions of English society were developed to deal with the gap left by the demise of church controls and ancient laws. Meanwhile, those who were gentlemen in name but not in behavior could get away with some rather extreme acts.

Around the start of the eighteenth century, the phenomenon acquired a generic name: the Mohocks. The name may have been derived from tales about savages in the New World. Turkey is also mentioned as a source. The name didn't change the activities much. John Gay wrote a play called *The Mohocks* about 1712, followed in about 1735 by Hogarth's *A Rake's Progress* etchings on the same theme. Hogarth's theme had to do with *individual* immorality, however. Sometimes the labels were merely names given to casual hell-raising, but it is definite that many of them were formal voluntary associations.

The most outrageous if not most notorious of the associations of the time was the Medmenhamites. "When Whigs and Tories, Dissenters and High-churchmen, scientists, and enthusiasts of all sorts were formally meeting in taverns and coffee-houses, what could be more natural than that extremists among the well-to-do, upper class libertines should organize clubs?"[41] This organization was the creation of Sir Francis Dashwood, a notorious rake and, significantly, a respected public official. The Medmenhamites prepared "an equivalent of the black mass and induced neophytes with a topsy-turvey religiosity."[42] Their vices were numerous. They were said to wear black gowns and to drink from a human skull. Unlike many other such organizations of rakes, they allowed women to be present and to be involved as participants and not necessarily as objects or victims. Other organizations did not allow women to be present; none allowed them to be full members.

The Terrible Club (no date available) seems to be a rather shallow mockery of the Medmenhamites. Characteristically, it did not so much seek to exceed in bizarre behavior, as to mock those whose excesses were notorious. It was said to meet monthly at midnight in the Tower of London. The members would dine, the president providing the main dish. Meat was cut with bayonets. They ate with hat, gloves, and swords in place. The beverage was "rack-punch, quickened with gunpowder."[43]

Organizations of rakes seem to have been differentiated along several dimensions. Though they all were devoted to violation of norms of proper society, each seemed to specialize in some particular sin. Some excelled in drink, some in gambling, some in dueling, some in sex. A second form of differentiation concerned drink. Each club had a favorite drink. The punch bowl, as discussed previously, was often the center feature of the table. When punch was introduced from India in the reign of Queen Anne, it became a favorite drink and for a time replaced coffee in some clubs. Each club seemed to have its own recipe and tried to excel all the others. In any case, it was not seemly to have the same punch as any other club. This search for variety and uniqueness of beverages and ceremonies in each organization is in extreme contrast to the standardization of rituals of the gilds.

In 1765 there emerged the *macaronis* and *jessamies*, which were more useless than evil. They did not scour nor duel. They "encouraged dallying with sin rather than embracing it as their fathers and older brothers had done."[44] They reveled in foppish clothes.

A pamphlet of 1675 heaped scorn on the earlier town gallant. Here is a sample of the vitriol of the anonymous author. "A Town-Gallant is a bundle of *Vanities* composed of *Ignorance*, and *Pride, Folly*, and *Debauchery*; a silly *Huffing* thing, three parts Fop, and the rest Hector; a kind of *Walking Mercer's Shop*. . . ."[45]

His vices, to summarize from another section, were love of clothes and the body, lust, opposition to marriage, whoring, obscenity, vile wit, profanity, gluttony, ignorance, drinking to excess, and atheism. He was, one might say, something of a generalist. But, to contradict our informant, who does seem prone to exaggeration, the rake was sufficiently rational to organize voluntary associations, though it is hard to imagine how they could be very stable ones if even a tenth of the claimed sins were true.

The Calves Head Club drank from the skull of a calf, symbolic of the beheading of Charles I. This theme of drinking from a skull was found in many clubs of the rakes for a century, and always seemed to be a controversial symbol. The Calves Head Club was not simply a club of rakes, however. Their intention was political action by means of vulgarization and obscenity, and in such organizations the political club and deviant club themes merge.

Edward (Ned) Ward, a notorious eighteenth-century scandalmonger, first published his exposé of the clubs in 1709.[46] The book went through many editions. The names of the clubs Ward talks about reveal something of their nature, though it is hard to see why these should all be called secret clubs, as Ward indicated. There were the Lying Club, the Thieves, the Beggars, the Broken Shopkeepers, the Basket Woman's, the Beau's, and the Mollies. The last appears to have been a voluntary association of transvestites or perhaps simply a group of men who gathered to mock women by caricature.

Another theme evident in the club life of England was the striving for uniqueness of purpose or name. The issue here is not so much deviance as simply the desire to be different, as noted regarding drinks. This theme appeared less than a decade after the coffeehouse movement was firmly under way. The first instance seems to be the establishment of the Club of Kings, made up of men whose last name was King. Charles II thought it was humorous and accepted honorary membership. The succeeding century brought a profusion of clubs that sought to outdo each other in the ingenuity of their names and goals.

The Fox Hunters Club was a grouping of those injured at hunting.[47] The Lazy Club met in their nightgowns. Their salutation was to be a yawn.[48] The Hum Drum Club met for the purpose of being quiet, to have mild conversations, and to smoke.[49] The Daffy Club seems to be a bit more seriously deviant, at least in the outcome, for they were devoted to gin drinking in pairs. Gin at the time was a potent drink, not only because of its alcohol but because it had a high lead content derived from lead pipes used in the distilling process, and gin drinkers were frequently subject to brain damage and sometimes death.

The Lookers-On Club, like the Hum Drum, specialized in being extremists in moderation.[50] They made numerous rules about moderation in the use of language, to the point of squelching members who utilized superlatives in speech. "We admit neither toasting nor singing upon any pretext, and it would be as great an offence to raise a horse laugh in a Quaker Meeting as to encourage any rude expression of joy among us."[51] In similar vein was the Silent Club of 1694, which took as its maxim "Talking spoils company."[52]

The Little Club, of members under five feet tall, was naturally followed by the Tall Club. There was also the Club of Ugly Faces, and the No Nose Club.

There were other drinking clubs mentioned by Ward (and again by Hindley, who often draws on Ward uncritically) that may have been genuine or perhaps Ward's own inventions. They sometimes seem to be caricatures, and too simply devoted to excesses to ring true. The same might be said, however, of the comical clubs mentioned above. At any rate, Ward tells of the Golden Fleece, a tipplers' club, and of the Everlasting Club. The latter organized themselves to keep their drinking going around the clock, and claimed to have done so between 1650 and 1666, with an excusable lapse from their commitments when the city burned down. They claimed to have begun again in 1667 and to have continued to 1700, interrupted seriously only for quarterly business meetings.

The differentiation between types of clubs that was a feature of the eighteenth century was described above primarily as that between types of institutions common to all societies (e.g., art, music), and secondarily between morally approved and deviant organizations. Deviance among gentlemen's clubs then became so widespread that they themselves began a further process of differentiation. The foregoing clubs may be distinguished sociologically into contracultural and value-inversion types. The Hectors, the Scourers, the Nickers, and their ilk were contracultural; that is, they enacted their values into roles that opposed and interfered with the cultural systems and relationships of nonmembers. The Medmenhamites and The Terrible Club by contrast seem to symbolize the inversion of cultural values by ceremonies, rituals, and encapsulated acts relating mostly to members. The types are probably not completely exclusive, and some may fall in between the two. The contracultural club represents a potential breakdown of voluntary associations in that it transforms the encapsulated internal activities into visible or external ones. In so doing, it also violates the limits to permission implied by the ancient principles of law. The value-inversion type, on the other hand, is related to the outside world only through the subjective interpretation of the individual. For such men as Dashwood, it seemed to offer a sort of catharsis and recreation.

The Hectors, the Scourers, and their contracultural ilk may have been responsible for a kind of transformation or diffusion of club life. They became feared rather widely, and many people apparently formed local clubs on individual streets to avoid going out at night. A rhyme from the era goes like this:

Prepare for death, if here at night you roam
and sign your will before you sup from home[53]

## Operative and Accepted Masons: Residual Gilds

The Masons are very instructive for the examination of the two eras, since they appear to be an example of the earlier medieval gild in the later era. However, the transformation that they underwent through time shows that they do in fact conform to the general outlines of this analysis. The history of the Masons is typical of other craft gilds in their origin, a pure craft gild in the mature phase, with a more enduring voluntaristic element than most craft gilds, and then a gradual division into a voluntary association and a labor association at the end of the era.

Writings on Freemasonry are voluminous. Few writers, however, have examined the relationships of the craft gild and the voluntary association with sufficient attention to organizational distinctions. Reliance here has been placed in the work of Conder, who seems more aware of the problems than most.[54] He cites a number of minutes and records of the London Masons' gild, of which he was a member. These records show mention of a "Fellowship of Masons" by the year 1472, when they received a grant of arms, followed by a change to the name Company of Freemasons in 1530.[55] The Masons were attached, as gilds, to religious houses in the sixteenth century, and so undoubtedly this is a conservative estimate as to the date of the first Mason's gild. Because Masons were often itinerant workers who moved from one building site to another, they lacked the stability of other workers who were rooted in a community. To provide the stability of employment that the other gilds had, they developed forms of identification—a kind of a union card, so that they would qualify for help in a new work place. This was accmpanied by secret signs and supporting rituals that made the Masons' gilds unique among medieval workers.

Conder's sources reveal use of a formal distinction between operative Masons (i.e., workers in stone) and "free and accepted", or simply "accepted," Masons by 1620. This distinction probably existed even earlier. All gilds at that time had procedures for accepting nonoperative members, and for many gilds that had already lost their economic monopoly, it was only in that form that the gilds had any significance anymore. The thing that made the Masons unique, as Freemasons, was that they already had a firmly established international fellowship of operatives, which was not true of any other gilds, and they had a basis for secret protocol that was well established before they came under criticism as a subversive or heretical organization.

There are several reasons why the Masons prospered as an operative organization and successfully set up the conditions for survival in altered form. The Masons were among the most highly trained and intellectual of the medieval craftsmen. Their work called for a knowledge of art forms, mathematics, and elementary physics. Their wide travel acquainted them with many cultures. Their contacts with architects and other learned men made it possible for them to draw many important people into honorary or accepted membership. The Masons readily developed a tolerant religious fellowship that made only moderate demands on its votaries, and made it possible to unite in one group people from a wide variety of backgrounds. It was well adapted to an age experimenting with deism and other new religious forms.

The fellowship of Freemasons seemed to draw wide support throughout Europe and then America, and at the same time it drew consistent attacks from established churches to which it was an intolerable threat. Starting in 1738, seven Popes have condemned Freemasonry. Protestant churches have also condemned it from time to time.


## New Forms in the Eighteenth and Nineteenth Centuries

Most of the kinds of voluntary associations that have been discussed before, continued into the modern era in some form. The period under discussion here in fact saw the gild return to the form of voluntary association, as all but a few craft gilds became property-owning nonprofit charitable societies and ceremonial organizations. Perhaps the most significant changes had to do with the adaptation of clubs to the problems of social strata to which they had previously been foreign. They were transformed from organizations of gentlemen in two ways: they were found as more exclusive small clubs of elites, particularly the inner circles of the House of Commons, and they were taken up by the newly emerging working classes as mutual-security organizations.

In 1797 Sir Frederick Eden conducted an official inquiry into the condition of the poor.[56] It was one of the earliest of a long line of such investigations. His commentary was addressed to the positive as well as the negative conditions, and he had much praise for the Friendly Societies, which had only recently been given official recognition. Eden says:

> If the merit of political institutions is to be appreciated from ancient precedent and long practice, there are few social contrivances, which have better claim, on this account to approbation and support, than those simple establishments called Benefit Clubs, or Friendly Societies whose object is to exemplify one of the wisest political maxims, "that, by an association of the *many*, the *few* may be assisted. . . ."[56]

Eden then cites some gild ordinances at length and recommends them to the Friendly Societies, which he sees as one of the most commendable ways for the poor to help each other and, once they are established, for parishes to use as a channel for charity. Perhaps the most revealing aspect of the report is the attitude present throughout, that Friendly Societies solve a problem *for the rich*, by organizing the poor. For example, Eden opposes making dues into taxes, since this would ruin voluntarism. His comment is also quoted in full, because it is the earliest use encountered in this research of the term "voluntary association" (the *Oxford English Dictionary* has 1849).[57] "Any attempt to combine these *voluntary* associations with parochial taxes, will, I am persuaded, do much harm; and lessen that sense of independence, which a member of a Benefit Club, totally unconnected with a Poor's Rate, now enjoys."[58]

Eden's ideology may not have been so unrepresentative of the actual public attitudes of the poor themselves. There is evidence that they spoke of self-reliance as one of the basic traits to be sought in members and encouraged by the clubs. The association itself was formed with a view to promotion of mutual confidence in those for whom self-reliance was acceptable. The later Friendly Societies, discussed at length by Baernreither, show an extremely strong ideology, which is essentially moralistic in tone.[59] There was explicit law among them about the prohibition of drinking—the contrast to the gilds and clubs could scarcely be more complete. The three attitudes to drink of gilds, clubs, and Friendly Societies may be conceptualized as, respectively, integration, indulgence, and prohibition. Prohibition in some cases gave way to temperance. Many of the nineteenth-century Societies were founded by Sunday schools or were actually part of them. Some, however, are said to have begun from the groups of friends gathered at a tavern or at a work place. In general, the societies were consistently similar to the Protestant sects in both attitudes and organization. Methodism seemed to have an affinity for Friendly Societies, perhaps because both relied on direct autonomous organizational action to solve problems, and shared similar attitudes about prudence, self-reliance, thrift, and drinking.

The reasons that the Friendly Societies prospered in the period of the industrial revolution may not have been the same as the reasons they began. A survey of societies registered with the government in 1883 revealed seventy-seven that were in existence as early as 1687.[60] Defoe mentions Friendly Societies in a 1697 essay.[61] The United General Sea Box of Borrowstouness Friendly Society traces its records to 1634, and the Sea Box Society of St. Andrews to 1643.[62] But since there were self-help tendencies in all eras of Britain's history, perhaps the dates are unimportant. They did not at any rate make enough of an impression to be a matter of much public record. In general, these were early precedents of a new type that did not reach maturity in the age of interest here. Baernreither claims there were 32,000 Friendly Societies in England in 1874, which would make it a major social institution then.[63]

By the nineteenth century the types of Friendly Societies had proliferated to cover a wide variety of needs of the working class. Some were simply social in nature, but sometimes with an added general purpose such as self-improvement. There were Dividing Clubs or Tontines (named after an Italian founder), which had an entrance fee and a subscription out of which there were payments for sickness and the remainder periodically divided. There were Deposit Friendly Societies, which had a regular savings provision, for which the membership meetings were sources of encouragement. The village and county societies often had a more comprehensive approach, with formal insurance provisions and the opportunity to draw on managerial skills of officials. Some of the later societies were simply insurance brotherhoods, with very large memberships and not a great deal of emphasis on fellowship.

The Friendly Societies were by their nature independent endeavors to provide security. Nevertheless, they often failed because of the unanticipated pitfalls of such organizational endeavors, and because a small unaffiliated organization had little ability to forcefully require members to fulfill their obligations. The sacred oath of the fraternity gave way to the personal ethical obligation of the working man, which might become a legal obligation under certain circumstances but which was more often than not simply a tragic loss to his fellow investors. Parliament was very slow to do anything about it, and even when laws were passed, they were erratically enforced. Another reason for failure was lack of knowledge of the actuarial basis of insurance. What this meant in social terms was that early members could not get their retirement pay unless they attracted new members, but they often failed to adapt and change their organization to be attractive to young men. It became obvious to many of them that they would gain a great deal by affiliation or by seeking support from the available organizations and individuals who could lend continuity and who had reserve resources to draw upon. With this in mind, some Friendly Societies were formed from among workers in factories or businesses. Some sought to gain a further measure of solidarity by drawing together people of other kinds of common affiliation, such as a church or from ethnic minorities. Some early Friendly Societies copied Masonic orders in the practice of secrecy. Others formed fraternal organizations in which the ritual eventually became more significant than the insurance provisions that had given rise to them.

The eighteenth-century idea of self-help and self-reliance was preceded by a number of reconstructions of the organization of benevolence. Actions in the reign of Edward VI forbade large expenditures of money for chantries and encouraged direct charity. The gilds continued the practices of charity, but as previously, found it more to their liking to give to the worthy, who were more easily regulated in closed institutions. Consequently, they frequently used the endowments that they received from their members to create schools and orphanages and the like, and this practice continued in the eighteenth and nineteenth centuries. The ascendancy of Protestantism was accompanied by development of new charitable societies that made direct appeals to the public rather than relying on the encapsulated financing of the gilds, which for the most part operated increasingly on the income from estates rather than on revenues from membership.[64]

The new working mens' associations of the seventeenth and eighteenth centuries may be summarily divided into two analytic types: the Friendly Societies and allied mutual organizations, and the charities. The former are voluntary associations; the later are eleemosynary (i.e., nonprofit) Formal Volunteer Organizations, the recipients of voluntarism and frequently closely affiliated with voluntary associations, but distinctly separate from them because they lack analytic group members in voluntary roles.

The new charities were accompanied by organizations that proposed to reform the poor. The two purposes were often directly coupled in one organization, a practice with which we are familiar in modern times. For example, the end of the seventeenth century saw the emergence of the Society for the Reformation of Manners, which aimed specifically at changing the character of lower-class life.

In the research for this study, an attempt was made to find reliable information on the precedents of the contemporary English workingmen's *social* clubs. The modern clubs often combine insurance and mutual-benefit features with purely recreational voluntary associations, and are closely related to the Friendly Society movement. Some, however, are simply concerned with a night a week at the club, which has for them the very practical advantage of lower prices for beer and a chance to select one's companions. There is no reason to assure that this motive is a new one, and therefore it may be that there existed lower-class copies of the clubs and privileged taverns of the seventeenth-century gentlemen. But nothing more than hints can be found from writers who mention them or assume they existed but who did not find them significant enough to investigate. Hindley mentions the Two Penny Club, which was composed of "artizans and mechanics."[65] He gives no date, however, and it may simply be contemporary (i.e., *ca.* 1825). The workingmen's social clubs may also be seen as a lower-class counterpart of the elite London residential clubs of St. James and Pall Mall.

The consumer's cooperative movement is a phenomenon of voluntarism that emerged in the nineteenth century in England. It was one of many kinds of endeavor of the time that aimed at economic reform, particularly at the lot of the poor. Among these were some that combined intentional co-residence and formal organization of a whole community on an integrated basis, such as the intentional cooperative communities of Fourier, King, and many others in the United States. The consumer's cooperative movement began with the weavers of Rochdale, who formally organized themselves for voluntary cooperation on a comprehensive basis. The new voluntary associations drew on the knowledge of means of voluntary organization that the Friendly Societies had developed. What they added was a formula for sharing risks and returns from actual distribution and later the production of goods. By so doing, they became involved in change of the economy, which was sensed and strongly resisted by those committed to corporate industrial organization and individual entrepreneurship.

The cooperative movement has been thoroughly analyzed in many publications and, therefore, will not be pursued further here. The same may be said of the labor union movement.

The gentleman's club continued into modern times, changing with the times and adapting to needs of other strata. It has taken several forms. One is essentially unchanged: the dining club of select membership, and the older and better. One such club is spoken of by its members as *The Club*, and one learns only by considerable search that it has a legal name, the Roxburghe.[66] This club was founded in 1764 (or soon joined) by such notables as Joshua Reynolds, Samuel Johnson, Edmund Burke, and Oliver Goldsmith. There are interesting records of the membership process in Boswell's notes about how Johnson helped him gain membership. The club's records also show that in spite of such distinguished company, the attendance in early years averaged only about one-third.[67]

A second form of the gentleman's club, and mostly an innovation of the nineteenth century, was the residential club. It had a mansion of some sort, and rooms for bachelor members, plus provision for diverse recreational and leisure activities such as cards, smoking, reading, drinking, or dining. Some of these clubs have endured for 150 years or more without much change. Most of them faced financial problems, caught as they usually were in a conflict between growing expenses and the undesirable solution of higher membership. Exclusiveness leads to higher per capita costs. Some of these clubs were based on a rather specialized membership, such as the Oriental, whose members at first were exclusively veterans of service in India. They sometimes created two classes of members: full privileged, and partial or nonresidents who had the privilege of social use of the premises, but did not crowd the facilities. It is perhaps this form of gentlemen's club that is responsible for the outsider's image of the British clubman. Numerically, it is insignificant. There are numerous alumni or veteran's clubs that are similar or are modeled after the residential club.

This coverage of the new organizations at the end of the era has not been complete. Attention has been given only to those more prominent types that replaced older kinds or had some continuity with them. Since the focus is sociological and not historical types, the omissions are not likely to be serious. Undoubtedly some injustice has been done, particularly to newer forms of endeavor in religion and to some independent charitable organizations whose histories have yet to be written. Voluntarism in modern Catholicism and Judaism has been ignored, since their organizations were introduced late in the era and had little continuity with the past. The missionary and tract societies of evangelical Protestantism, the Roman Catholic Society of Jesus, and others would undoubtedly reveal some new dimensions worth future sociological consideration.

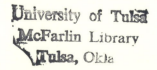

## Notes

1. Thomas H. S. Escott, *Club Makers and Club Members* (London: T. Fisher Unwin, 1914), p. 17.

2. Crane Brinton, "Clubs," in Edwin R. A. Seligman, ed., *Encyclopaedia of the Social Sciences*, 15 vols. (London: Macmillan, 1948), III, p. 574.

3. Robert Joseph Allen, *The Clubs of Augustan London* (Cambridge, Mass.: Harvard University Press, 1933), p. 6.

4. John Timbs, *Club Life of London*, 2 vols. (London: Chatto and Windus, 1865), I, p. 3.

5. Escott, *Club Makers and Club Members*, p. 21.

6. Edgcumbe Staley, *The Gilds of Florence* (New York: Benjamin Blom, 1967), p. 373.

7. Allen, *The Clubs of Augustan London*, pp. 8-9.

8. Samuel Johnson treats "club" as a verb: "to club, to pay a common reckoning." Samuel Johnson, *A Dictionary of the English Language*, 2 vols. (London: W. Strahan, 1755), no pagination.

9. It seems almost contrived to treat such an apparently trivial topic analytically. The social definition of drink however, is far from a trivial matter. The analytical category here is the nature of resources for support of voluntarism.

10. Timbs, *Club Life of London*, II, p. 1. In the original, the drink is spelled "coffa." James Spedding, Robert Leslie Ellis, and Douglas Denon Heath, eds., *The Works of Francis Bacon*, 15 vols. (Boston: Brown and Taggard, 1861), V, pp. 26-27. See also note 13.

11. Charles Hindley, *Tavern Anecdotes and Reminiscences, etc.*, (London: William Cole, 1825), p. 276.

12. Edward Bramah, *Tea and Coffee* (London: Hutchinson of London, 1972), p. 12.

13. Ibid., p. 43. E. S. De Beer, ed., *The Diary of John Evelyn* (London: Oxford University Press, 1959), p. 11, entry for May 29, 1636. Evelyn writes of a Greek, Nathaniel Conopios, whom he saw drink "Coffè," "which custome came not into England til 30 years after."

14. Hindley, *Tavern Anecdotes and Reminiscences*, p. 276.

15. Bramah, *Tea and Coffee*, p. 41.

16. Timbs, *Club Life of London*, II, p. 14.

17. Bramah, *Tea and Coffee*, p. 45.

18. Ibid., p. 47.

19. Timbs, *Club Life of London*, II, p. 22.

20. Bramah, *Tea and Coffee*, p. 20.

21. Allen, *The Clubs of Augustan London*, p. 14.

22. Lewis S. Feuer, *The Scientific Intellectuals: The Psychological and Sociological Origins of Modern Science* (New York: Basic Books, 1963).

23. Martha Ornstein, *The Role of Scientific Societies in the Seventeenth Century*, 3rd ed. (Chicago: University of Chicago Press, 1938). First published, 1913.

24. Perhaps history does repeat itself in the matter of differentiation of associations. At the time of writing, alchemy is making a comeback, and of course through voluntary associations.

25. H. A. F. Crewdson, *The Worshipful Company of Musicians* (London: Constable, 1950), p. 15.

26. Eric Mackerness, *A Social History of English Music* (London: Routledge and Kegan Paul, 1964), p. 39.

27. Ibid., pp. 40-42.

28. Ibid., p. 47.

29. Reginald Nettel, *Seven Centuries of Popular Song: A Social History of Urban Ditties* (London: Phoenix House, 1956), p. 96.

30. Mackerness, *A Social History of English Music*, p. 114.

31. Dennis Brailsford, *Sport and Society, Elizabeth to Anne* (London: Routledge and Kegan Paul, 1969), p. 14.

32. Ibid., p. 42.

33. Ibid., p. 53.

34. Keith Warner, "Major Conceptual Elements of Voluntary Associations," in David H. Smith, Richard D. Reddy, and Burt R. Baldwin, eds., *Voluntary Action Research: 1972* (Lexington, Mass.: Lexington Books, 1972), p. 75.

35. A modern empirical study of this issue is presented in Jack C. Ross, "Toward a Reconstruction of Voluntary Association Theory," *British Journal of Sociology* 23, 1 (March 1972): 20-32.

36. Allerdyce Nicoll, *British Drama*, 5th ed. (London: George C. Harrap and Co., 1962), p. 247.

37. Arnold Williams, *The Drama of Medieval England* (Kalamazoo, Mich.: Michigan State University Press, 1961), p. 2.

38. Ibid., p. 52.

39. Nicoll, *British Drama*, p. 41.

40. Louis C. Jones, *The Clubs of the Georgian Rakes*, (New York: Columbia University Press, 1942), p. 14.

41. Ibid., p. 1.

42. Ibid., p. 3.

43. Hindley, *Tavern Anecdotes and Reminiscences*, p. 124.

44. Jones, *The Clubs of the Georgian Rakes*, p. 8.

45. Anonymous, *The Character of a Town Gallant; Exposing the Extravagent Fopperies of Some Vain Self-conceited Pretenders to Gentility and Good Breeding* (London: Printed for W. L., 1675), p. 1.

46. Ned Ward, *The History of Clubs: in XXIV Chapters*, 2nd ed. (London: J. Phillips, 1710).

47. Hindley, *Tavern Anecdotes and Reminiscences*, p. 125.

48. Ibid., p. 126.

49. Ibid., p. 127.

50. Ibid., p. 130.

51. Ibid.

52. Ibid., p. 131.

53. Timbs, *Club Life of London*, I, p. 39.

54. Edward Conder, Jr., *Records of the Hole Crafte and Fellowship of Masons With a Chronicle of the History of the Worshipful Company of Masons of the City of London* (London: Sonnenschein and Co., 1894).

55. Ibid., p. 8.

56. Sir Frederick Eden, *State of the Poor*, 3 vols. (London: J. Davis, 1797), I, p. 590.

57. Oxford University Press, *The Compact Edition of the Oxford English Dictionary*, 2 vols (New York: Oxford University Press, 1971), II, p. 3655.

58. Eden, *State of the Poor*, I, p. 631.

59. Josef Maria Baernreither, *English Associations of Workingmen*, English edition, enlarged and revised by the author, trans. Alice Taylor (Detroit: Gale Research Co., 1966).

60. Ibid., p. 160.

61. P. H. J. H. Gosden, *Self-Help Voluntary Associations in the 19th Century* (London: B. T. Batsford, 1973), p. 4.

62. Ibid., p. 6.

63. Baernreither, *English Associations of Workingmen*, p. 162.

64. William Joseph Kahl, *The Development of London Livery Companies* (Boston: Harvard Graduate School of Business Administration, 1960), p. 23.

65. Hindley, *Tavern Anecdotes and Reminiscences*, p. 135.

66. Mounstuart E. Grant Duff, *The Club, 1764-1905* (London: privately printed, 1905).

67. Ibid., pp. 1-10.

# 6 *Restatement of the model*

Ⅰn Chapter 1, certain aspects of voluntary associations were defined that were judged to be appropriate for investigation of the phenomenon in a wide range of societies. These topics were *existence, prevalence, variety, purposes,* and *consequences.* A nine-variable model was adopted that was proposed as a way of explaining the two most basic ones, existence and prevalence. No model or theory was proposed to explain variety, purposes, and consequences, which were supplementarily investigated in the process of applying the model regarding existence and prevalence to eleven types of societies.

The societies investigated proved to be quite uneven as to availability of data, and not all of the nine variables could be systematically applied to each type. Therefore presentation was geared to a case study of each society, rather than following each variable. In this chapter we return again to the variables of the model, and a recapitulation of what was learned from their application to each society.

It was suggested in Chapter 1 that the "model" was only provisional, because it did not specify the interrelation of all the parts. Some of the relationships were discussed, but not worked out in detail. Now that the case studies have been presented, the individual elements ("hypotheses") of the model may be modified by the findings, and more complete statements about the relationships of elements attempted.

Communication

The first hypothesis about communication was that greater prevalence of voluntary associations would be associated with greater per capita interior volume of communications. Per capita volume was defined as "the ratio of the total number of intercommunications initiated and received by members of the network to the total number of individuals comprising the network."[1]

This was reformulated to state that a high volume of communication was necessary but not sufficient for existence of voluntary associations because other factors might extinguish voluntarism even when communication was good. A multiple-element model of this sort implies, of course, that each part is necessary but not sufficient. The Arunta was the simplest society encountered; their economy resulted in population dispersion over a wide territory, relatively low-level communication, and negligible development of associations. There were, however, many societies with much greater volume of communications that had weak associational development, such as the Polynesian Island sample. Volume of communication is, therefore, a rather insignificant element in model reconstruction: it indicates the existence of other things but by itself reveals little of interest, and so we may more efficiently go directly to the things it represents. Volume of communication would be a representative metric in comparative numerical analysis of societies that were similar on a number of other variables (e.g., comparison of peasant societies).

To look at the problem another way, the city obviously presents the condition in which people are faced with the fewest difficulties of communication owing to physical separation alone. The city-state of Athens was a case in which concentration of people did result in a large volume of communication and resultant voluntary associations. Chinese cities, in contrast, produced quite the opposite effect. Concentrated Hindu villages had associations, but not voluntary associations.

If volume of communication is tenuous as a necessity for voluntary association existence, it is even more so regarding **prevalence**.

Prevalence, of course, implies existence plus certain other conditions.

Connectivity and permanence were identified as two variables concerning necessary prerequisites for communication in networks. It was seen in the case of the Plains Indians that long periods of separation were not a barrier to formation of voluntary associations. Members expected to meet each summer and to communicate intensely, and relevant communication links were made stronger by kinship. The most instructive negative case was that of the ancient Hindus, in which the restrictions of caste inhibited communication between individuals of different castes.

There may be permanent communication links with a high degree of connectivity without such links' leading to voluntary associations. This condition is most often realized when the links exist between persons of different social rank. High rank typically increases control of communication. This situation existed in Tahiti, in which rank consciousness was extreme; in peasant societies, there were adequate links between peasants of equal rank but there were expectations that links with nonpeasants were the decisive ones. Social ranking may either be thought of as a diffuse and undifferentiated total quality attributed to *persons* regarding all conceivable societal values, or it may be articulated with differentiated *values* regarding the same person. In Tahiti we encountered an extreme example of the first case, in which each person was ranked the same on all variables and no self-differentiation was possible as the basis for the emergence of alternate communication links between ranks. The royalty thus dominated all communications between people of the same rank. By contrast, in Rome, economic and social ranking systems were differentiated from religious ranking, and as a result, communication was easily achieved between people of different social and economic ranks and so religious voluntary associations for burial were prevalent, either among people of the same or different social and economic ranks.

Among the Nupe the importance of age as a determinant of social rank was responsible for a high level of linkage between equals. When coupled with a high valuation of obligations to specified kin, the *communication* conditions for voluntary association formation were created. In certain of the Plains Indian tribes, a similar phenomenon was encountered; the result was age-strata voluntary dance associations.

In China, Rome, and Athens the extended family became a formal multigenerational organization, with common cultic observance. This common identity was a basis for multiple communication linkages of a permanent nature; under certain added circumstances, this led to religious voluntary association.

The cultural synthesis of Judaism in Babylonian exile, and the following period coupled with ecological concentration, led to a high volume of internal communication and association formation.

Common occupation creates a likelihood of high communication volume. Vicinal organization of gilds was found in almost every case of common market-oriented occupation. This ecological factor is so ubiquitous that it is easily overlooked. Although it is also associated with other factors, such as common religious identity and civic status, a high density of communication linkages is one of the most consistent correlates of gild formation. Recruiting of sons to gild membership is a related dimension.

In modern societies with a fairly high rate of migration, voluntary associations may be still common, if the volume of communication in the city is adequate. Among primitive societies, migration may have other kinds of consequences. Among the Nupe a cumulatively high rate of migration to distant jobs tended to break down the basis of obligations that supported age-grade voluntary association. Communication in primitive societies thus acquires its significance only over long periods of stable residence; modern voluntary associations may flourish based on member replacement and more immediate realization of rewards, and a high volume of communication between statuses rather than the same individuals.

## Goals and Interests

The communications variables were purely social in conception. In comments made about them, certain modifiers were mentioned, particularly cultural aspects; goals and interests, by contrast, are cultural necessities for existence and prevalence of voluntary associations. Goals and interests differ as to specificity. The former here indicates a greater degree of formal definition and precision; interests may be defined as more diffuse and continual immediate orientations to kinds of ends. What I have in mind is something akin to Max Weber's distinction between *zweckrational* and *wertrational* types of action. The distinction, however, is not easy to make in research of this type. We are concerned, following Smith's formulation, with the degree of differentiation and the number of goals and interests pursued in the society.

It was stated that in order for a number of groups, and hence associations, to exist, there must be differentiated goals and interests or kinds of them shared by sets of individuals of a network. Single-purpose organizations were relatively rare in this study, and when they occur now must be seen as a result of a high degree of differentiation of goals in modern societies coupled with the existence of other factors in the model that make it feasible to develop organizations narrowly oriented to such ends. The multiple-purpose organization was formerly quite common. The medieval English gild was the most thoroughly studied of these multiple-purpose organizations. It is obvious, however, that the distinction between single purpose and multiple purpose was not always clear; it might be proposed, in fact, that insofar as organizations develop satisfactory mechanisms of coordination, all organizations have a single purpose at the highest coordinative level. It is necessary, therefore, to add some comment about the internal structure of "multiple-purpose" voluntary associations.

Multiple-purpose voluntary associations existed and were prevalent when the culture had values that supported and sustained coordinative functions through a leadership role or roles without destroying the motivation of voluntarism. The most pervasive and consistent values were common religion, usually supported by identification of and loyalty to a specific patron deity or saint, conferring sanctified coordinative ability on individuals who were qualified by reason of status and behavior.

A second source of multiple-purpose voluntary associations was the fact that solidarity developed through association under oath of obligation implies enactment of the responsibilities associated with such solidarity in the culture. In medieval Christianity the concept of the organic unity of Christendom implied that a body meeting in the name of Christ should enact his precepts; in time, these were functionally isolated and coordinated as specified roles under an official. The later clubs, by contrast, enacted more individualistic ethics. In Athens the values of friendship led to clubs of friends who enacted multiple purposes, but less systematically.

It was shown that the modern tendency is to create separate voluntary associations for specific kinds of single purposes, and to distinguish associations as to voluntarism and nonvoluntarism. In the older societies analyzed here, that sort of distinction was rare, and voluntarism and nonvoluntarism were found in the same association, particularly in the gild. Generally, it may be concluded that existence of an eponym or hagionym indicates a multiple-purpose organization, though there may be idiosyncratic reasons for such a symbol and other sources of multiple purposes.

Where the society as a whole has a high degree of sharing of goals, the voluntary association may be formed so that certain sets of persons may distinguish themselves for pursuit of those goals. The Jewish synagogue is one example; the different Cheyenne military societies furnish another.

It must be concluded that Smith's statement (considered as an hypothesis) is false. There may be numerous voluntary associations with a relatively small number of differentiated goals as long as there are cultural values that support differentiation of groups of people for these similar goals. This statement may then be related to the conclusions about the communications variables: multiple-purpose organizations are more likely when connectivity and permanence of communication networks are high, as is the case when they are supported by ecological concentration, common religion or ethnicity, or some other sources of multiple synthesis in the community.

## The Collective Action Orientation

It was hypothesized that voluntary association prevalence would be greater for increase in permission for collectivities, degree of instigation, resources for collective action, and rewards from action. Permission refers to a system input from authorities. The remaining three refer to personal qualities, or to actions mediated through members. For a model that is analytically tidy, permission should be classified with the communication variables, since it is obviously a matter of the purely social level of analysis. Communications would then be the social level, goals and interests cultural, collective action personal or psychological.

The majority of our case studies were of societies that took the form of a state, and in each case, permission was a major issue. Permission was divided into two aspects—civil liberties and civil rights being, respectively, the right to be different and the right to be the same. To be most useful for analytical purposes, the concept of permission needs to be distinguished from those aspects of social organization, particularly stratification, that inhibit communication. Permission, then, is analytically relevant once it is established that voluntary associations are possible on other grounds. In the case of Rome, permission as a civil right was an issue at the origin of the Empire, though the civil right and civil liberty of the association had been granted in the earliest laws. Attempts were made to suppress them at times in Athens, though Athenians too had a tradition of civil liberty. In some peasant societies, the existence of secret societies indicates that the rudiments of association formation existed but permission was not given. Permission may not be present, owing to a specific political authority, the most obvious case, but also because important members of a society diffusely and generally disapprove, as was the case with permission for Nupe women who met every other criterion for voluntary association prevalence, and in other societies, for women generally. On the positive side, the Cheyenne had a high level of respect for their women and supported their right to voluntary associations.

Another means of withdrawing permission was cooptation. The best example was that of the Roman Empire in its waning years. The Hindu royalty managed control of gilds through a slightly different mechanism. The Chinese emperors attempted control of neighborhood associations through registration. African primitive states sometimes attempted control of voluntary associations (fraternities) through the surreptitious sharing of power with them, or suppression in other cases.

In summary, permission takes its place as the last (chronological) stage of our model: after all other conditions of existence, and particularly of prevalence (or in the case of fewer multiple-purpose organizations, virulence), are well established and they are seen as politically dangerous, suppression may occur. By contrast, effective voluntary assocations create one important basis of effective operation of governance and distribute control and problem solving among the citizens, providing a pluralist force that vexes and inhibits tyrants.

Outright suppression or formal grants of permission are only the most obvious final acts; less obvious and ultimately more important are the numerous ways in which rulers and the societies they rule bring into existence conditions that support growth of citizens who are capable or organizing and acting through voluntary associations— qualities that were identified as degree of instigation, resources for collective action, and rewards from action. Methodological difficulties with identification of such personal qualities were stated in Chapter 1.

"Instigation" refers to the tendency and ability of individuals and organizations to form more. Where the conditions of communication permanence and connectivity prevail, as outlined above, the likelihood is high that parents will induct their children into similar organizations and prepare them to accept that mode of action. Instigation is significant as a problem in times of rapid change, where values of parents are not obviously appropriate to the following generation. The societies considered all had devices of training or inducing youth into adult associations. The age-grade associations of the Africans were the most formal of these. Apprenticeship to gilds was also prominent. By contrast, monastery membership was often presented to women as a matter of no choice, while males more often chose monastic life voluntarily. The clubs of seventeenth-century England made no attempt to train people to membership, and each generation created its own unique methods, usually based on personal qualities that were unique but possibly stimulating to members.

As mentioned in Chapter 1, resources for collective action are hard to distinguish from instigation. But for most of our sample, the instigation variable was less significant than the resources. That is, there was a tendency to continue single organizations over long periods of time, rather than form new ones. The multiple-purpose organization is more capable of adapting to changing conditions, and some multiple-purpose gilds endured for many centuries. Where such conditions prevail, succeeding generations need only be prepared for accepting what they find. Gilds and fraternities proved to be highly absorptive and probably retarded social change in all societies in which they were found; single-purpose organizations are more adapted to change, though that adaptation may lead to their demise and creation of new ones from the ashes of the old.

It was mentioned that resources were made more readily available to persons and their organizations by the nature of the ties to other organizations. Since the voluntary association is not ordinarily economically productive, its resources are strengthened by its ties to others that may provide them. These ties typically include those of the sources of communication connectivity, but are not necessarily limited to them. The Cheyenne received such resources from the fact that the man lived with his wife in her own father's band but belonged to his own father's voluntary association, thus providing an integrative bond. Nupe work groups established exchange obligations with certain kin who provided ceremonial and practical support. The Chinese filial obligations provided the solidarity necessary for organizational unity. The Athenian customs of friendship provided a firm bond for the club, and established enmity relations with others that added further internal unity through conflict. In the most complex study attempted, that regarding the fraternities and gilds, clubs and sects of England, it was proposed that ideal-typical psychological reasons could be identified—respectively, fear of purgatory (gild and fraternity) and hedonism (clubs) as motivational sources of organizational solidarity.

The idea of rewards concludes the set. The reasoning here is that members must see that they gain more by cooperative action than alone. There is a danger in research that the circular nature of this argument will be ignored, and that we will not establish the independent nature of the variables—it might cavalierly be claimed that the existence of voluntary associations proves that people gained more together than alone. The chances are that most people will not be able to make such a calculation, but will accept the association for what it immediately offers and will simply hope it works out. Such is the case with the innumerable African and Asian rotating credit associations, which have a high rate of failure.

The multiple-purpose voluntary association offers a more complex analytical problem regarding rewards than Smith probably had in mind in his original formulation based on single-purpose associations. The problem of the possibility of death may have been the dominant reason for formation of voluntary associations among Romans, English fraternities, Chinese family associations, and others, yet death is only certain ultimately and not as to time; therefore the mutual aid, feasting, and fellowship were always surplus rewards balanced against the ultimate penalty. It was the uncertainty of death, and the solidarity of one's fraternal members to provide properly for it, that gave such a strong basis to such organizations. By contrast, nonfraternal death provisions and insurance provisions have virtually eliminated this motive from modern life, and forced the emergence of more immediate rewards as a basis of organizational prevalence.

The club provides the strongest contrast. The qualities of membership were developed outside the organization, not in it. A person must be a gentleman to enter. His rewards were not in the future but in the present. Rewards must be more immediate to have significance—life, not death, was the source of meaning. Paradoxically, it was not change in the imminence of death that led to the club era, for plagues in the club era were as devastating as before and death as great a possibility; the change in the apprehension of death seems to have been due to changes in its meaning in religion and secular philosophies.

## Variety, Purpose, Consequences

These three topics were introduced as general categories to orient analysis, without any intent to develop a model to explain their occurrence. They, therefore, call for no systematic summary. It is sufficient to point out some of the ways that these topics were used throughout and to suggest their significance for further research.

In general, ancient civilizations and primitive societies had in common the fact that emerging community problems were solved by new voluntary associations formed in traditional ways. In sixteenth-century England, voluntary associations, for the first time, became consistently creative, leading to emergence of new goals from within. Voluntary associations produced a surplus of goals.

As societies become large and more complex, specialization typically emerges and results in separate institutionalization of certain kinds of problems and their solution. This phenomenon was illustrated in our analysis of English society with particular force in the emergence of universities around the year 1000 A.D., a thing for which there was no immediate precedent. It was also illustrated by the separate analysis of the institutionalization of drama, music, and sports. Though these things had been separately institutionalized before, never had they been so independent. It was shown that voluntary associations did not immediately succeed as a social form in the field of music and drama, awaiting development of suitable resources such as skills, technology of printing, and availability of leisure among the emerging middle class.

The relation between purposes and consequences is the basis of evaluation. Formal evaluation was a rather foreign concept to most of the people of the eras involved. Some evaluation was implicit. Roman and Athenian authorities did not always appreciate the clubs, and their suppression was the result. The popularity and expansion of dancing clubs among Plains Indians signifies their success. Among many other societies, there is a more confusing picture. The Nupe and other African states continually encountered disillusionment with their organizations under the impact of modernization, but seemed to have no alternative but to try again.

The systematic evaluation of consequences of voluntary association is in the long run a matter of philosophy of government and of society itself—topics that have only been touched on, but which may be seen as ultimately of greater importance than those undertaken here.

## Notes

1. David H. Smith, "Modernization and the Emergence of Volunteer Organizations," in David H. Smith, ed., *Voluntary Action Research: 1973* (Lexington, Mass., Lexington Books, 1973), p. 58. I assume that communication and intercommunication are identical concepts here.

# *Appendix*

Interdisciplinary Search on Voluntary Associations[1]

There are a number of commonsense everyday categories of human affairs that do not fall easily into the classification of academic departments, but which give rise to specialized studies through institutes or associations. For example, poverty, leisure, recreation, aging, and voluntarism are all topics of research at the present time involving coordinated investigation carried out through interdisciplinary associations composed of specialists from a variety of academic backgrounds. The job of developing bibliographies is typically a high priority of such agencies, but these efforts commonly founder on problems of differentiated disciplinary vocabularies. More often than not, the individual researcher finds the interdisciplinary bibliographies too general, or more to the point, the vocabularies are unique to each discipline and impede or make impractical genuine interdisciplinary efforts.

This essay is the report of one attempt to organize an interdisciplinary search, with the object of retrieval of information on voluntary associations in different societies at different times, in all relevant disciplines. The writer is a sociologist, with some training in political science and social work. The fields of search included sociology, political science, history, religion, anthropology, and to a lesser extent law, architecture, theater and costume, folklore, medicine,

music, art, sport and recreation, journalism, and some distinct sub-
categories of history such as local history, amateur history
publications, public records, and so on.

The essay is in a sense more the record of a personal attempt at
creation of a new role definition, than a finished or detailed product.
It began with the not very startling observation, of a purely theoretical sort, that a way of seeing was a way of not seeing—a cliché that had
been worked up into some very elegant formulations by recent
writers on the sociology of knowledge. The obvious problem was to
develop a practical and effective way of seeing what I was blind to.
The essay itself is in the tradition of the study of sociological craftmanship in the sociology of sociology. I had in mind such works as
those of Phillip Hammond's *Sociologists at Work*[2] and C. Wright
Mills's "On Intellectual Craftmanship."[3]

The first stage in deciding on an approach came when the
sociological references in standard voluntary association books and
articles had been read and their sources traced. The next move I had
planned, to standard anthropological literature, met with poor
results, until I accidentally discovered that an entirely different
terminology was being used to identify the materials. The conclusion
had to be that there must be a way of looking for materials that
anthropologists knew which was economical and systematic.

The endeavor, stated more abstractly, seemed to consist of two
parts: recognizing and questioning the assumptions of my role as a
sociologist in order to prepare the way to think like some other sort of
specialist; and learning the technical vocabulary, indexing, and
bibliography practices of the source discipline.

The attempt at role re-creation resulted in the discovery of about
ten times as large a universe of references as were previously available to me as a sociologist. Whether this kind of ratio can be expected
from every endeavor of this sort or if it is true only for this one
remains to be seen when others try something of the same kind. For
what it is worth, here is the way I then proceeded analytically to
understand the search procedure.

I first discovered what not to do. I discovered very early in the
game that it does *not* help very much to talk to colleagues in each
discipline, unless they are very specialized in the field of concern. I

encountered enthusiastic interest, but also soon found that after an hour of systematic library work *without* help, I knew more about *my* interest in *their* field than they did. The numerous errors and false leads encountered by asking for help led me to abandon collegial brain-picking as an interdisciplinary method. Maybe it would work if there were a closer relationship with such a specialist—such as marriage. My wife objected.

It was soon discovered that subject matter indexes in the prominent journals in various disciplines are not similarly organized. Some major journals have no subject matter index on a cumulative basis. Partial bibliographies were accessible through the journal indexes of the *American Sociological Review* and the *American Journal of Sociology*. The *Dissertation Abstracts* are helpful, but repetitive of otherwise accessible items. *Psychological Abstracts* produces some useful material, but proved not as good as the cumulative indexes of the major sociology journals. *Sociology Abstracts* lacks the time depth in this field to be very useful. I found the organization of cumulative indexes in journals in other fields to be of very little use.

In all cases, even in sociology, it became obvious that a general theoretical understanding of the way concepts were used in each discipline was necessary before the practical coverage, if I was not to overlook major areas of knowledge. The general model follows.

Concepts may be distinguished abstractly in published work, at three levels.[4] Level 1 may be called the elementary data language level. It involves the move from precept to concept in the identification of behavior by an observer. It typically involves understanding the culture of the behavioral event. I will call it the *object vernacular*.

Level 2 is the *native* nonspecialized vocabulary of the researcher or observer, into which he must translate level 1 if he and his immediate audience of his own culture are to understand it. The move from 1 to 2 is often a matter of metaphor or analogy. This process of transfer is the focus of many problems, particularly in anthropology, because it involves issues of personal identity of the researcher.[5] I shall call it the *subject vernacular*. Note that both 1 and 2 assume the observer as reference role.

Level 3 is the *technical*. It is designed to communicate with a professional reference group, is normative in nature and coded, partially formal or written and partly not. Some aspects of the technical language can be quantified. I will not take up here the issue of process of technicalization of the level 2 language, though within the time span of existence of sociology it is considerable, and even more so among the older disciplines with which I am concerned. An example of technicalization is the redefinition of the word "voluntary" for purposes of precise use in this study. The reverse of technicalization is vulgarization. For this paper, the main issue is not technicalization, but the logic of the research procedure in each discipline. Also, it should be pointed out that I am concerned only with the way research is reported, which is a different issue from the way it is done in the field or in the armchair. Otherwise there would have to be attention to the differences at level 1 between connotative and denotative concepts, perception and conception, and so on.

## RESEARCH PROCESS MOVES

|  | From (1) | To (2) | To (3) |
|---|---|---|---|
| *Sociology* | | | |
| (a) Hypothetical deductive variety | Level 3 (proposed theory) | Level 1 or 2 (operationalization) | Level 3 (verified theory) |
| *History* | | | |
| (b) | Level 1 | Level 2 (situated explanation) | Level 3 (general explanation) |

Let us consider first some of the things that happen in the process of research in sociology and history, the pair of disciplines in which the contrasts in the use of concepts seems to be the greatest—this is also the pair of disciplines that contributed the most material for the study.

Of course, the table oversimplifies and truncates much of the work in each field. But let us consider the significance of the six cells as a way of starting to understand interdisciplinary information retrieval. The level of conceptualization is typically very different in history and in sociology. One rarely encounters concepts classified in cell 2b that lead to data in 1b, though modern historians tend toward consciousness of sociological methodology, as was once the case in reverse direction when sociology was very young. Instead, cell 2b tends to be organized in terms of the vocabulary of 1b. For example, historians who write about Greek voluntary associations tend to identify Greek organizations by name in Greek (1b), and then classify them as either *erani* or *thiasi*. Later, synoptic historians note the analogy of the *thiasi* with the American mutual-benefit club (2b), but do not usually tie this to a more abstract concept at level 3. Similar approaches were found in the literature of ancient Rome, India, and China, where the chaos is later ameliorated somewhat by Max Weber's imposed ideal types (which are subject vernacular terms elevated to level 3 by denotative specification). Level 3b is rarely encountered in historical studies, except in the synoptic writers, such as Crane Brinton's treatment of clubs in the *Encyclopedia of the Social Sciences*. Synoptic historians tend to merely refine level 2 subjective vernacular.

Historical studies are best approached with level 2 in mind, and the best way to do that, until bibliographical research is attempted in a certain field, is to go to sociology for level 3, and draw up a list of key concepts to use at level 2. The single best source for this purpose is Murray Hausknecht, *The Joiners*.[6] In a reflexive sense, what I am saying is that sociologists ought to be conscious of what they tend to do automatically.

A comparison of sociological and anthropological approaches is not quite so striking. Again, at the risk of oversimplification, a rough classification may be made for sensitizing purposes.

Parts of the diagram are superfluous. I have found almost no sociological research on voluntary associations of functionalist genre, though functionalist treatment of voluntary associations in textbooks, such as Rossides's recent text, are plentiful.[7] Generally, the explanation seems to be that functionalists treat voluntary associations in a

## RESEARCH PROCESS MOVES

|  | From (1) | To (2) | To (3) |
|---|---|---|---|
| *Sociology* |  |  |  |
| (a) Hypothetical-deductive | Level 3 | Level 1 or 2 | Level 3 |
| (b) Functional | Level 3 | Level 1 or 2 | Level 3 (functional explanation) |
| *Anthropology* |  |  |  |
| (c) Ethnographic | Level 1 (case study typical) | Level 2 | Usually none or level 3 |
| (d) Classical | Level 1 | Level 1 | Level 3 (functional explanation) |
| (e) Modern functional | See b, sociological functionalism |  |  |
| (f) Modern anthropological explanation) | See sociology, all varieties |  |  |

purely theoretical manner, drawing data from survey research done in other theoretical bases (or on no theoretical basis at all). The avoidance of study of voluntary associations by functionalists is an interesting topic for a student of the sociology of sociology.

Anthropological ethnography concerning voluntary associations seems to fall into two main groups. Historical ethnography is the work of travelers or explorers, missionaries, merchants, and the like. It is a rich source of materials, but must be treated for bibliographical purposes like the historical sources—there were no technical concepts that allow a taxonomic search.

Professional ethnography has the same conceptual tools as late-functional anthropology, and in fact is often indistinguishable. To limit ethnography to description, as the etiology of the work implies, is to stop short of explanation. Ethnography in anthropology seems to serve the same purpose for anthropology that survey research does for sociology: it provides an empirical base for analytical work. My impression is that it is the most poorly defined division of anthropology.

A substantial portion of the ethnography on the Plains Indians bridges historical and professional ethnography. Materials were gathered around 1915 by early professional ethnographers writing for a critical professional reference group, but the materials utilized recollections of very old informants, such as aged Indians or explorers.

Work on political science, for the purpose of this paper, may be divided into modern behavioral political science, which is practically identical with political sociology so far as theory and methodology are concerned, and the older theoretical-historical approach. Behavioral political science tends to try to bridge the sociological and the older vocabularies, and so the subject vernacular is found.[8]

Theoretical political science shares much of its vocabulary with philosophy, law, and earlier, with religion. Thus sixteenth-century works by such writers as Althusius and Grotius can be searched under vocabularies common to religion and philosophy, but Gierke, who is a nineteenth-century interpreter of both (translated in the twentieth century with still further modifications in vocabulary), moves to the object vernacular "corporation," giving it a technical denotation.

Twentieth-century legal and political philosophers tend to feature terms such as "pluralism" and "association" with occasional reference to "corporation": each is a second-level term raised to the third level. As theoreticians, they ignore level 1, which makes theorizing easier.

Contemporary voluntary association analysts in religion tend toward a technical vocabulary drawn from sociological writers, especially Ernst Troeltsch (who drew on Max Weber), and more recently James L. Adams. There is, however, a strong mix with the traditional seminary patois, and one must search under "free church" as well as "sect" and "cult," and in church history works for the object and subject vernacular items (e.g., Schwenkfelder; then sect, Anabaptist, Schwenkfelder). Confusing as religious writings are to the nonspecialist, religionists have among the best-kept records and the search is very rewarding.

Vocabulary development within sociology itself has undergone technicalization, but the early pioneers' commitment to sociology as a general science led to use of an abstract vocabulary from the start. Although the distinctions made above about the relation of concept and research procedure are generally valid, they do not always help identify the way that we approach literature in practice. It helps to work with a distinction between survey research (hypothetical-deductive or ethnographic) and community studies, because the types are recognizable from the titles. The monumental American pioneer efforts at community studies (Lynd, W. L. Warner, Drake, and Cayton) used either object vernacular or technical level concepts to refer the reader to their material. That is, one looks under "voluntary associations" to get to some second-level concept, of which there appear to be about twenty in common use (see table at end). This isn't much different from survey research (typically of a later date), which tended, however, to start with "voluntary association," technical level operationally defined, and lump the results under the object vernacular headings or simply as a count of memberships. In any case, they are usually cross-listed, and the problem is not locating material, but its meaning (which I shall not take up here).

A final note on concept finding in current sociology. The Association of Voluntary Action Scholars has attempted a vocabulary synthesis, which may in time lead to adoption of "formal voluntary organization" as the technical term, of which voluntary association would be a certain component. This move has not yet born fruit.

Reference to the past still requires imposed systems. The table that follows is an attempt at a key word charting in a sample of the areas mentioned above. Its use may, I hope, lead more sociologists to explore some very rewarding topics outside their own discipline.

After about 1650, the growth of new forms is rapid and includes literary chambres, scientific societies, many varieties of social clubs, new forms of fraternity, the modern lodge movement, the Friendly Societies, and the workingman's club. Each can be easily fitted into the patterns outlined in the table.

## Notes

1. This is a modified version of a paper given to the Atlantic Association of Sociologists and Anthropologists Annual Meeting, Charlottetown, Prince Edward Island, March 1972.

2. Phillip Hammond, ed., *Sociologists at Work* (New York: Basic Books, 1964).

3. C. Wright Mills, "On Intellectual Craftsmanship," in Llewellyn Gross, ed., *Symposium on Sociological Theory* (Evanston, Ill.: Row, Peterson and Co., 1959), pp. 25-53.

4. This may be compared to a similar statement by Lachenmeyer. "Any science can be conceptualized as a dual information transfer. The first information transfer is between men and the events that are the subject matter of their science. The second is between men as scientists about these events." The author concludes that sociology is not a science. Charles Lachenmeyer, *The Language of Sociology* (New York: Columbia University Press, 1971), p. 1.

5. Since sociology and anthropology seem to be converging on many theoretical issues and the target research groups seem also to be merging, it may be the case that we will witness a convergence such that in another few decades the major difference between the two might be that anthropologists will be those who are best trained at the subject-object interpersonal level and the sociologists will be those best trained at data-handling levels. In sum,

we would differentiate at the methodological level rather than at the topic or theory level as now.

6.  Murray Hausknecht, *The Joiners* (New York: The Bedminster Press, 1962).

7.  Daniel Rossides, *Society as a Functional Process* (Toronto: Mc-Graw-Hill Co. of Canada, 1968).

8.  The shortcomings of the typology are evident here. The technical vocabulary of one generation may become the subject vernacular of the next.

# EXAMPLES OF STUDIES BY CONCEPT-LEVEL

|  | 1st Level | 2nd Level | 3rd Level |
|---|---|---|---|
| Sociology survey research (example: Hausknecht, *The Joiners*) | American Legion<br>VFW<br>DAV<br>Jewish War Veterans<br>Catholic War Veterans<br>DAR<br>Native Sons of the Golden West<br>AMVETS<br>Gold Star Mothers | Veterans military patriotic | Voluntary associations |
|  | Eleven names | Health organizations related to health | Voluntary associations |
|  | Eighteen names | Civic or service | Voluntary associations |
|  | Eight names | Political or pressure group | Voluntary associations |

| 1st Level | 2nd Level | 3rd Level |
|---|---|---|
| Seventeen names | Lodges, fraternal, secret societies, mutual benefit (and auxiliaries) | Voluntary associations |
| Eight names | Church, religious | Voluntary associations |
| Eight names | Economic, occupational, professional (other than health) | Voluntary associations |
| Seven names | Cultural, educational, college allumni (other than health) | Voluntary associations |
| Fourteen names | Social sports, hobby, recreational (except church connected) | Voluntary associations |

| | 1st Level | 2nd Level | 3rd Level |
| --- | --- | --- | --- |
| Anthropology, British, modern. Kenneth Little, *West African Urbanization* | Advanced Babua Womens' | Cultural | Voluntary associations |
| | Evolués | | |
| | Old Achimotan | | |
| | Old Bo Boys | | |
| | People's Educational | | |
| | One name | Political | Voluntary Associations |
| | Three names | Tribal and womens' | Voluntary associations |
| | One name | Dining | Voluntary associations |
| | Four names | Social and sports | Voluntary associations |
| | Four names | Recreational companies | Voluntary associations |
| | Five names | Syncretist cults, benefit and Christian Societies | Voluntary associations |

|  | 1st Level | 2nd Level | 3rd Level |
|---|---|---|---|
| Sociology Community Studies: examples, R. & H. Lynd, Ch. 17-19, *Middletown*, and Ch. 7. *Middletown in Transition*. | About 30 names | Club: civic, church, child rearing riding, study, literary, working men's | Leisure associa- tion |
|  | Three names | Lodge | Leisure associa- tion |
|  | Four names | Union | Leisure associa- tion |
|  | Four names | Church: choirs Sunday schools, sororities | Leisure associa- tion |
| Historical example: medieval histories in general (a) early (i.e., post Roman) | Innumerable names in vernacular | *Collegia* | — |
|  | English nouns | *Frith* | — |

|  | 1st Level | 2nd Level | 3rd Level |
|---|---|---|---|
| (b) *Ca.* 1000 A.D. | Innumerable names in vernacular | Guild, gild, gield, gyle, gilhalla, gwul, goel, gouil, feill, feil, feighl, gulde, Germane verb forms: gylden, gildan, geldan | Guild, gild in later summary writings |
|  | Scandinavian pre-Christian | Maegth, aets, Geschlecther, farae | — |
|  | English, French names, some Italian, German, etc. | Peace associations | Listed under gild at times, indiscriminate |
|  | Italian, then other European | schola | University |
|  | Saint's names | fraternity, sodality, confraternity | Voluntary association or gild by later writers. Eponym |

|  | 1st Level | 2nd Level | 3rd Level |
|---|---|---|---|
| (c) Late medieval, transition to late era | E.g., The Court of Good Company (1400) | Club | Voluntary associa- tion (named 1791) |
| | Other Club names | Club | Club |
| | Many English names | Coffee- house | Club |
| | Rota | Rota | Political club |

# Annotated bibliography
# to appendix

Adams, James L. "Bibliography." In *Voluntary Associations: A Study of Groups in Free Societies, Essays in Honor of James Luther Adams,* edited by D. B. Robertson. Richmond, Va.: John Knox Press, 1966. This work is a good key to religious writing on voluntary associations.

Althusius. Works not easily accessible in English. See Gierke for book notes.

Brinton, Crane. "Clubs." In *Encyclopaedia of the Social Sciences,* edited by Edwin R. A. Seligman, Vol. 3. 15 Vols. London: Macmillan, 1948. Broad historical treatment, with stress on Europe and United States.

Drake, St. Clair, and Cayton, Horace. *Black Metropolis.* 2 vols. 1945 Reprint. New York: Harper Torchbooks, 1962. In the Warner tradution, combining a series of historical and empirical studies.

Gierke, Otto. *National Law and the Theory of Society 1500 to 1800.* 2 vols. Boston: Beacon Press, 1957.

———. *Political Theories of the Middle Ages.* Boston: Beacon Press, 1958. Both volumes useful mostly for extensive notes and bibliography on source for study of law and political theory on associations and corporations.

Grotius. See Gierke for book notes.

Hammond, Phillip, ed. *Sociologists at Work.* New York: Basic Books, 1964.

Hausknecht, Murray. *The Joiners: A Sociological Description of Voluntary Association Membership in the United States.* New York: Bedminster Press, 1962. A skilled integration of national studies. Extensive bibliography, which is now out of date.

Lachenmeyer, Charles. *The Language of Sociology.* New York: Columbia University Press, 1971. Technical analysis of the language of sociology.

Little, Kenneth. *West African Urbanization: A Study of Voluntary Associations in Social Change.* Cambridge: University Press, 1965. One of a great many British sociological and anthropological studies in

Africa that have a much higher degree of integration than do American studies.

Lynd, Robert S., and Lynd, Helen M. *Middletown.* New York: Harcourt, Brace and Co., 1929.

————. *Middletown in Transition.* New York: Harcourt, Brace and Co., 1937. Two classics, now of historical interest as period pieces, and example of the heroic chaos era in research methodology.

Mills, C. Wright. "On Intellectual Craftsmanship." In *Symposium on Sociological Theory,* edited by Llewellyn Gross. Evanston, Ill.: Row, Peterson and Co., 1959.

Rossides, Daniel. *Society as a Functional Process.* Toronto: McGraw-Hill Co. of Canada, 1968. Functionalist integration of voluntary association studies in an introductory text.

Warner, W. Lloyd, and Lunt, Paul. *The Social Life of a Modern Community.* New Haven: Yale University Press, 1941. More empirical than the Lynd volumes, and more encyclopedic, but not of much use as access to other works or to theory.

Weber, Max. "Max Weber's Proposal for the Sociological Study of Voluntary Associations." Translated by Everett Cherrington Hughes. *The Journal of Voluntary Action Research,* I, 1. Winter 1972. Dates from 1910. A programmatic essay. Weber considers gilds in several works, the volumes on China and India being good representations of the ideal-typical method applied to voluntary associations.

# Bibliography

Items from the appendix are placed in an "Annotated Bibliography" following the appendix.

Abbott, Frank Frost. *The Common People of Ancient Rome.* New York: Bilbo and Tannen, 1965.

Abram, A. *English Life and Manners in the Later Middle Ages.* London: George Routledge and Sons, 1913.

Adams, James Luther. "Foreword." In *Voluntary Action Research: 1972,* edited by David H. Smith, Richard D. Reddy, and Burt R. Baldwin. Lexington, Mass.: Lexington Books, 1972.

Adams, Jeremy duQuesnay. *Patterns of Medieval Society.* Englewood Cliffs, N.J.: Prentice-Hall, 1969.

Albright, W. F. *From the Stone Age to Christianity.* 2nd ed. Baltimore: Johns Hopkins Press, 1957.

Allen, Robert Joseph. *The Clubs of Augustan London.* Cambridge, Mass.: Harvard University Press, 1933.

Anderson, Robert T. *Traditional Europe: A Study in Anthropology and History.* Belmont, Calif.: Wadsworth Publishing Company, 1971.

————. "Voluntary Associations in History." *American Anthropologist,* 73 (March 1971).

Auboyer, Jeannine. *Daily Life in Ancient India, From Approximately 200 B.C. to 700 A.D.* Translated by Simon Watson Taylor. New York: The Macmillan Co., 1965.

Baernreither, Josef Maria. *English Associations of Workingmen.* English ed., enlarged and rev. by the author. Translated by Alice Taylor. Detroit: Gale Research Co., 1966.

Banton, Michael. "Voluntary Associations: Anthropological Aspects." In *International Encyclopaedia of the Social Sciences,* edited by David L. Sills, Vol. 16. 17 vols. New York: The Macmillan Company and the Free Press, 1968.

Baron, Salo. *A Social and Religious History of the Jews*. 10 vols. New York: Columbia University Press, 1952-1965.

Baron, Salo, and Blau, Joseph L., *Judaism: Postbiblical and Talmudic Period.*Indianapolis: Bobbs-Merrill Co., 1954.

Bishop, Morris. *The Middle Ages*. New York: American Heritage Press, 1970.

Bloch, Marc. *Feudal Society*. 2nd ed. Translated by L. A. Manyon. London: Routledge and Kegan Paul, 1962.

Boak, A. E. R. "Late Roman and Byzantine Guilds." In *Encyclopaedia of the Social Sciences*, edited by Edwin R. A. Seligman, Vol. 7. 15 vols. London: Macmillan, 1948.

Bode, Jerry G. "The Voluntary Association Concept in Twentieth Century American Sociology." In *Voluntary Action Research: 1972*, edited by David H. Smith, Richard D. Reddy, and Burt R. Baldwin. Lexington, Mass.: Lexington Books, 1972.

Brady, Robert. *A Complete History of England, etc.* 2 vols. London: Samuel Lowndes, 1685.

Brailsford, Dennis. *Sport and Society, Elizabeth to Anne*. London: Routledge and Kegan Paul, 1969.

Bramah, Edward. *Tea and Coffee*. London: Hutchinson of London, 1972.

Brentano, Lujo. "On the History and Development of Gilds." In *English Gilds*, by J. Toulmin Smith. London: Trubner, 1870.

Brinton, Crane. "Clubs." In *Encyclopaedia of the Social Sciences*, edited by Edwin R. A. Seligman, Vol. 3. 15 vols. London: Macmillan, 1948.

Brown, G. Baldwin. *From Schola to Cathedral: A Study of Early Christian Architecture and its Relation to the Life of the Church*. Edinburgh: David Douglas, 1886.

Burgess, John Steward. *The Guilds of Peking*. New York: Columbia University Press, 1928.

Cagnat, R. "Sodalicium, Socalitas." In *Dictionnaire des Antiquités Grecques et Romaines*, edited by Charles Daremberg and Edmund Saglio, Vol. 5. 5 vols. Graz: Akademische Druck, 1969.

Calhoun, George Miller. *Athenian Clubs in Politics and Litigation*. Austin, Texas: Univeristy of Texas Press, 1913.

Carcopino, Jérômé. *Daily Life in Ancient Rome: The People and the City at the Height of the Empire*. Translated by E. O. Lorimer. Edited by Henry T. Rowell. New Haven: Yale University Press, 1940.

Chang, Chung-Li. *The Chinese Gentry: Studies on Their Role in Nineteenth Century Chinese Society*. Seattle: University of Washington Press, 1955.

Chapple, E. D., and Coon, C. S. *Principles of Anthropology*. New York: Holt, 1942.

Chesneaux, Jean. *Popular Movements and Secret Societies in China 1840-1950*. Stanford, Calif.: Stanford University Press, 1972.

Clune, George. *The Medieval Guild System*. Dublin: Brown and Nolan, 1943.

Cockeram, Henry. *The English Dictionarie*. Menston, England: The Scholar Press, 1968.

Codrington, Robert Henry. *The Melanesians*. Oxford: The Clarendon Press, 1969.

Conder, Edward, Jr. *Records of the Hole Crafte and Fellowship of the Worshipful Company of Masons of the City of London*. London: Swan Sonnenschein and Co., 1894.

Connor, Walter Robert. *The New Politicians of Fifth Century Athens*. Princeton, N.J.: Princeton University Press, 1971.

Coote, Henry Charles. *The Ordinances of Some Secular Guilds of London from 1354 to 1496*. London: Nichols and Sons, 1871.

————. "The Ordinances of Some Secular Guilds of London, 1354-1496." *Transactions of the London and Middlesex Archaeological Society* IV, 28 (1875).

Crewdson, H. A. F. *The Worshipful Company of Musicians*. London: Constable, 1950.

Daraul, Arkon. *Secret Societies*. London: Tandem Books, 1965.

De Beer, E. S. *The Diary of John Evelyn*. London: Oxford University Press, 1959.

Dill, Samuel. *Roman Society from Nero to Marcus Aurelius*. London: Macmillan and Co., 1904.

Drekmeier, Charles. *Kingship and Community in Early India*, Stanford, Calif.: Stanford University Press, 1962.

Duckat, Walter. *Beggar to King: All the Occupations of Biblical Times*. Garden City, N.Y.: Doubleday and Co., 1968.

Eberhard, Wolfram. *Conquerors and Rulers: Social Forces in Medieval China*. 2nd rev. ed. Leiden: E. J. Brill, 1970.

Eden, Sir Frederick. *State of the Poor*. 3 vols. London: J. Davis, 1797.

Edwards, John, and Booth, Alan. *Social Participation in Urban Society*. Cambridge, Mass.: Schenkman Publishing Co., 1973.

Eisenstadt, S. N. "The Protestant Ethic Thesis." In *The Sociology of Religion*, edited by Roland Robertson. Harmondsworth, Middlesex: Penguin Books, 1969.

Ellis, William. *Polynesian Researches*. London: Henry G. Bohn, 1853.

Feuer, Lewis S. *The Scientific Intellectuals: The Psychological and Socio-*

logical Origins of Modern Science. New York: Basic Books, 1963.

Forrest, Denys. *The Oriental: Life Story of A West End Club*. London: B. T. Batsford, 1968.

Gamble, Sidney D. *Ting Hsein: A North China Rura Community*. New York: Institute of Pacific Relations, 1954.

————. *North China Villages: Social, Political, and Economic Activities Before 1933*. Berkeley and Los Angeles: University of California Press, 1963.

Gasquet, Abbot. *Parish Life in Medieval England*. 2nd ed. London: Metheun and Co., 1907.

Geertz, Clifford A. "The Rotating Credit Association: A 'Middle-rung' in Development." In *Social Change: the Colonial Situation*, edited by Immanuel Wallerstein. New York: John Wiley and Sons, 1966.

Goldman, Irving, *Ancient Polynesian Society*. Chicago: University of Chicago Press, 1970.

Gordon, C. Wayne, and Babchuck, Nicholas. "A Typology of Voluntary Associations." *American Sociological Review* 24, 1 (February 1959).

Gosden, P. H. J. H. *Self-Help Voluntary Associations in the 19th Century*. London: B. T. Batsford, 1973.

Grinnell, George Bird. *The Cheyenne Indians: Their History and Ways of Life*. 2 vols. New York: Cooper Square Publishers, 1928.

Gross, Charles, *The Gild Merchant*. 2 vols. Oxford: At the Clarendon Press, 1890.

Grote, George. *A History of Greece*. New ed. 10 vols. London: John Murray, 1907.

Hahn, Herbert. *The Old Testament in Modern Research*. Philadelphia: Fortress Press, 1966.

Hartson, Louis D. "A Study of Voluntary Associations, Educational and Social, in Europe During the Period from 1100 to 1700." *Pedagogical Seminary*, Vol. 18, 1911.

Herlihy, David. "Guilds." In *The New Catholic Encyclopedia*, edited by William J. McDonald, Vol. 6. 15 vols. New York: McGraw-Hill Book Co., 1967.

————, ed. *Medieval Culture and Society*. New York: Walker and Co., 1968.

Herskovits, Melville J. *Dahomey, an Ancient West African Kingdom*. Locust Valley, N.Y.: Augustin, 1938.

Hindley, Charles. *Tavern Anecdotes and Reminiscences of the Origin of Signs, Clubs, Coffee Houses, Streets, City Companies, Wards, etc.*

*Intended as a Lounge-Book for Londoners and their Country Cousins. By One of the Old School.* London: William Cole, 1825.

Hobsbawm, Eric. *Primitive Rebels* New York: Frederick A. Praeger, 1963.

Hoebel, E. Adamson. *Man in the Primitive World.* New York: McGraw-Hill Book Co., 1958.

*The Holy Bible, Authorized King James Version.* London: William Collins Sons and Co., 1958.

*The Holy Bible, Revised Standard Version.* New York: Thomas Nelson and Sons, 1951.

Hone, William. *Ancient Mysteries Described, Especially the English Miracle Plays Founded on Apocryphal New Testament Story, etc.* London: Published by the author, 1823.

Hsiao, Kung-Chuan. *Rural China, Imperial Control in the Nineteenth Century.* Seattle: University of Washington Press, 1960.

Hu, Hsien Chin. *The Common Descent Group in China and Its Functions.* New York: The Viking Fund, 1948.

Hull, Richard W. *Munyakere: African Civilization Before the Batuuree.* New York: John Wiley and Sons, 1972.

Jensen, Alan F. *Sociology: Concepts and Concerns.* Chicago: Rand McNally and Co., 1971.

*The Jerusalem Bible*, Readers Edition, Garden City, N.Y.: Doubleday and Co., 1968.

Johnson, Arthur Harvey, *The History of the Worshipfull Company of Drapers.* 5 vols. Oxford: At the Claredon Press, 1914-1922.

Johnson, Harold Whetstone. *The Private Life of the Romans.* Chicago: Scott, Foresman, and Co., 1932.

Johnson, Samuel. *A Dictionary of the English Language.* 2 vols. London: W. Strahan, 1755.

Jones, Louis C. *The Clubs of the Georgian Rakes.* New York: Columbia University Press, 1942.

Jones, P. E. *The Worshipfull Company of Poulters of the City of London: A Short History.* London: Oxford University Press, 1965.

Kahl, William Joseph. *The Development of London Livery Companies.* Boston: Harvard Graduate School of Business Administration, 1960.

Keesing, Felix M. *Social Anthropology in Polynesia.* London: Oxford University Press, 1953.

Kerri, James Nwannukwu. "Anthropological Studies of Voluntary Associations and Voluntary Action: A Review." *Journal of Voluntary Action Research* 3, 1 (January 1974).

Kersey, John. *Dictionarium Anglo-Britannicum.* Menston, England: The
    Scholar Press, 1969.
Kirby, Richard M. "Voluntary Action in Developing Countries: Types,
    Origins, and Possibilities." *Journal of Voluntary Action Research* 2, 3
    (July 1973).
Knowles, David. *The Religious Orders in England.* Cambridge: Cambridge
    University Press, 1950.
Kramer, Stella. *The English Craft Guilds: Studies in their Progress and
    Decline.* New York: Columbia University Press, 1927.
Lacroix, Paul. *France in the Middle Ages.* New York: Frederick Ungar
    Publishing Co., 1963.
Lambert, J. M. *Two Thousand Years of Guild Life.* Hull: A. Brown and
    Sons, 1891.
Lécrivain, Charles. "Thiasos." In *Dictionnaire des Antiquitiés Grecques et
    Romaines,* edited by Charles Daremberg and Edmund Saglio, Vol. 5. 5
    vols. Graz: Akademische Druck, 1969.
Lipset, Seymour Martin. *Political Man.* Garden City, N.Y.: Anchor Books,
    1960.
Lipset, Seymour Martin, and Bendix, Reinhard. *Social Mobility in Industri-
    al Society.* Berkeley and Los Angeles: University of California Press,
    1960.
Llewellyn, Karl Nickerson, and Hoebel, E. Adamson. *The Cheyenne Way:
    Conflict and Case Law in Primitive Jurisprudence.* Norman, Okla.:
    University of Oklahoma Press, 1941.
Lods, Adolphe. *The Prophets of Israel.* New York: Dutton, 1937.
Lowie, Robert H. *Societies of the Arikara Indians.* New York: The Trustees,
    the American Museum of Natural History, Anthropological Papers,
    1915. XI, 8.
————. *Plains Indians Age Societies.* New York: The Trustees, the Ameri-
    can Museum of Natural History, Anthropological Papers, 1916. XI,
    13.
————. *Societies of the Kiowa.* New York: The Trustees, the American
    Museum of Natural History, Anthropological Papers, 1916. XI, 11.
————. *Primitive Societies.* London: Routledge, 1921.
Mabogunje, Akin L. *Urbanization in Nigeria.* London: University of
    London Press, 1968.
Mackerness, Eric. *A Social History of English Music.* London: Routledge
    and Kegan Paul, 1964.
Malinowski, Bronislaw. *Argonauts of the Western Pacific.* New York: E. P.
    Dutton and Co., 1961.

Martindale, Don. *American Society.* Princeton, N.J.: D. Van Nostrand Co., 1960.

————. *Social Life and Cultural Change.* Princeton, N.J.: D. Van Nostrand Co., 1962.

Massignon, Louis. "Islamic Gilds." In *Encyclopaedia of the Social Sciences,* edited by Edwin R. A. Seligman, Vol. 7. 15 vols. London: Macmillan, 1948.

Maybon, Pierre B. *Essai sur les Associations en Chine.* Paris: Plon-Hourrit, 1925.

Mommsen, Theodore. *De Collegiis et Sodaliciis Romanorum.* Kiliae: In Libraria Schwersiana, 1843.

Murrie, James R. *Pawnee Indian Societies.* New York: The Trustees, the American Museum of Natural History, Anthropological Papers, 1914. XI, 7.

Myrdal, Gunnar. *An American Dilemma.* 2 vols. New York: McGraw-Hill Book Co., 1964.

Nadel, S. F. *A Black Byzantium: The Kingdom of the Nupe in Nigeria.* London: Oxford University Press, 1942.

Nettel, Reginald. *Seven Centuries of Popular Song: A Social History of Urban Ditties.* London: Phoenix House, 1956.

*The New English Bible.* Oxford: At the University Press, 1970.

Nicoll, Allerdyce. *British Drama.* 5th ed. London: George C. Harrap and Co., 1962.

Ornstein, Martha. *The Role of Scientific Societies in the Seventeenth Century.* 3rd ed. Chicago: University of Chicago Press, 1938.

Orozo, Guillermo Moreda. "Fishermens' Guilds in Spain." *International Labor Review* 94, 5 (1966).

Oxford University Press. *The Compact Edition of the Oxford English Dictionary.* 2 vols. New York: Oxford University Press, 1971.

Painter, Sidney. *Medieval Society.* Ithaca: Cornell University Press, 1951.

Palisi, Bartolemo. "A Critical Analysis of the Voluntary Association Concept." In *Voluntary Action Research: 1972,* edited by David H. Smith, Richard D. Reddy, and Burt R. Baldwin. Lexington, Mass.: Lexington Books, 1972.

Paul-Louis. *Ancient Rome at Work.* New York: Barnes and Noble, 1965.

Pfeiffer, Robert H. *Introduction to the Old Testament.* New York: Harper & Row, 1948.

Previte-Orton, C. W. "The Italian Cities Till c.1200". In *The Cambridge Medieval History,* edited by H. M. Gwatkin et al., Vol. 5. 8 vols. Cambridge: At the University Press, 1929.

Rabinowitz, Louis Isaac. "Hevra." In *Encyclopedia Judaica*, edited by Cecil Ròth and Geoffrey Wigoder, Vol. 8. 16 vols. Jerusalem: The Macmillan Company, 1972.

Rashdall, Hastings. *The Universities of Europe in the Middle Ages*. 2 vols. Oxford: At the Clarendon Press, 1895.

————. "The Medieval Universities." In *The Cambridge Medieval History*, edited by H. M. Gwatkin et al., Vol. 6. 8 vols. Cambridge: At the University Press, 1929.

Redfield, Robert. *The Little Community, and Peasant Society and Culture*. Chicago: University of Chicago Press, 1960.

Riley, Henry Thomas. *Memorials of London Life*. London: Longmans, Green and Co., 1868.

Rivers. W. H. R. *Social Organization*. New York: A. A. Knopf, 1929.

Robertson, D. B., ed. *Voluntary Associations: A Study of Groups in Free Societies, Essays in Honor of James Luther Adams*. Richmond, Va.: John Knox Press, 1966.

Robertson, H. M. *Aspects of the Rise of Economic Individualism: A Criticism of Max Weber and His School*. New York: Kelley and Millman, 1959.

Rose, Arnold M. *Theory and Method in the Social Sciences*. Minneapolis: University of Minnesota Press, 1954.

Rose, Arnold M., and Rose, Caroline B. *Sociology: The Study of Human Relations*. 3rd ed. New York: Alfred A. Knopf, 1969.

Ross, Jack C. "Toward a Reconstruction of Voluntary Association Theory." *British Journal of Sociology* XXIII, 1 (March 1972).

Ross, Jack C., and Andersen, Raoul R. "Occupational Pluralism: Expansive Strategies in Barbering." *Sociological Review* 20, 2 (May 1972).

Ross, Jack C., and Wheeler, Raymond H. "Structural Sources of Threat to Negro Membership in Voluntary Associations in a Southern City." *Social Forces*, 45 (December 1967).

Sahlins, Marshall D. *Social Stratification in Polynesia*. Seattle: University of Washington Press, 1958.

San Nicolò, Mariano. "Guilds in Antiquity." In *Encyclopaedia of the Social Sciences*, edited by Edwin R. A. Seligman, Vol. 7. 15 vols. London: Macmillan, 1948.

Scheler, Max. *Ressentiment*. Edited by Lewis A. Coser. Translated by William Holheim. New York: The Free Press of Glencoe, 1961.

Sellin, Ernst, and Fohrer, Georg. *Introduction to the Old Testament*. Translated by David E. Green. Nashville: Abingdon Press, 1968.

Service, Elman. *Primitive Social Organization.* New York: Random House, 1971.

———. *Profiles in Ethnology.* New York: Harper & Row, 1971.

Sills, David L. "Voluntary Associations: Sociological Aspects." In *International Encyclopedia of the Social Sciences,* edited by David L. Sills, Vol. 16. 17 vols. New York: Macmillan Company and the Free Press, 1968.

Simmel, Georg. *The Sociology of Georg Simmel.* Translated and edited by Kurt Wolff. Glencoe, Ill.: The Free Press, 1950.

Skinner, Alanson. *Societies of the Iowa, Kansa, and Ponca Indians.* New York: The Trustees, the American Museum of Natural History, Anthropological Papers, 1915. X1, 9.

Smith, Arthur H. *Village Life in China.* New York: Fleming H. Revell Co., 1899.

Smith, Constance, and Freedman, Anne. *Voluntary Associations.* Cambridge, Mass.: Harvard University Press, 1972.

Smith, David H., "Modernization and the Emergence of Voluntary Organizations." In *Voluntary Action Research* edited by David H. Smith, Lexington, Mass.: Lexington Books, 1973.

———, ed. *Voluntary Action Research: 1974.* Lexington, Mass.; Lexington Books, 1974.

Smith, David H.; Reddy, Richard D.; and Baldwin, Burt R.; eds. *Voluntary Action Research: 1972.* Lexington, Mass.: Lexington Books, 1972.

Smith, J. Toulmin, ed. *English Gilds.* London: N. Trubner, 1870.

Smith, Lucy T. "Introduction." In *English Gilds,* edited by J. Toulmin Smith. London: N. Trubner, 1870.

Spedding, James; Ellis, Robert Leslie; and Heath, Douglas Denon, eds. *The Works of Francis Bacon.* Boston: Brown and Taggard, 1861.

Spencer, Baldwin, and Gillen, F. J. *The Northern Tribes of Central Australia.* Oosterhout, Netherlands: Anthropological Publications, 1969.

Spier, Leslie. *The Sun Dance of the Plains Indians.* New York: The Trustees, the American Museum of Natural History, Anthropological Papers, 1921. XVI, 7.

Staley, Edgcumbe. *The Gilds of Florence.* New York: Benjamin Blom, 1967.

Stenton, Doris Mary. *English Society in the Early Middle Ages, 1066-1307.* Harmondsworth, Middlesex: Penguin Books, 1967.

Stow, John. *A Survey of the Cities of London and Westminster and the Borough of Southwark, etc.* 6th ed., 2 vols. Edited by John Strype. London: 1754.

Thompson, Alexander Hamilton. "The Monastic Orders." In *The Cambridge Medieval History*, edited by H. M. Gwatkin et al. 5 vols. Cambridge: At the University Press, 1929.

Thrupp, Sylvia. *The Merchant Class of Medieval London (1300-1500)*. Chicago: University of Chicago Press, 1948.

Timbs, John. *Club Life of London*. 2 vols. London: Chatto and Windus, 1865.

Tsu, Yu Yue. *The Spirit of Chinese Philanthropy*. New York: AMS Press, 1968.

Unwin, George. *The Gilds and Companies of:London*. 4th ed. London: Frank Cass and Co., 1963.

Vaux, Roland de. *Ancient Israel: It's Life and Institutions*. New York: McGraw-Hill Book Co., 1961.

Vinogradoff, Sir Paul. "Foundations of Society (Origins of Feudalism)." In *The Cambridge Medieval History*, edited by H. M. Gwatkin et al. Vol. 2. 5 vols. Cambridge: At the University Press, 1929.

Wallis, Louis. *The Bible is Human*. New York: Columbia University Press, 1942.

Waltzing, Jean Pierre. *Etude Historique sur les Corporations Professionelles chez les Romains Depuis les Origines Jusqù à la Chute de l'Empire d'Occident*. 4 vols. Louvain: Paters, 1895.

Ward, Ned. *The History of Clubs: In XXIX Chapters*. 2nd ed. London: J. Phillips, 1710.

Warner, W. Keith. "Major Conceptual Elements of Voluntary Associations." In *Voluntary Action Research: 1972*, edited by Daid H. Smith, Richard D. Reddy, and Burt R. Baldwin. Lexington, Mass.: Lexington Books, 1972.

Warner, W. Lloyd. *A Black Civilization*. Rev. ed. New York: Harper and Brothers, 1958.

Weber, Max. *The Religion of China*. Translated and edited by Hans H. Gerth. Glencoe, Ill.: The Free Press, 1951.

————. *Ancient Judaism*. Translated and edited by Hans H. Gerth and Don Martindale. Glencoe, Ill: The Free Press, 1952.

————. *The Religion of India*. Translated and edited by Hans H. Gerth and Don Martindale. Glencoe, Ill.: The Free Press, 1958.

————. *The Sociology of Religion*. Translated by Ephraim Fischoff. Boston: Beacon Press, 1964.

————. *Economy and Society*. Translated by Ephraim Fischoff et al. Edited by Guenther Roth and Claus Wittich. 2 vols. New York: Bedminster Press, 1968.

Webster, Hutton. *Primitive Secret Societies: A Study in Early Politics and Religion.* New York: Octagon Books, 1968.

Westlake, H. F. *The Parish Gilds of Medieval England.* New York: Macmillan, 1919.

White, Paul E. "Resources as Determinants of Organizational Behavior." *Administrative Science Quarterly* 19, 3 (September 1974).

Williams, Arnold. *The Drama of Medieval England.* Kalamazoo, Mich.: Michigan State University Press, 1961.

Wischnizer, Mark. *A History of Jewish Crafts and Guilds.* New York: Jonathan David, 1965.

Wissler, Clark. *General Discussion of Shamanistic and Dancing Societies.* New York: The Trustees, the American Museum of Natural History, Anthropological Papers, 1916. XI, 12.

# Index

NOTE: The following abbreviations are used in the index. AV = King James Bible (Authorized Version); FVO = formal voluntary organization; JB = Jerusalem Bible; NEB = New English Bible; OT = Old Testament; RSV = Revised Standard Version; VA = voluntary associations.

*Abashieni*, 54
Abbott, Frank Frost, 109, 112, 132
Abby, 141, 185; music schools in the, 222
Abram, A., 202
*Accademia dei Lincei*, 219
*Accademia del Cimento*, 219
*Académie Royale des Sciences*, 219
Act of Conveyance, 136, 139, 141
Act of Toleration, 157
Actors, 103
Adams, James Luther, 24, 274
Adams, Jeremy duQuesnay, 169, 203
Affection, in collective action, 18
Africa, 20, 130, 145
Africanus, Leo, 53
*Agape*, 89, 94
Age-grades. *See* age ranks
Age ranks: associations in, 56-57; and cohorts, 38; control by, 54; grades of, 47, 66; mutual aid in, 54; of Plains Indians, 38, 40
Albright, W. F., 133
*Album*, 141; Roman, 116

Alchemy, 252
Ale, 171, 208
Alexander the Great, 86
Algonkian, 32
Allen, Robert Joseph, 206-207, 251-52
Alms, 151
Althusius, 273
Amateurism, 230
*American Journal of Sociology*, 269
American Legion, 35
American Red Cross, 68
*American Sociological Review*, 269
Analytical group members, 10-11, 248
Anam, 49
Ancient societies, research list, 71
Anderson, Robert T., 60, 70, 201-202
Anglican, 158
Anglo-Saxon, 152, 171
Anne (Queen of England), 239
Anthropology, 70, 267, in Africa, 55; and Bible, 117; kinship in, 120; among peasants, 61; research in,

22, 27-28, 273; sources for, 8, 267
Apollo Club, The, 208
Apothecary, 209
Appius Claudius Caecus, 112
Apprenticeship, 189; in India, 87
Arabs, 128
Aranta. *See* Arunta
Arapho, 32
Archaeology, 51; on Bible, 117
Archery, 197, 227-28
Architecture, 23, 267; and masons, 244
*Archon*, of *genos*, 93
Arikara, 40-41
Ariori, 47, 69; as VA, 47
Aristocracy, Roman, 112-13
Army volunteers, 121
Art: study of, 267; in Tahiti, 46
*Arte*, 116
Arunta, 29-31, 45, 67, 255
Asaph, 119-121
Asceticism of secret societies, 83
Ascription in VA, 75
Ashbea, 118
Asoka, Emperor, 89
Assimilation, Roman, 112
Assizes: of ale, 171; of bread, 171
Associations, 6, 11, 101; area, 78;
    ascribed, 28; burial, 117; Chinese,
    72-73, 78; compound, 78;
    compulsory, 78; concept of, 274;
    cooperative, 79-80; credit, 81;
    differentiation of, 259; familial,
    104; general, 78; institutions and,
    61, 86; instrumental, 108;
    intermediate, 231; markets, 53;
    membership in, 75, 78; military,
    30-35; mutual aid, 82; and
    pluralism, 86; specific, 78; in
    Tahiti, 46; tribal, 30, 33-34; strata

in, 34, 75; sworn, 79. *See also* VA
Association of Voluntary Action
    Scholars, 274-75
Assyria and Israel, 123
Athabaskan, 32
Athens, 91-99, 103, 146; civil
    liberties in, 260; civil rights in,
    260; clubs of, 259;
    communications in, 255, 257;
    family in, 257; friendship in, 259,
    262; and Rome, 109; VA of, 257
Athletics in Tahiti, 46
Atlantic Association of Sociologists
    and Anthropologists, 275
Attic city states, 91
Auboyer, Jeannine, 87, 130
Augustine, Saint, 162
Augustus, Emperor, 107
Authority, 71, 146; of church, 151
AV. *See* King James Bible
Ayre, The, 225

Babchuck, Nicholas, 160, 202
Babylonian exile, 117, 123; and
    Israel, 123
Bachelor house, 49
Bacon, Francis, 209
Baernreither, Josef Maria, 246, 253
Bailiff and gilds, 58
Bakers, 165, 172; of England, 171
Baking, 102, 119, 124
Baldwin, Burt R., 8, 10-11, 14,
    24-25, 134, 202
Ball Players, the, 103
Bamako, the, 63
Band, 28-30; associations of, 48;
    institutions of, 28, 48; mobility of,
    29, 33; size of, 29, 38; tribal, 32
Bandits, 84
Bankers, gild of, 79

Banks Islands, VA of, 50
Banton, Michael, 28, 47, 50, 67, 70
Bantu, history of, 51-52
Barbers, 162, 187-88, 192, 210, 213; caste of, 90; Jewish, 199; of Norwich, 186-87; Roman, 103
Barber-surgeons: clothing of, 149; and lepers, 148
Baron, Salo, 122, 133-34
Basket Woman's Club, the, 240
Bastons of Cornhill, London, 211
Batak, of Sumatra, 49
*Bath-asheba*, 118
*Bauggildi*, 167
Beadles, 151
Beau's Club, the, 240
Becket, Saint Thomas, 192
Beer, 171, 208, 213
Beggars, 196
Beggars Club, the, 240
Beguines, 150
Belgium, 150
Benchers, 170
Beliefs, in collective action, 18
Bendix, Reinhard, 67, 159, 202
Benedictines, 161
Bequests, to *collegium*, 107
Berdache, 37
Beverly, England, 180
Bevis Marks, London, 199
Bible, the Holy, and drama, 233
Biography, as research source, 23
Birmingham, England, 184
Bishop, Morris, 136, 200, 203
Bishops: gilds and, 187-88; indulgences and, 194; *soke* and, 187
Blackfoot, 32
Blau, Joseph L., 122, 133-34
Bloch, Marc, 168, 203

Blow, John, 223
Boak, A. E. R., 98, 121
Bode, Jerry G., 24
Bonds, security, 81
Booth, Alan, 26
Bornu, 52-53
Borough, 144; charters, 180; gild merchant in, 179-80; growth of, 184; laws of, 180
Botticelli, 207-208
Bourgeois, petits, 84
Bourne, Randolph, 114
Boxer Rebellion, 84
Bowls (game), 229
Boyle, Robert, 219
Boy Scouts of America, 6, 12, 68
Brady, Robert, 140, 200
Brahman, 86
Brailsford, Dennis, 252
Bramah, Edward, 213, 251-52
Branle, 224
Bravadoes, the, 238
Bread, 171-72
Brentano, Lujo, 168, 203
Brewers, 102, 209
Bridesmaids, 103
Brinton, Crane, 251, 271
Britton, Thomas, 226, 232
Broken Shopkeepers Club, the, 240
Broker, 88
Bronzesmiths, 124
Brotherhood of St. Thomas Becket, 179
Brown, G. Baldwin, 105, 132
Buddhism, 89; heterodox, 83; millenarian, 83
Buglers, the, 238
Bull, John, 223
Bullroarers, 50
Burford, England, 181

Bureaucracy, Chinese, 79, 82;
    church, 116; military, 71;
    primitive, 51; Roman, 116
Burgess, John Stewart, 79-80, 129
Burgesses, 181, 183; in gilds, 168
Burgher, 79. *See also* Burgesses
Burial, 113; in Athens, 96; *genos*, 92;
    insurance, 81; place of, 75; among
    Romans, 108; shrine, 74
Burke, Edmund, 249
Butchers, 124
Butlers, 162
Byrd, William, 223-24
Byzantine, 166

Caddoan, 32
Caffein, 214
Cagnat, H., 101, 131
Calhoun, George Miller, 97, 131
Calvinism, 157, 227
Cambodia, tribes of, 49
Cambridge University, 162, 218-19,
    222, 229, 234-35
Canal repair, 78
Candles, at death, 176
Canons regular, 161, 222
Canterbury, England, 181, 192
Capitalism, 157
Capitularies, 168
Carcopino, Jérôme, 110, 132
Carpenters, 102, 185
Case studies, 19
Castanet players, 103
Caste, 45, 71, 85, 87, 125, 130; and
    brokers, 88; in community, 90;
    taboos, 89; in villages, 90
*Castle of Perseverance*, 235
Cathedral, 141, 185, 222
Catholic. *See* Roman Catholics
Cayton, Horace, 274

Cellini, Benvenuto, 208
*Cercles d'amusement*, 103
Chang, Chung-Li, 129
Chantry, 141, 248
Chapel, 144, 167
Chapel Royal, 223
Chapple, E. D., 61, 70
Chapter of Paternoster Row, the,
    211
*Charashim*, 118
Charing Cross, London, 211
Chariot builders, 124
Charisma: of club leaders, 154; of
    Pawnee leaders, 42; routinization
    of, 42
Charity: at Corpus Christi, 195;
    Jewish, 117
Charlemagne, 164-65
Charles I, 154, 229, 236
Charles II, 219, 236, 241
Chaucer, Geoffrey, 191, 207
Checkerboard makers, 103
Cheshire Cheese, the, 211
Chesneaux, Jean, 83, 130
Chesterton, G. K., 223
Cheyenne, 7, 31-43; military VA,
    259; resources of, 262
*Chia*, 73-74, 76
*Ch'i hsien hui*, 80
Chiefdom: definition of, 43;
    economics of, 43-44; hierarchy of,
    43; leadership of, 43, 51;
    primitive, 27; of Tahiti, 45-46, 48;
    voluntarism of, 48
Children, age-grades, 56
Children of the Aruska. *See*
    Contraries
China, 72-85, 87, 145, 271;
    bibliographies of, 129; family in,
    257, 263; and India, 86, 90;

medieval, 72; modern, 72; permission and, 260; VA of, 257

Christianity: in China, 83; Constantine and, 105; in India, 90; research on, 117; trade and, 55; unity of, 259; VA in, 117

Chronicler, the, 120

Chronicles, Book of, 118-20

Church, 135; clubs and, 205; fraternities and, 147-48; gilds and, 147; membership in, 13, 161; monasteries and the, 160; music in, 222, 225; parish, 141; voluntary, 158

Church, Protestant: associations of, 117; Masons and, 244; Puritans and, 225

Cicero, 103

Cimon, 206

Cinque-ports, 184

Cistercians, 162

Citizenship, 79, 174

City: assimilation to, 113; Chinese, 79; fortified, 125; and gilds, 125; the Occidental, 79; the primitive state and, 51

City-state, 71, 91

Civil liberties, 17, 260

Civil rights, 17, 260

Clan, 86, 118; associations and, 109; Chinese, 73, 78

Clan-gild, 120

Class struggle, in Rome, 100

Claudius, 165

Clergy: drama and, 233; pay of, 147; roles of, 147

Clients, Roman, 112

*Clientes*, 110-11

Clodius, 107

Club, clubs: activities, 141; adult, 40; alumni, 250; Apollo, 208; Catch, 232; charity of, 40; of Charlemagne, 165; of Cheyenne, 35-36; Chinese, 80; coffeehouse, 155, 211-13, 215; contracultural, 242; dancing, 32, 38, 40, 48, 264; data on, 139-40; definition of, 5, 179, 251; for drama, 237; emergence of, 205-208; endurance of, 154; English, 21, 75; exclusive, 5-6; finance of, 155; first, 206; gentlemen's, 136, 249-50; ghosts and, 48; gilds and, 154, 208; glee, 232; goals of, 154; Greek, 206, 259; *Hetairiai* as, 97; instigation of, 206, 262; Kiowa, 40; madrigal, 226; male only, 50; medieval, 135; members of, 153-55; mutual benefit, 271; Occleve's, 206; permission for, 206; pictures of, 213; political, 215-16; property of, 155; Quill Decorators', 35-36; religion in, 48, 141; residential, 6; resources of, 206, 263; rewards from, 206; ritual in, 48; roles in, 175; Roman, 103; Rota as a, 215-16; rules in, 155; science, 217, 221; secularism of, 205; sex of members, 5-6; solidarity in, 153-54; strata, 244; *thiasos* as a, 96; value inversion in, 242; as a verb, 179; of veterans, 250; and war, 40; women and, 5-6, 41-42, 156; workingmen's, 136, 248; of youth, 40

Club, The, 249

Clubhouse, 50-51

Club of Kings, the, 241

Club of Ugly Faces, the, 241

Clune, George, 140, 200

Cluny, 162, 192
Cobblers, 192
Cockeram, Henry, 205
Cocoa Tree, the, 214
Codrington, Robert Henry, 49,
    69-70
Coercion of membership, 13
Coffee: and digestion, 210; history
    of, 208-211; recipe for, 211
Coffeehouses, 154-55, 239, 241;
    admission to, 212; closed, 216;
    first, 210; location of, 211; science
    and, 221
Cognition, facilitative, 18
Cohort, 38; age and, 42; of *ena*, 56
Colbert, 220
Collective action orientation, 16-17,
    144, 259-60
Collective work in gild shops, 58
College, 141; in England, 170;
    Pontifical, 102; Roman, 101
*Collegia. See collegium*
Collegiates, voluntarism of, 162
*Collegium*, 165-66, 188; army and,
    103; *arte*, 116; *artificium* as, 101;
    assimilation, 110; burial and,
    105-106; changes in, 110; class
    and, 116; compulsory, 101-102,
    116; cooptation in, 116; in
    England, 166; *fabrorum* and, 161,
    165; gilds resemble, 116; groups
    and, 113; Jews and, 105; *opificim*,
    102, 111; organization of, 106-107;
    personal, 106; religion and, 116; in
    Rome, 101; *sodalicium* and, 104;
    for youth, 104
Colonialism: in Africa, 54, 56;
    administration and, 73
*Comitia curiata*, 112, 115
Commerce, Saharan, 52

Commoners, in Tahiti, 45
Common Ground Association, the,
    77
Commonwealth, era of the, 226-27
Commune, 72, 79, 87
Communication, 260; among the
    Arunta, 255; in bands, 31; and
    caste, 90; among the Cheyenne,
    32; in the city-state, 98; definition
    of, 10; hypothesis on, 255;
    permanence of, 14; rank and, 256;
    volume of, 14-15, 19, 85, 255
Community: *arte* as, 116;
    associations in, 73; of Essenes,
    122; the Jewish, 124, 127;
    participation in, 12; the Roman,
    108; structure of, 108
Complexity, 59; and clubs, 48;
    continuum of, 27-28; integration
    and, 66; primitive, 51; test of
    hypothesis, 64-65; theory of, 28,
    61, 71; tribal, 31
Conder, Edward Jr., 201, 243, 253
Confraternity. *See* Fraternity
Confucian, 73, 77, 82
Connectivity: of Athenian society,
    98; and communication, 15, 19
Connor, Robert W., 92, 131
Conopios, Nathaniel, 251
Consciousness of kind, 69-70
Consequences, 137, 215, 254, 264;
    evaluation of, 264; purposes and,
    264
Conspiracies, Roman, 104
Constantine, Emperor, 105
*Constitutiones Olenensus*, 165
Contraries, 36, 41
Control, social, 12; by age-grades,
    54; economic, 30; religious, 31,
    45, 54; by kin, 54; by secret

societies, 54; by tradition, 54; in *tsu*, 74; of VA, 100; by violence, 48

*Conversi*, 162

Cook, Captain James, 44

Cooks, 162

Coon, C. S., 61, 70

Cooperatives, 9, 69, 249

Cooperative Crop-watching Association, 78

Coote, Henry Charles, 150, 166, 201, 203-204

Copper workers, 102, 124

Cordwainers, 102

Corinthians, Book of, 105

*Corpora*, 101

Corporation: concept of, 101; gild and, 135; phases of, 164

Corpses, transportation of, 106, 132, 178

Corpus Christi: drama, 234-35; feast, 177

Court: Athenian, 96-97; musicians', 165; Royal, 154

Court of Assistants, 190

Court of Good Company, The, 206

Covenant, doctrine of, 117, 123, 157

Covent Garden, London, 211

Craft gild. *See* Gild, craft

Crafts: African, 87; Indian, 87; Islamic, 55

Credit assurance, 72. *See also* Associations, credit

Cree, 32

Crewdson, H. A. F., 221, 252

Cromwell, Oliver, 140, 225

Crop-watching, 72, 78

Crow, 34

Crusades, 192

Cults, 95, 103, 119; fertility, 47; gild

and, 124; Hindu, 89; organization of, 124; Roman, 102

Curator, 104

*Curatores Honorati*, 107

*Curia*, 111-12

Curriers, 102


Daffy Club, The, 241

Dagobert, King, 165

Dahomey, 55, 59

Dancing, 43, 103; associations for, 39, 57; among Cheyenne, 37-38; as "property," 39. *See also* Clubs, dancing

Danube, trade route, 166

Daraul, Arkon, 131

Dashwood, Sir Francis, 239, 242

David, as king and psalmist, 120, 126, 165

Death, meaning of, 146

Debate, in club, 141

Declaration of Sports, The, 229

Decorating, 102

Decorum, in *collegium*, 106

Decurions, of *collegium*, 107

Definitions, pluralistic, 9-10

Defoe, Daniel, 246

Delphi, Oracle of, 95

*Deme*, 93, 123, 126

Democracy, 9; Athenian, 98; Ibo, 54; primitive, 59; Roman, 108; and VA, 17, 28, 59

Deposit Friendly Societies, 247

Derby, England, 226

Deviance and differentiation, 242

Deviants, 31, 45; in clubs, 237; dates of, 238; in taverns, 238; transvestites in club of, 240; types of, 137

Deuteronomy, Book of, 121

*Dharma*, 87, 89
Differentiation: and Athenian
    society, 98; and complexity, 27;
    moral, 242; VA and, 65
Dill, Samuel, 106, 132
Diocletian, 106
Dionysian, 95, 103
*Dissertation Abstracts*, 269
Dividing Clubs, 246
Division of labor, 32. *See also*
    Differentiation
Documents, medieval, 138
Dog Soldiers of Cheyenne, 34-35, 43
Dominance, 31; of chiefs, 57; by
    males, 49; physical, 48; among
    primitives, 57
Dominicans, 162
Doxies, 196
Drake, St. Clare, 274
Drama, 233, 264; associations for,
    22, 78; companies, 233;
    fraternities, 233; gild sponsorship
    of, 234; medieval, 233-34;
    research and, 23; VA and, 233. *See
    also* Dramas, church
Dramas, church: of the Advent, 233;
    of the Annunciation, 233; of the
    Assumption, 233; of Corpus
    Christi, 234; of the Nativity, 233;
    of the Resurrection, 233; of *quem
    quaeritis*, 233
Drapers, 188
Drayton, Michael, 208
Drekmeier, Charles, 86-87, 130
Drink, 251; ale as a, 208; beer a
    common, 208; chocolate a new,
    214; in clubs, 239; cocoa becomes
    a popular, 214; coffee discovered
    as a, 208; cost of, 214; gin a
    dangerous, 241; milk not a

common, 209; porter as a, 209;
    sack a common, 209; tea as a,
    213-14; wine a luxury, 209
Duckat, Walter, 124, 127, 134
Duff, M. E. G., 253
Dunstan, 161
Dyers, 58, 102, 125
*Dzolo. See Ena*

Easter Monday, 228
East India Company, 178-79
Eastland Company, 178
Eberhard, Wolfram, 72, 129
Economy: and associations, 80; and
    social organization, 48
Ecology, 44
Economists, liberal, 140
Eden, Sir Frederick, 245, 253
Edgar, King of England, 161
Education, Jewish, 117
Edward I, 182; and Jews, 198
Edward VI, 139, 206, 247-48
Edwards, Daniel, 210
Edwards, John N., 26
*Egbe. See Ena*
Egypt, 128; and Israel, 123
Eisenstadt, S. N., 157, 201
Elective affinity, concept, 85
Eleemosynary, 101
Elementary data language, 269
Elite, Roman, 105
Elizabeth I, 135, 139, 179, 194, 206,
    224-25, 227, 229-30, 235
Ellis, Willial, 44, 69
El Mansur, 53
Elyot, 226
Embroiderers, 58
Emperor: and patronage, 111;
    Roman, 104, 109
Empire, 104, end of Roman, 106; of

Gana, 52; of Mali, 52; Roman, 110-11; of Songhai, 52; VA in, 116

Employers, 12

*Emporoi*, 98

*Ena*: age sets of, 56; behavior control in, 57; collective work of, 57; leadership of, 56; membership in, 56

Ends-means relation and voluntarism, 76

England, 173, 182, 184, 190-91, 193, 197-98, 208, 210, 223, 226, 240, 249, 262-63; drama of, 234; gilds of, 125; musicians of, 221; Normans and, 136; Rome and, 171; specialization of, 264

Enterprizes, 176

Environment, consequences of, 31

Ephors, 146

Epistomology, 39

Eponyms, 119, 195, 259

*Erani*, 92, 95-96, 271

*Eranos. See Erani*

Essenes, 122

Esteem, in stratification, 75

Esther, Book of, 121

Ethnic groups in Rome, 112

Ethnography, 273

Ethiopia, 210

Etzioni, Amitai, 11, 25, 231

Eunuchs, Chinese, 83, 113

Europe, 87, 130

Evaluation of VA, 264

Evelyn, John, 210, 251

Everlasting Club, The, 241

Everyman, 235

Exemplary charisma. *See* Charisma

Existence, 137, 144, 215, 254. *See also* VA, existence in

Exogamy, 32

Ezra, Book of, 120

Fairs, 182

*Familia. See* Family, Roman

Familism and China, 71

Family: Athenian, 92; associations, 73, 83, 109; Chinese, 72-73; Indian, 86; religion of the, 73, 109; Roman, 109, 114; urban, 126

*Farandole*, 224

Farming, collective, 57

Farr, Thomas, 210

*Fasci*, 63-64

Feasts, 263; in China, 81; Christian, 89; in India, 89-90

Feelings, in collective action, 18

*Fei*, 84

*Feighal*, 167

*Feil*, 167

*Feill*, 167

Fellowship of *Eranos*, 92

*Ferme*: definition of, 172; as a mechanism, 173

*Feste du Puy*, 196, 223, 232

Festivals, Roman, 107, 112

Fetish lodge, 37

Feudalism: in China, 80; oath of, 145

Fielding, Henry, 94

Fifth Monarchy Men, 158

*Filles de Joie*, 156

Fines, in *collegium*, 106

*Firma burghi*, 181, 183

Fishermen, 165, 234

Fishmongers, 172, 185, 190

Flattery, among Romans, 108

Flexed Leg Association, 34

Florentine, 167

Flutists, 102

Fohrer, George, 119, 134

Folklore, study of, 267

Folkmoot, 171
Food distribution and stratification, 45
Football, 228
Foreigners, 182
Foreigns. *See* Foreigners
Forestalling, policy of gild merchant against, 182
Formal Voluntary Organizations, 11-12; model and, 14-15; prevalence and, 14. *See also* FVO
Formal Volunteer Organizations, 121-22; Friendly Societies as, 248; prevalence of, 14; Royal Society as an example of, 217
Forrest, Denys, 24, 201
Fortune Theatre, the, 236
Fourier, F. M. C., 249
Fowlers, 124
Fox, George, 158
Fox Hunters Club, The, 241
Fox, Sherwood, 9, 24
France, 87, 168, 171, 184, 219, 223
Francis of Assisi, Saint, 163
Franciscan, 162, 193
Fraternity, fraternities, 101, 135, 141, 220; affiliations of, 141; in Africa, 59; authority and, 187; beadles in the, 151; behavior and, 151; benefits of the, 145; burial by the, 141, 152; charity of, 147, 191; Chinese, 79; and church, 147; and club, 205; continuity of, 166; Corpus Christi, 195; dates, 136; death and the, 146; deviance and the, 146; drama and the, 141; emergence of, 205; ethics of the, 146; family and the, 152; feasting in the, 141; feudal origins of the, 136; the *frith* and, 168; German,

167-68; gild and, 167-68, 177, 183; insurance and, 147; Jewish, 117; and kin, 152; of knights, 193; mechanisms and, 173; motives of, 262; multiple purpose, 141; mutual aid in, 141, 147, 152; oath in, 145; of Old Testament, 122; parish, 176, 184; patron saints of the, 149; pilgrimages and, 191; property of, 149; purgatory and the, 146; religion of the, 141; rotating credit associations and, 145; size of, 141; student, 170; the Sun Dance, 37; tribal, 54; usury, 147; voluntarism of the, 191; women in the, 150
Fraternity of Our Lady's Assumption, 195
Fraternization, 88
Freedman, Anne, 3, 5, 7, 23-24
Freedmen, 112-13
Freedom: city as source of, 181; mechanisms of, 174
Freedom of association, 18; Cheyenne principle of, 36; Roman, 36
Freemasons, 166, 215, 243-44. *See also* Masons
Friars Minor, 162
Friars Preachers, 162
Friendly Societies, 136, 245-46; cooperatives and, 249; insurance in, 247; Masons and, 247; Methodism and, 246; Parliament and the, 247; taverns as meeting places of, 246
Friendship: Greek, 94; *hetairiai*, 96
*Frith*, 80, 152, 167-69, 171
*Frith-bohr*, 169
*Frith*-gild, 168

*Fu Manchu*, 84

Functionalism, 273

Funerals: in age-grade associations, 57; of *collegium*, 106

FVO, 18, 248. *See also* Formal Voluntary Organizations

Galileo club member, 219

Gamble, Sidney D., 77-78, 80, 129-30

Games, medieval, 228

Gana (Ghana), 52, 80

Gasquet, Abbot, 140, 200

Gatekeeper, concept of, 88

*Gbe*, 59

Geertz, Clifford, 80, 129

*Gegylde*, 167

*Ge-harashima*, 118

*Geld*, 167

*Geldan*, 167

*Geldonia*, 167

*Gene. See Genos*

*Gennetai. See Genos*

*Genos*, 94-96; and *gens*, 109; numbers of, 93; and *Tsu*, 92

*Gens*, 104; clients in, 112; functions of, 109-110; and *Genos*, 109

Gentleman, gentlemen, 152, 206; actors and, 154; ages of, 153; of Chapel Royal, 223; clothing of the, 155; clubs of, 238, 245, 263; debts of, 156; definition of, 152; deviants and, 238, 242; drama and, 237; dramatists and, 153; musicians and, 153; religion of, 152; roles of, 154, 207; and work, 152

Gentry: and cricket, 229-30; defined, 81

George, the (tavern), 211

Germany, 168, 219-20

Ghana. *See* Gana

Ghetto, 125, 128

Ghosts, concern of clubs, 48

Gibbons, Orlando, 223

Giddings, Franklin, 69

Gideon, voluntary army of, 7, 121

Gield, 167

Gierke, Otto, 273

Gild, gilds, 135, 199, 220; adulterine, 172; African, 52-53, 55, 203; apprentices in, 189; archaeology and, 86; art of, 156; *arte* and, 116; Athenian, 92-97; in Bible, 118, 122; and burgesses, 144; capitalism and, 115, 140; caste and, 87; chapels of, 185; chaplains of, 151; charity of, 147-48; charters, 176-78; Chinese and European, 79; church and, 147, 185; city, 125; and clans, 120-21; clubs and, 208; collegiate, 162; *collegium* and, 116; commerce, 79; communications, 257; compulsory, 102; continuity of, 166; councils of, 116; courts of, 151, 190; and cults, 124; definitions of, 25, 141-42, 173; as drama sponsors, 234, 236; drinks of, 209; economics of, 164; employees of, 190; endowments of, 148; English, 21, 258; European, 58, 79, 138, 166; family and, 58, 152; *ferme* and, 174; Florentine, 167; fraternal origins of, 141, 170, 177; freedom and, 175; Friendly Societies and, 245; funds, 188; *geldonia* and, 165; German, 168; of goldsmiths, 119; halls of, 138, 183; historians of,

206; histories of, 138, 206; in India, 87, 126, 180; Islamic, 91, 166; Jewish, 22, 123, 124-26, 197-99; journeymen of, 189; of Kalendars, 168; kinship and, 55, 58; leadership, 126; leagues of, 55; and lepers (lazars), 148; literacy in, 80; liturgy of, 88; livery of, 149; loans by, 147; locations of, 125; magicians in, 123; markets and, 87, 153; Masons (Freemasons) and, 243; masters of, 189; Mediterranean, 52; meetings of, 185; membership of, 177; mobs and, 130; motives of, 262; multiple purpose, 258; music of, 222; of musicians, 120, 224; name variants of, 167; among the Nupe, 56; officers of, 189-90; organizations of, 228; origins of, 165, 205; patrons of, 185; of Pawnee shamans, 43; powers of, 58, 79, 87, 185; prevalence of, 262; priests of, 190; professional, 79; prophets and, 119; provincial, 79; psalms of, 120; as quasi-VA, 142; ranking of, 138; records of, 138-40; in reform, 140; religion and, 58, 97, 179; roles in, 175, 189-90; Roman, 101, 124, 164-65; saints and, 119; signs of, 149; of singers, 120; size of, 52; in sports, 228; *sreni* as, 87; standards, 146; suppression of, 164; Tahitian, 46; taxation of, 58; usury and, 147; as VA, 79, 97-98; village, 125; voluntarism of, 52, 58, 120, 126-27, 141-42; of Waits, 222
*Gilda mercatoria*, 87, 102, 164. *See also* Gild merchant, the

*Gildan*, 167
Gild, craft, 79, 87, 164, 176, 178, 183, 187; authority of, 187-88; distribution of, 185; emergence of, 183; membership of, 182; merchants and, 188; oaths of, 187; rules of, 188; as VA, 187-89; vicinal distribution of, 187. *See also* Gild, gilds
Gild of the Holy Trinity, 196
Gild, merchant, 79, 87, 115, 176, 178, 183; and craft gild, 188; use of livery, 191; voluntarism of, 189; wealth of, 189
Gild merchant, the (*gilda mercatoria*), 164, 176; charities of, 180; charters of, 180; and craft gilds, 183; economics of, 180; end of, 184, 199; membership of, 181-82; and merchant gild, 183; monopolies of, 180-82; religion of, 180
Gild of St. Michael on the Hill, 176-77
Gillen, F. J., 67
Gladiators, Roman, 103
Globe Theatre, the, 236
Glovers, 188
Goals, 257-58; commitment to, 12; differentiation of, 14, 19, 46, 85, 90, 98-99, 139; and dispositions, 10; group, 10; kinds of, 16, 37, 100; pluralistic, 154; religious, 154-55; secular, 154-55; shared, 259; of *tsu*, 74; of VA, 108
God, Jewish, 105
Gods: of Greeks, 91; of Romans, 104
*Goel*, 167
Golden Fleece Club, The, 241
Goldman, Irving, 44, 47, 69

Gold-smelters. *See* Gold workers
Goldsmith, 118; as Roman occupation, 103; wealth of the, 189. *See also* Gold workers
Goldsmith, Oliver, 249
Gold workers, 102
Golf, 229
Gordon, C. H., 124, 160
Gordon, C. Wayne, 202
Gosden, P. H. J. H., 253
*Gouil*, 167
Government: of Athens, 92; of Rome, 113
Gratification, 31
Gravediggers, 58
Great Britain: Guild Socialism in, 21; liberalism in, 21; VA study in, 20. *See also* England
Greece, 71, 102-103, 141; drama in, 235; eponyms in, 119; and India, 86; and Israel, 121-22; and Jewish culture, 128; and Rome, 115-16; VA of, 271
Green Crop Association, 77
Green Ribbon Club, The, 216
Gregory, Pope, 161
Gresham College, London, 218
Grinnell, George Bird, 67-68
Gross, Charles, 138, 181-82, 184, 200-201
Gros Ventre, 32
Grote, George, 131
Grotius, 273
Group: definition, 10; existence of, 16; goals of, 10, 16; organized, 10; *sangha*, 86; VA as, 66; voluntary, 10
Guild, 118, 142; Israelite, 124, Roman, 107; temple singers and, 119. *See also* gild

Guild Socialism, 140. *See also* Great Britain
*Gulde*, 167
*Guru*, 89
*Gyldan*, 167
*Gyle*, 167
Gymnasium: in Athens, 122; in Jerusalem, 122

Hagionym, 119, 259
Hahn, Herbert, 133
Hallmoot, 171
Hammond, Phillip, 268, 275
Handel, G. F., 226
*Hansa. See* Hanse
Hanse, 167, 178; as verb, 178
Harem, Chinese, 83
Harrington, James, 215
Harrow, 228
Hartson, Louis, 202-203
Harvest, 72
Hasidaeans, 122
Hatmakers, 58
Hausknecht, Murray, 271, 276
*Havurah*, 128
Haxey Hood (village game), 229, 232
Hay dealers, 103
*Hebrah, Kaddisha*, 198
*Hebroth*, 198
Hectors, the, 238, 242
Hedonism, 136; and science, 217-21
Hellenism, 121, 128; gilds of, 92. *See also* Greece
Heman: in gild, 121; temple singer, 119-20
Henry I, 172
Henry III, 184
Henry V, 200
Henry VIII, 136, 139, 165, 196, 227

Herdsmen, in gilds, 124
Herlihy, David, 200, 202-203
*Hermandades*, 192
Herskovits, Melville, 55, 70
*Hetairai*, 131
*Hetairia*, 92, 104, 115-16, 206
*Hetairiai*: as associations, 96; as
    conspiracies, 96, 98-99; and
    subversion, 97. *See also Hetairia*
*Hetairoi*, 98, 131
Heterodoxies, 89
*Hevra Kaddisha*, defined, 128
Hidatsa, 38, 41
Hincmar, Archbishop, 168
Hindley, Charles, 241, 249, 251, 253
Hindu, 88-89, 126
Historians, amateur, 140
History, 267, 270-71; social, 23
Hobsbawm, Eric, 63-64, 70
Hoccleve. *See* Occleve
Hoebel, Adamson, 30, 34, 38, 67-68,
    70
Hogarth, William, 238
Hogglers, 197
*Hoi amphi. See Philoi*
*Hoi peri. See Philoi*
Homer, 95
Honan, 77
Hone, William, 204
Honor, 173
Hooke, Robert, 219
Hopei, 77
Horse: function of in plains
    economy, 33; racing, 230
Hospices, 192
Hospitallers, the, 192-93
Hostels, 170; Chinese, 80
Houseboat builders, 124
House of Commons, 245
Household, Roman, 109

*Hsiao*, 76
Hsiao, Kung-Chuan, 129
*Hsing*, 73-74
Hudson's Bay Company, 178
Hu, Hsien Chin, 129
*Hui kuan. See Hui kwan*
*Hui kwan*, 80
Hull, Richard W., 54, 70
Humanism, 25
Hum Drum Club, The, 241
Hunting: in bands, 29, 48; in
    primitive states, 51; tribal, 32
Husbandmen, 166
Husting, the, 171
Hypotheses, 259-60

Ibadan, 54
Ibo, 54, 63
Ideal type, 218; club member, 152;
    fraternity, 171, 176; gild, 171;
    hedonism as an, 262; method and
    the, 136, 140; music VA as an, 226;
    purgatory as an, 262; in sources,
    138; subject vernacular and, 271
Identity, in definition, 10
Ideology. *See* methodological
    problems
*'igareth kakelaf*, 198
*Ignobilis*, 103
*Iliad*, 98
Ile Ife, 52, 54
India, 85-91, 125, 130, 239, 250, 271;
    and China, 86, 90; and Rome, 102
Indulgence, in drinking, 246
Ine, King, 169
Information retrieval, 21, 267, 271
Information transfer, 275
Inner barristers, 170
Inns of Chancery, 170
Inns of Court, 170, 235

Instigation, 17, 19-20, 98, 144, 260; and children's membership, 251; and clubs, 206; concept of, 17; definition of, 18; limits to, 85; and Romans, 102

Institutions and organizations, 86

Insurance, 247; and clubs, 248; and fraternities, 147

Integration, 85; of associations, 35, 49; of castes, 90; and complexity, 27, 66; definition of, 40; and drinking, 246; of military units, 40; VA and, 112-13

Interests, differentiation of, 14

Interlude, the, 235

Iowa tribes, 41

*I-po Hui*, 77

Ireland, 182

Iron, in technology, 52

Islam, 54-55, 128, 164, 197; gilds of, 90, 166; and India, 91; in Mediterranian, 52; spread of, 53, 167

Israel, 71, 122-23, 125; captivity of, 124; and gilds, 125; and Greece, 121; and Rome, 121

Italy, 166, 171, 207, 219-20, 223, 235

Ivory, 52-53, 64

James I, 154, 229, 236-37

James II, 194, 226

Jason, 121-22

JB. *See* Jerusalem Bible

Jeduthun, 119-21

Jensen, Alan, 203

Jeremiah, Book of, 119

Jerusalem, 122

Jerusalem Bible (JB), 117-18, 121, 133-34

Jessamies, the, 240

Jesus of Nazareth, 105, 122, 126

Jews, 133, 141; and China, 83; and gild merchant, 181; and gilds, 125, 164, 197-98; and India, 90; merchants and, 128; monarchs and, 113; piety of, 122; *ressentiment* of, 89; sects and, 105

Joab, 118

John the Baptist, 186

Johnson, Arthur Harvey, 200, 204

Johnson, Harold Whetstone, 109, 132

Johnson, Samuel, 5, 24, 154, 201, 211, 240, 251; dictionary of, 179

Joint liability association, 80

Jones, Inigo, 236

Jones, Louis C., 153, 201, 253, 257

Jones, P. E., 181, 204

Jonson, Ben, 154, 208

Joseph, Saint, 126, 185

Journalism, study of, 268

Journeymen, 150, 189

Jousting, 227

Judah, 118

Judaism, 117-28; in Babylon, 257; eras of, 117; gilds and, 117; and Greece, 122; Rome and, 122. *See also* Jews

Judges, Book of, 121

Judith, Book of, 121

Jugglers, 103

Julius Caesar, 104, 107

Juries, of Athens, 99

Kahl, William Joseph, 138, 164, 200, 253

Kalends, 168

Kanem, 53

Kano, 53-54

Karmathian Brotherhood, 54, 166, 197

*Kartabhajars*, 89
Katanga, 51
*Kedeia. See* Marriage, Athenian
Kenya, 54
Kerri, James Nwannukwu, 26
Kerry, John, 205
King, kings: bailiff of, 171; and clubs, 216; despotism of, 54; use of *ferme*, 181; and gilds, 58; Israelite, 126; *moots* of, 171; early Roman, 112; sports of, 227; in Tahiti, 46. *See also* Monarchs
King James Bible (AV), 117-19, 133-34
Kings, Book of, 119
Kings Society, The, 197
Kingston Upon Hull, England, 195-96
Kinship, 29-30, 32-33, 44; affines in, 110; cognates and, 110; and gilds, 151-52; Greek, 93-94; primitive, 29-30, 32-33, 44; Roman, 109; strata and, 45; study of, 22; VA of, 65, 84
Kiowa, 32, 34, 40-41
Kirby, Richard M., 61, 70
Knights of Alcantra, 192
Knights of Dobrin, 192
Knights of the Holy Sepulcher, 192
Knights of Montesa, 192
Knights of the Sword, 192
Knowles, David, 202
Korah, 119-21
Korea, gilds of, 80
Koumintang, 84
Kramer, Stella, 138, 200
Kublai Khan, 76
*Kula* ring, 9, 68
*Kung K'an I-po Hui*, 77-78

Laadah, 118
Laborers, 197
Lachenmeyer, Charles, 275
Lacroix, Paul, 166, 202
Lambert, J. M., 164-65, 202, 204
Late Drinkers Club, the, 103
Latin, in drama, 234
Law: field of, 267; Roman, 101; vocabulary of, 273
Lazars. *See* Lepers
Lazy Club, the, 241
Leadership: charismatic, 121; of gilds, 126; military, 54; of peasants, 61-62; role, 258; in *sreni*, 90; in *tsw*, 74. *See also* VA, leadership
Leather workers, 58
Lécrivain, Charles, 95, 131
Leeds, England, 184
*Leges conviviales*, 208
Leibniz, Baron von, 220
Leicester, England, 226
Leisure. *See* Methodological problems
Lepers (lazars), fraternities and, 148
Levellers, the, 158
Levirate, 127
Levites, 120
*Li*, 76
Liberalism. *See* Great Britain
Linen-workers, 118
Lipset, Seymour Martin, 28, 67
Literati, Chinese, 81
Literature, as a research source, 23
Lithuania, 198
Little Club, the, 241
Liturgy of gilds, 88
Livery, London companies, 189, 191
Llewellyn, Karl N., 34, 67-68
Lloyd's, 211

Loans by gilds, 147
Lobby, 173
Locksmiths, 165
Lodge, 30; communal, 49; for secret society, 84; and VA, 49
Lods, Adolphe, 133
Lombardy, 165
London, 170, 172, 183-84, 188, 194, 199, 207, 211, 213, 216, 218, 236, 243, 249; bridge, 194; drapers, 177; fire, 138; *frith*, 171; gilds, 169; Hanse, 167; Tower of, 239
Londonderry, 130, 194
Lookers-on Club, the, 241
Lord Mayor, 191, 232
Lothair, Emperor, 165
Louis XIII, 220
Lowie, Robert, 39-40, 67-69
Ludgate Hill, London, 211
Luther, Martin, 227
Luxury, Romans and, 103
Lying Club, the, 240
Lynd, Robert and Helen M. Lynd, 274

*Maat*, 123
Mabogunje, Akin L., 70
Macaronis, the, 240
Maccabees, Book of, 121, 134
Mackerness, Eric, 252
Madrigal, development and nature of, 225
Madrigal Society, the, 226
Mafia, 63-64
Magic: Cheyenne, 37; peasant, 62
*Magistri*, 107
Mahal, 119
Malchiah, 118
Malchijah, 119
Mali, 52

Malinowski, Bronislaw, 9, 24, 69
Mana, 45
Manchester, England, 184
Mandan, 38, 41
Mandarins, 77, 83
Mao, 72, 84
Mareshah, 118
Market, 69; empire and, 54; gild and, 87
Mariners, gilds of, 234
Market town, designation as, 184
Martindale, Don, 69, 86, 130
Marriage, 32; Athenian, 94; in *genos*, 93; and rank, 44-45; Roman, 111
Marx, Karl, 21
Mary (Queen of England), 139, 206
Masons: accepted, 243; in London, 243; operative, 243; and popes, 244; skills of, 244
Mass, 139, 141
Massignon, Louis, 166, 203
Mastery of nature, concept of, 48
Mau-Mau, 59
Maybon, Pierre B., 73, 129
Medicine bundle, 41
Medicine Hat, 37
Medicine man, 41
Medicine, study of, 269
Medieval, concept of the, 136-37
Medmenhamites, the, 239, 242
Meetings, behavior in, 151
Meistersingers, the, 223
Melanesians, 43-44, 69
Membership: numbers of, 16; size of, 106; in *tsu*, 74
Mende, the, 59, 63
*Mercatorum*, 101
Mercenaries, 193
Merchant, 118; the Jewish, 128;

religion of, 95; the Roman, 115. *See also* Gild, merchant

Merchant Adventures, the, 142, 178-79

Merchant gild. *See* Gild, merchant

Merchant's Gild of St. George, the, 179

Merchant town, designation as, 184

Mermaid Tavern, the, 208

Methodism, 136, 158; and Friendly Societies, 246

Methodological problems: drama as a, 21; and ideology, 21-22; interdisciplinary, 21; leisure and, 22; bias against music as, 21; and bias against religion, 21. *See also* Research

Metics: occupations of, 123; organizations of, 123; Roman, 112

Migration: influences on, 76; and VA, 76

Miles' coffeehouse, 215

Military: bands, 31; and bureaucracy, 71, 100; careers, 114; Cheyenne, 32; conquest, 53; and phratry, 93; politics, 115; Roman, 114; Spartan, 91

Militia of gild, 88

Milk, as medieval drink, 209, 214

Mills, C. Wright, 268, 275

Minnesingers, 223

Minnesota, 32

Mishnah, the, 117

Missionaries, 8; African, 55; biases of, 69, 73

Mithraism and *collegium*, 105

Mobs, 104

Model, 14, 19, 27, 45, 85, 98, 102, 154, 254, 258, 261, 269. *See also* Communication, permanence of;

volume of; Connectivity, and communication; Differentiation; Instigation; Payoffs; Resources

Modernization and peasantry, 61

Mohocks, the, 238

Mois of Siam, the, 49

Mollies, the, 240

Mommsen, Theodore, 102, 106, 132

Monarch, values of, 226-27. *See also* King

Monastery, 222, 261; culture of, 161; destruction of in England, 136; and knights, 159; as quasi-VA, 159-63; and sects, 159; theory of, 163

Monks, 141, 160; in gilds, 181

Monopoly, 102

Monotheism, 104-105

Monteverdi, 225

Mooney, James, 36

Morality plays, 235

Morocco, 53

Morris dance, 224, 228

*Mos*, 123

Moslems, in China, 83. *See also* Islam

Motivation, 18

Mountain societies, 81

Multiple purpose organizations and age-grades, 56

Mums, the, 238

Murie, James R., 67-68

Music, 233, 264; associations for, 22, 57, 224; in clubs, 141; as field of study, 268; in gilds, 222; of Tahiti, 46. *See also* Methodological problems, bias against; music as

Musicians, 189; classified, 221-22; gilds of, 119

Mustering gate, 118
Mutual aid, 52, 147, 168, 197, 263; in
    age-grades, 54; in gilds, 55;
    Jewish, 117; in secret societies,
    84; *tsu*, 63, 74
Mutual security organizations, 167
Myrdal, Gunnar, 108-109, 132
*Mystai. See Thiasos*
Mystery (Mastery): equivalent to
    craft, 181; laws on, 183

Nadel, S. F., 55, 70
Naga of Assam, 49
Naples, Italy: gilds in, 164
*Naukleroi*, 98
Nazi Germany, 17
NEB. *See* New English Bible
*Nebiim*, 123
*Negotiatorum*, 101
Negroes, American, 108
Nehemiah, Book of, 118, 120
Netherlands, 223
Nethinims, 116
Nettel, Reginald, 226, 252
Network, 10, 14-17
Newemeyne, the, 197
New English Bible (NEB), 117-18,
    133-34
New Guinea, 44
Newspaper, 212
Newton, Isaac, 218, 221
New Zealand, 44
Nickers, the, 238, 242
Nicoll, Allerdyce, 233, 252
Nigeria, 56
Nile River, 51
*Nobilitas*, 115
Nobles: patronage, 154; purgatory
    and the, 146; religion of the, 144
No Nose Club, the, 241

Nonprofit, 101
Norms: in gilds, 52; voluntarism, 69
Norwich, England, 186-88
Numa, King, 101-102, 168
Nupe, 55-59, 63, 116; age ranks of,
    256; communications of, 256;
    migration of, 257; modernization
    of, 264; obligations of, 256, 262;
    resources of, 262

Oath, 173, 258-59; of burgesses, 144;
    obligations and, 145
Obedientaries, 162
Obits, 146
Object vernacular, 264, 274
Oblates, 119
Obligations: Athenian, 93; Chinese,
    110; feudal, 173; of fraternity
    members, 151; oaths of, 145
Occleve, 206-207
Occupation: and *collegium*, 102; and
    gild, 124; Romans and, 102-103; of
    subcastes, 125; in Tahiti, 46
Occupational community, 163
Oduduwa, 52
Offices, naming of, 107
Ogboni association, 59
*Oikos*, 92
Ojibwa, 32
Old Testament, 117, 119-120, 122,
    124, 133. *See also* names of
    specific books
Oligarchs, the, 97
Operationalism, 7
*Opificum*, gilds of, 185. *See also*
    *Collegium*
Opportunity cost, 19, 160
*Ordo*, 107
Organization: boundaries of, 10;
    changes in, 135; definition of, 10;

intermittent, 230-31
Oriental Club, the, 250
Ornstein, Martha, 219, 252
Orozo, Guillermo Moredo, 165, 202
Ostracism and *hetairai*, 97
OT. *See* Old Testament
*Otiosi*, 219
Oxford University, 162, 170, 218,
    222, 229, 235

Pacifism, 105
Pageant wagons, 234
Painter, Sidney, 186, 204
Palestine, 125
Palisi, Bartolomeo, 3, 23
Pall Mall, London, 229; clubs of, 249
*Panchayat*, 90
*Pao-chia*, 77
Paris, 170, 220
Parish, 184; clerks, 189, 223;
    fraternities, 197
Parliament: Act of 1388, 176, 186; as
    club, 216
Parsons, Talcott, 11, 25
Pastry makers, 103
*Pater*, 110
Patronage, patron, 104-105, 186;
    and *clientes*, 110; *collegium* and,
    107, 113; Roman, 110; VA and,
    113; voluntarism and, 132
*Patroni*, 107. *See also* Patronage
*Patronus. See* Patronage
Paul-Louis, 102, 116, 131, 133
Pawnee, 41-42
Payoffs, 19; of collective action, 17;
    definition, 18; of FVO, 14, 17
Peace associations, 169
Peace of God, 169
Peasants, 60-64; and complexity, 60;
    of China, 80; land use by, 62;

leadership of, 62; marketing by,
    62; modernization and, 61; strata
    of, 62; and tribes, 61
Peking, 80
Pepys, Samuel, 154, 199, 215, 226
Perception: in collective action, 18
Perfumers, 103
Periwig, 213
Permanence: Athenian
    communication and, 98;
    communication and, 16, 19. *See
    also* Communication
Permission, 14, 17-19, 28, 64, 71,
    85, 144, 216, 236, 242; Athens
    and, 98; in bands, 31; among
    Cheyenne, 260; civil liberties and,
    260; civil rights and, 260; clubs
    and, 206; legal, 173-74; and
    location, 125; Nupe women and,
    260; secret societies and, 60, 260;
    in Tahiti, 46
Perruke, 213
Persia, 105, 128
Peter, Saint, 185
Pfeiffer, 120, 134
Pharisees, 122
*Philoi*, 94
Philosophy, vocabulary of, 273
Phratry, 86; deities of, 95; Roman,
    114
Phylae, 93. *See also* Tribe, Athenian
Physicians, Roman, 103
Piety, filial, 73
Pilgrimage, 74, 81, 141
Plains Indians, 31-32, 37-38, 40, 42,
    66, 273; communications of, 256;
    VA of, 256-57
Plantagenets, 223
*Plebes*, 107, 113-14, 116
Pluralism: and aristocracy, 116;

crude, 86; goals and, 154; membership, 154; Roman, 115; the use of the term, 274
Plutarch, 97, 102
Poetry: in clubs, 141; in taverns, 207
Poland, 198
*Polis*, 93; loyalty to, 94; politics in, 94
Political science, 267, 273
Politics: Athenian, 99; of *hetairia*, 192
Polynesia, 43, 45, 48-49, 69, 255
*Pontife* brothers, 194
Pontifical college. *See* College, Pontifical
Popes: and clubs, 216; and knights, 193
Poro association, 59
Porters, 165
*Potestas*, 110, 174
Potters, 102, 124-25
Poulters, 172
Power, 9; of chiefs, 50; of gilds, 79
*Praesides*, 107
Precepts, 194
Prefect, Book of the, 166
*Prefecti*, 107
Pressure group, 108
Prevalence, 19-20, 85, 99-100, 137, 144, 215, 254-56, 258-60. *See also* VA, prevalence
Previté-Orton, C. W., 132
Priests, 120, 124; of band, 30; Chinese, 83; gilds of, 168; Greek, 94; Roman, 102
Primitive, concept of the, 51
Productivity: and associations, 49; of chiefdom, 49; and complexity, 27; of tribe, 49
Professionalism, 230

Prohibition of drinking, 246
Property: common-owned, 74; educational use, 74; fraternal, 149; and *genos*, 92; in relief, 74; religious use of, 74
Prophets, 119; emissary, 162; exemplary, 162
Protestantism, 159; and capitalism, 157; and charity, 248; ethic of, 157; pluralism of, 155; secularism and, 155; and voluntarism, 135
Provençal, 224
Psalms, Book of, 119-20; of David, 120
*Psychological Abstracts*, 269
Public Discussion Association, 77
Public Welfare Association, 77
Punch (drink), 239
Purgatory, as a motive in gild formation, 145-46
Puritan, 158, 225, 229
Purpose, 137, 215, 254, 264; and consequences, 264

*Quaestor*, 104, 107
Quakers, as VA, 158
Quasi-Voluntary Associations (Q-VA), 142; definition, 13, 160; Islamic, 55; knightly orders as, 192; monasteries as, 159-63; the Nupe and, 58; *tsu* and, 76, 81
*Quem quaeritis*, drama, 233
Quill Decorators. *See* Club, clubs, Quill Decorators'
*Quinquennales*, 107
Quiros, Pedro F. de, 44

Rabbi, the, role of, 127
Rabinowitz, Leon Isaac, 134
Rag dealers, Roman, 111

Raids: military, 35; vengeance, 35

*Rake, The*, 240

Raleigh, Sir Walter, 154, 208

Rank: achieved, 47; ascribed, 47; of persons, 256; and values, 256

Ranters, the, 158

Rashdall, Hastings, 203

Rationality, 76, 89, 145; Israelite, 126; and religion, 152; of tribes, 126

Recreation: in age-grades, 56; study of, 268

Reddy, Richard D., 8, 10-11, 14, 23, 25, 134, 202

Redfield, Robert, 61, 70

Regional republics, 86

Regrating, in gild merchant, 182

Rehabites, 124

Religion: as academic field, 267; associations of, 78; of burgesses, 144; burial and, 108; Cheyenne, 37; Chinese, 83; in clubs, 48, 141; concept of, 136-37; craft gilds and, 184-86; cultic, 83, 103; deism as, 152; in England, 139; and exercise, 227; in family, 45-46, 73, 109; of gentlemen, 152; of gilds, 58; Greek, 94; heterodox, 83; Israelite, 123; of nobles, 144; organization of, 104; orthodox, 83; and political science, 273; primitive, 28; of Roman patricians, 144; of secret societies, 83; social control by, 48, 54; in *thiasos*, 92, 98; and VA, 224; values and, 82. *See also* Methodological problems

Republican era, Roman, 104, 107

Research: biases, 21; interdisciplinary, 267; methods, 8, 19, 137-44; process model of, 272; survey, 273. *See also* Methodological problems

Resources, 19, 144, 206, 251, 260; collective action, 17-18; distribution of, 11; FVO and, 14, 17

Restoration, the, 225

Revised Standard Version (RSV), 117-18, 133-34

Rewards, 13, 74, 144, 206, 260, 262; in nonvoluntary associations, 19; psychic, 12-13; in VA, 85

*Ressentiment*, 89, 131

Reynolds, Sir Joshua, 155, 249

Richard II, 181, 186

Riley, Henry Thomas, 197, 204

Ritual: in clubs, 48; Jewish, 125; and young, 33

Rivers, W. H. R., 69

Roaring Boys, the, 238

Robertson, D. B., 133

Robertson, H. M., 146, 201

Rochdale weavers, 249

Role, roles, 221; of agents, 88; in Ariori, 47; in city, 79; in clubs, 79; communication and, 15; contranormative, 36; differentiation of, 37; failure of, 207; functional, 189; hunting, 38; leadership, 258; military, 38; penetrating, 175, 189; of scholars, 81, 218; of sociologist, 268; and values, 242; voluntary, 12; of women, 38

Roman Catholics, 6, 157-58, 199; change and the, 135; in England, 155; and fraternities, 159; and gilds, 159; medieval, 146; and

Rome, 166; and saints, 119; and
   sports, 227
Rome, 54-55, 71-72, 100-16, 128,
   141, 161, 165, 169, 185, 219, 271;
   Athens and, 109-10, 112; burial in,
   256; and China, 109-10, 113; civil
   liberties in, 260; civil rights in,
   260; communication in, 257;
   cooptation into gilds in, 260; death
   as motive in, 256, 263; democracy
   in, 100; eponyms in, 119; gilds of,
   125, 164, 167, 178; government
   of, 113; and Israel, 121-22; metics
   and, 112; military in, 114;
   permission in, 260; ranking in,
   256; republican, 72, 100; royal era
   in, 100; social organization of, 100;
   voluntarism of, 68
Rose, Arnold M., 9, 25, 86, 130
Rose, Caroline, 86, 130
Rosee, Pasqua, 210
Rose Theatre, the, 236
Ross, Jack C., 26, 200-201, 252
Rossides, Daniel, 271, 276
Rota, the, 215-16
Rotating credit association, 80, 145,
   263
Roxburghe, the, 249
Royal Exchange, the, 211
Royal Society, the, 217-19
Royalty: African, 53; Roman, 112;
   wealth of the, 53
Roysters, the, 238
RSV. *See* Revised Standard Version
Rumsey, Judge, 210
Russia Company, the, 178-79

Sadduccees, 122
Sahlins, Marshall D., 69
St. Albans, England, 230

St. James, London, 249
St. Lawrence Jewry (London
   church), 199
St. Michael on the Hill, 187
St. Paul's Cathedral, London, 211
Saints and gilds, 119
Salisbury, England, 226
Salt, African trade in, 52-53
Salvation Army, 132
Samaritans, 122
*Sangha* and the *hui*, 86
San Nicolò, Mariano, 98, 131-32
Santiago de Compostella, 192
Scandinavia, 164
Scheler, Max, 131
Scherer, Ross P., 160, 202
*Schola*, 105, 170
Scholars, Chinese, 74, 82
Schurtz, Heinrich, 69
Science, 219; coffeehouses for, 217;
   and hedonism, 217-21;
   sociological research as, 7
Scientific analyses in clubs, 141
Scourers, the, 238, 242
Scriveners, 189
Sculptors, 103, 124
Sea Box Society, the, 246
Seamen's gilds, 196
Secrecy, 49; violations of, 50
Secret associations. *See* Secret
   societies
Secret societies: African, 59;
   asceticism and, 83; in bands, 50; of
   boatmen, 84; in chiefdoms, 50;
   Chinese, 83-84; and clans, 83; and
   clubhouses, 49; control of, 54; and
   crime, 63, 84; family and, 83;
   functions of, 59-60; gilds and, 83;
   Islam forbids, 55; Italian, 63;
   mutual aid of, 84; among peasants,

63, 66, 84; permission and, 66, 260; and petit bourgeois, 84; in primitive state, 66; religious, 38; Sicilian, 63; of soldiers, 84; Spanish, 63; Taoist, 85; of totems, 31; of villages, 83; voluntarism of, 51, 63-66

Sects: Chinese, 83; Essenes as one of ancient, 122; Hindu, 89-90; Jewish, 105; and monasteries, 159; Pharisees among the, 122; Sadduccees among the, 122; Samaritans among the, 122; and VA, 159

Secularism, 135

Sefawa dynasty, 52

Seignory, 173

Self-assignment, 13, 25

Sellin, Ernst, 119, 134

Seminary, 274

Senate, Roman, 115

Sentiments: in collective action, 18; in VA, 20

Seraiah, 118

Servian, 114

Service, Elman, 27, 63, 66-68, 70

*Sesterces*, 106-107, 111

Sewing, 102

Sex: and associations, 48; determinism, 69-70; and licentiousness, 47

Shakespeare, William, 154, 208

Shamans, 41; gild of, 43; Pawnee, 43

*Shang* dynasty, 73

*Shansi*, 77-78

*Shantung*, 77-78

*She*, 76-78

Sheffield, England, 226

Shelah, 118

Shepherds, 166

Shipwrights, 234

Shoemakers, 102

Shoreditch, England, 236

Shoshone, the, 34

Shrove Tuesday, 227-28

Sib, 86

Sierra Leone, 59

Silent Club, the, 241

Sills, David, 5, 24, 167

Silversmiths, 124

Simmel, Georg, 13, 25

Singers, gild of, 120

Siouan, 32

Skidi. *See* Pawnee

Skills, in collective action, 18

Skinner, Alanson, 67-68

Skinners, 125; London gild of, 195

Slavery: in *collegium* membership, 106; and markets, 53; production and, 102; Roman, 112; and trade, 52-53

Sluggards, the, 103

Smith, Arthur H., 78, 80-81, 129-30

Smith, Constance, 3, 5, 7, 23-24

Smith, David Horton, 5, 8, 10-11, 14-19, 23, 25-26, 134, 202, 258-59, 263, 266

Smith, J. Toulmin, 178, 186, 204

Smith, Lucy, 168, 203-204

Smiths (occupation), 102; *collegium* of, 107

Smith, William, 131, 189

Social control. *See* Control, social

Social mechanism: definition of, 172; freedom as a, 174-75; an honor as a, 173; *soke* as a, 174

*Società delle Cene Poetiche*, 207

Social history. *See* History

Social science, Biblical, 117

Socialization, in the band, 30

*Societas*, 101

Societies, primitive: migration of, 257; structure of, 17

Societies, secret. *See* Secret societies

Society de la Calza, 207

Society Islands. *See* Tahiti

Society of Jesus, 250

Society for the Reformation of Manners, 248

Society of Shipup, 197

Sociology, 267-71; American, 20; definitions in, 7; historical, 4, 20-21; research in, 7; VA studies in, 274

*Sociology Abstracts*, 269

Sociology of Knowledge, 268

Socrates, 94

*Sodalicium*: and assimilation, 112; and burial, 106; and *collegium*, 104, 106; and cults, 104; definition of the, 101; and *gens*, 104; of groups, 113; and mobs, 104; organization of, 106; religion in the, 110; Roman, 101; and worship, 104

*Sodalitas. See Sodalicium*

Sodality, 101, 104; English, 141

*Sode. See Ena*

Soho, London, 211

*Soke*, 181; definition of, 174; and *ferme*, 174

Soldiers and Mithraism, 105

Solomon, 126

Solon, law of, 95-96

Songhai, 52

Soteriology, 89

Sovereignty, 12

Spain, mutual aid in, 64

Sparta, 91

Spencer, Baldwin, 67

Spier, Leslie, 37, 68

Spinners, 150

Spinning, 102

Spinsters, 150

Sport, study of, 268

*Sreni*, 87-90

*Stabile Emporium*, 179. *See also* Staplers, the

Staley, Edgcumbe, 203, 251

Staple, the, 179

Staplers, the, 142, 178-79

State, 130; definition of, 71; military, 114; modern, 60; organization of, 62; and secret societies, 62. *See also* State, primitive

State, primitive, 27-28, 51-60; agriculture in the, 51; the city in the, 51; economy of the, 51; history of the, 51-55; hunting and the, 51; permission in the, 261; preindustrial, 60; villages in the, 51

Status and esteem, 75

Stenton, Doris Mary, 173, 204

Stoolball, 229

Stow, John, 170, 203

Strand, London, 211

Stratification: Athenian, 99; of merchants and gilds, 53; peasant, 62; Roman, 108, 114-15

Street cries, 23

Strongbox, 188

Stuart kings, 225

Students, 103; of London Inns, 170

Subcaste, 125; government, 90; mobility of the, 90; recruitment to the, 90. *See also* Caste

Subchiefs, 45

Subject vernacular, 269

Sudan, 53

Suicide, of scholars in China, 82

Sun Dance, Cheyenne, 37

Sunday schools, 246

*Sung* dynasty, 73

Surgeons, 189

Sweepers, 90

*Sylva Sylvarum*, 209-10

Synagogues, 117, 259; in Babylonian era, 127; establishment of, 126; fraternities and, 128; and rabbis, 127; VA and, 126-27

Synoecism: definition, 123; Roman, 112

*Synomosiai. See Hetairiai*

*Synthytai. See Thiasos*

Syrian, 164

Tabu, in Tahiti, 45-46

Taghaza, 53

Tahiti: communication in, 256; geneologies of, 44; history of, 44; strata of, 44

Tailors, 58

Tall Club, the, 241

Tallis, Thomas, 224

Talmud, the, 198

Tanners, 102

*Tao*, 123

Taoism: heterodoxy of, 83; and secret societies, 83; and voluntarism, 85

Taverns, 207; and clubs, 239; signs of, 23; women in, 212

Taxes, 80, 211; of burgesses, 144; club dues and, 245; effects of, 126; farming of, 126

Tea, 214; Asian trade in, 213; and coffee, 213

Teams, athletic, 228-29

Technicalization, 269-70, 274

Teleology, transcendance of, 14

Temne, 63

Templars, the, 192-93

Temple servitors, 118, 120

Tennis, 229

Terrible Club, the, 239, 242

Theater: Chinese, 72; costumes of, 23; Elizabethan, 237; as a field of study, 267

Theatre, The, 236

Themistocles, 206

*Theraputae*, the, 122

*Thiasi*, 271. *See also Thiasos*

*Thiasoi*: freedom and, 95

*Thiasos*, 92. *See also Thiasi*

Thieves Club, the, 240

Thomistic thought, 218, 235

Thompson, Alexander Hamilton, 162, 202

Three Choirs Festival, the, 226

Thrupp, Sylvia, 146, 176, 201, 204

Timbuktu, City of, 53-54

Timbs, John, 103, 132, 200, 210, 251, 253

Tityre-Tus, the, 238

Tobit, Book of, 121

Tocqueville, Alexis de, 66

Tolls, 172, 181. *See also* Taxes

Tontines, the, 246

Tools, of the primitive state, 51

Tories, in clubs, 216

Totem: society of the, 29-30; tribal center of, 29

Trade: in copper, 52; European and African, 53; in gold, 52; of horses, 52; of ivory, 52; routes of, 52; of salt, 52; in slaves, 52

Traders, 124
Traditional Europe, Anderson's concept of, 200
Transvestites. *See Berdache*
Triad Societies, the, 83-84
Tribes: in Athens, 93; councils of, 33; of India and China, 85; primitive, 27, 30, 32-43
*Tribus*, 111, 123, 126
*Trinodas Necessitas*, 194
Trobriand Islands, 68-69
Troeltsch, Ernst, 117, 274
Trope (drama form), 233
Truce of God, 169
*Tsu*, the: definition of, 73; economic security of, 80; goals of, 74; organization of, 73-75; orthodoxy and, 77; rewards from, 75; sanctions of, 75; strata of, 75; as VA, 75-76
Tsu, Yu Yue, 80, 130
Tuckers, 197
Tudors, 194, 224. *See also* Elizabeth I; Henry VIII; Edward VI; Mary (Queen of England)
Turkey (country), 210, 238
Two Penny Club, 249

Unions, 6
United Association, the, 77
United General Sea Box, 246
United States of America: constitution of, 17; democracy in, 9; memberships of organizations in, 4, 66; VA study in, 20
University, the, 218, 220; gilds in, 170; intermittent VA in, 232; origins of, 170; sports in, 228
Unwin, George, 138, 146, 165, 200-201

Upright men, as medieval deviants, 196
Urbanization: African, 57; Israelite, 126
Urban, Pope, 195
Usury, 147
Uto-Axtecan, 32
Utter barristers, 170
Uxorilocal, 33

VA (voluntary associations): absence of, 28, 31; access to, 150; African anthropology and, 55; amateurism and, 233; American biases as to, 3-4; Ariori as, 47; in Athens, 92, 94; bands, existence in, 64; in Banks Islands, 50; breakdown of, 242; for burial, 117; changes in, 42, 116; chartered, 68; Cheyenne, 35-36; chiefdoms, existence in, 64; Chinese minority, 83; Chinese social structure and, 85; Christian, 105, 116; in city, 79; and class, 100; and clubhouses, 50; and collective work, 57; *collegium* as, 102; comparative method and, 136; and complexity, 27-28, 64; consequences of, 14; cooperatives as, 64; craft gilds as, 187; critiques of, 3; for dancing, 43; definitions of, 6, 8-9, 12; differentiation and, 4-5, 65; discipline in, 75; earliest, 4; economics of, 132; *eranos* as, 92; existence of, 4, 14, 28, 100, 154; experience in, 3, 7; expressive, 65; fraternal, 53, 79, 135; Friendly Societies as, 248; friendship and, 99; functions of, 9, 19, 28, 63; *gens* and, 113; gilds and, 97-98, 102, 144; goals of, 5, 9,

14, 108; Greek religion and, 92; *hetairia* as, 92; heterodox, 84; history of, 164; in hunting, 41, 43; ideal types of, 140-41; inequality in, 108; integration in, 112; instrumental types, 65; Judaism and, 117-128; Knights of the Holy Sepulcher as, 192-93; leadership of, 42; for leisure, 230; medial types, 173; membership in, 75, 81, 108; Methodism and, 158; military, 35-36; Mithraic, 105; for mutual aid, 84; of Negroes, 108; new, 135; Oblates as, 119; official, 41-42; Old Testament and, 4; patronage and, 113; among peasants, 61-62, 64, 66; permission and, 266; political, 128; power source, 54; prevalence of, 4, 14, 85, 100, 124, 154; primitive, 49, 55, 64, 66; research and, 3; Roman, 100, 112; role differentiation and, 37; rural, 69; sanctions due to, 65; scale of, 28; of scientists, 220; secondary nature of, 17; secret societies and, 63; and sects, 122, 135, 159; sex equality in, 156; strata and, 41, 66; suppression of, 59, 100; synagogue as, 117, 125-27; term, 245, 274; theory of, 82; and *thiasos*, 92; transformation of, 244; in tribes, 64-66; and *tribus*, 113; and *tsu*, 74-75; of unequals, 107; unofficial, 42; variety of, 14; village and, 63; and voluntary economy, 69; war and, 41, 43. *See also* Associations; Quasi-Voluntary Associations
Values, 13

Variety, 137, 215, 254, 264
Varnas, 130
Vaux, Roland de, 133
Vedas, era of the, 86
Venice, Italy, 207
Veterans, 103
Vicinal: craft gilds, 184; organization, 118-19; Roman, 103
Villages: caste dominance of, 90; Chinese, 90; gilds in, 125; Hindu, 90; peasant, 27-28; in primitive state, 51; skills in, 52
Villeins, 181
Vinogradoff, Sir Paul, 192, 204
Vintners, 209
Virilocality, 33, 73
Vishnuite, 89
Visions, 39
Voluntarism, 31, 65, 160, 267; in anthropology, 55; Athenian, 99; definition of, 6, 12-13; economic, 29; and freedom, 13; of gilds, 58, 126, 189; and humanism, 25; and India, 86; Islamic, 55; and patronage, 132; and peasants, 61; phases of, 75; of protestantism, 250; of religion, 161-62; restriction of, 116; in the *she*, 77; in Tahiti, 47; and taxes, 245
Voluntary: definition, 6, 85; fire department, 68
Voluntary action, 8, 12, 121; prevalence of, 17
Voluntary associations. *See* VA
Volunteer army, of Cheyenne, 122. *See also* Army, volunteer
Vulgarization, 270

Wach, Joachim, 160, 202
Wage labor, 57; effects of, 53-54

Waits, 222-23
Wales, 182
Wallis, Louis, 44, 133
Waltzing, Jean Pierre, 101, 103, 131-32
War: god of, 47; influence of, 76; rational-legal form of, 34; Roman, 114; in Tahiti, 45
Ward, Edward (Ned), 208, 240, 253
Warner, W. Keith, 3, 17, 24-25, 203, 252
Warner, W. Lloyd, 67, 274
Warriors, 123-24; Cheyenne, 42; Iowa (tribe), 41
Watch gate, 119
Watermen, 165
Wealth, Roman, 113
Weavers, 125, 172, 189; mat and basket, 58
Weaving, 102, 124
Webbers, 197
Weber, Max, 21, 85, 88-90, 117, 119, 121-23, 129-31, 146-47, 152, 157, 159, 201, 258, 271, 274
Webster, Hutton, 49, 69-70
*Wed*, 169
Weddings, in age-grade associations, 57
*Wergeld*, 167
*Wertrational*, 258
Westlake, H. F., 197, 203-204
Westminster, 211
Whigs, 154; clubs of, 216
White Lotus Societies, 83-84
White, Paul E., 25
William I, 20
Williams, Arnold, 252
Wills, 144
Winchester, England, 180-81
Wind River, 34

Wine, 209, 213
Wine-making, 102
Wischnizer, Mark, 134
Wisconsin, 32
Wissler, Clark, 43, 67-68
Wolff, Kurt, 25
Women: in age-grade associations, 56; Cheyenne, 260; Chinese, 73; in clubs, 208; fraternities, 150; in gilds, 150, 181; Nupe, 260; sociability theories of, 69-70; in sports, 230; in taverns, 212-13
Women's societies. *See* Club, clubs, women and
Worship: ancestor, 75; cultic, 104; eroticized, 90; phallus, 89; in *she*, 76; in temples, 78
Wrestling, 228; in Tahiti, 46
Wright, N., 225
Wyndrawers, 197

Yahweh, 105
YMCA, 80
York, England, 180, 195, 234
Yoruba, 52, 63, 121, 123

*Zweckrational*, 258

# About the Author

Jack C. Ross is associate professor of sociology at Memorial University of Newfoundland, Canada. His special interest is the study of social organizations through historical sociology, and he has written many articles on the subject for scholarly journals. With Raymond H. Wheeler, he was co-author of *Black Belonging: A Study of the Social Correlates of Work Relations among Negroes*, published by Greenwood Press in 1971.